FOUR MAJOR WARS of LOUIS XIV

1. 1667-1668 ... War of Devolution*

   Claiming wife's inheritance of Spanish Netherlands

   Triple Alliance of Holland, England & Sweden fought to preserve "balance of power" ... checked Louis

   Treaty of Aix-la-Chapelle preserved greater part of Sp. Neth for Spain - but gave France Charleroi, Tournai & Lille

2. 1672-1679 ... Franco-Dutch War

   To destroy Dutch trade & get Sp. Neth.

   Led to war with Emperor, German States, Spain & finally England.

   Treaty of Nimwegen (1678-1679) caused Spain to cede Franche-Compte & several Belgian fortresses

3. 1689-1697 War of the League of Augsburg or War of the Palatinate

   In America King Wm's War (led it, between French & English colonists.

   Louis started it by seizing Palatinate 1688
   France won land victories ... lost at sea

   Treaty of RYSWICK caused Spain to give up Loraine to its duke - but keep Alsace. acknowledged Wm III King of England.

   1685 Louis revoked Edict of Nantes.

4. 1702-1713 War of Spanish Succession

   In colonies called "Queen Anne's War"

   Charles II of Spain died - left Spain to Louis' grandson Phillipe of Anjou.

-over-

But Emperor Leopold I (1658-1705) was also a Hapsburg & nearest male relative of Charles II

—

Europe's delemma: to prevent either France or Austria from getting too strong...

Leopold & Wm formed the Grand Alliance — Austria, England, Holland, Brandenberg-Prussia, Hanover & the Palatinate, Portugal & Savoy.

Aim: to put Emperor's second son the Hapsburg archduke Chas. on Spanish throne.

—

Marlborough & Eugene of Savoy won great land victories. But Tories came to power & fired Marlborough. Leopold died & archduke Chas succeeded him. Thus his claim to Spain was as menacing as Philip of Anjou's.

Treaty of Utrecht 1713

1. Philip - King of Spain providing crowns of France & Spain would never be united
2. Austria indemnified with Naples, Milan Sardinia, Sp Neth,
3. France gave England Newfoundland, Nova Scotia & Hudson's Bay
4. Spain gave England Minorca & Gibraltar & monopoly of slave trade in Spanish America
5. Elector of Brandenberg recognized King of Prussia
6. Duchy of Spain became a Kingdom

THE SUNSET OF THE SPLENDID CENTURY

Also by W. H. Lewis

THE SPLENDID CENTURY

I. THE DUC DU MAINE

The Sunset of the Splendid Century

THE LIFE AND TIMES OF
LOUIS AUGUSTE DE BOURBON
DUC DU MAINE
1670–1736

W. H. LEWIS

NEW YORK
William Sloane Associates, Inc.

Printed in Great Britain

TO JANE McNEILL

Contents

Illustrations

(The above illustrations are reproduced by permission from the originals in the Bibliothèque Nationale, Paris.)

Foreword

In a very loose sense this book might be regarded as a sequel to *The Splendid Century*, published in 1953. But as it is a story complete in itself, I should prefer to say that it is the France of Louis XIV seen from a different angle. In *The Splendid Century* I dealt with classes rather than individuals, with problems of government and policy, rather than with private lives. Here, I have endeavoured to complete the picture by telling the life-story of the Duc du Maine, Bastard of France, against a lightly sketched background showing the rise, triumph, and decline of Louis XIV, and the repercussions which followed on his death.

Readers who know the period may perhaps be a little surprised at the choice of the Duc du Maine as the central figure, but there was a reason for his selection. We have enough, perhaps too much history as seen through the eyes of its makers, and we certainly know too little about most reigns as they appeared to the minor characters who lived through them. Now the Duc du Maine, in spite of his peculiar status, was a very ordinary man, and in writing his biography I have, I think, given a picture of the life of any typical rank and file member of Louis XIV's higher aristocracy. I selected Maine precisely for his ordinariness; a more prominent figure would not have served my purpose so well.

Anyone who writes about the past is at once faced with the baffling problem of money, and it may be confessed at once that the question of its conversion into any intelligible figures presents almost insuperable difficulties. To attempt any real comparison between the cost of living today and that in the seventeenth century would require a lifetime of research by a monetary expert, and I can offer the reader no better assistance than the very rough conversion table on which I worked myself:

1 livre (silver)	=1 franc (17th cent.)	=1 franc (1914)	=10d. (1914)
6 " "	=1 crown "	=6 " "	=5s. "
4 crowns "	=1 louis (gold) "	=24 " "	=20s. "

In conclusion, I wish to express my gratitude to the Director of the Bibliothèque Nationale, Paris, for his assistance in procuring me the illustrations for this book; to my friend Gervase Mathew and to my brother Dr. C. S. Lewis for their patience in listening to several chapters of it in manuscript; and to my friend Joy Davidman for her great kindness in correcting the proofs.

W. H. LEWIS

Headington, Oxford
October, 1954

THE SUNSET OF THE SPLENDID CENTURY

1. Love and Lust

It is curious to reflect that for more than half the century which bears his name, Louis XIV is either unborn or a nonentity.

Historians tell us that he reigned from 1643 until 1715, which is true enough in its way, but it affords a more accurate picture of the period if we say that Cardinal Mazarin[1] reigned from 1643 until his death in 1661 and was succeeded by Louis XIV. And Mazarin's reign was as absolute as that of Louis XIV was to be; here was no wise and tactful elder statesman guiding and forming a youthful king for the government of a great heritage, but a greedy, ambitious foreigner, intent on making a vast fortune, squeezing France in velvet-gloved hands of iron, whose king was merely the most distinguished of his victims. Until his death freed Louis, the king had not only no power, but not even enough influence to beg a position for a friend, and few courtiers thought it worth while to pay any attentions to the shabby, silent, penniless youth who was called the King of France. Mazarin himself, so far from showing him any deference, failed to treat him with common civility; if Louis' presence was needed for some piece of formal business, the cardinal sent for him as he would for a clerk, and when Louis appeared, would raise himself an inch or two from the seat of his chair by way of acknowledging his sovereign's presence. "How long I could have tolerated it if he had not died," said Louis many years later, "I do not know." The answer appears to be that he would have been compelled to tolerate it as long as his mother, Anne of Austria,[2]

[1] Mazarin, Giulio, Cardinal, born 14th July 1602 at Piscina, Italy; captain, Papal infantry, 1620–5; Nuncio to France, 1634–6; naturalized French citizen, 1639; Cardinal, 1641; Prime Minister of France, 1642–61; died 9th March 1661.

[2] Anne of Austria, Queen of France; Anne Maurice, daughter of Philip III of Spain and of his wife, Margaret of Austria, born Valladolid, 22nd September 1601; married Louis XIII, 9th November 1615; bore future Louis XIV, 5th September 1638, and Philippe de France, Duc d'Orlèans ("Monsieur"), 20th September 1640; died of cancer, 20th January 1666.

was alive, for in her lay the secret of Mazarin's retention of power in spite of the hatred felt for him by half France and the ruinous civil war of the Fronde, for which his presence in the country was made the pretext. The relationship between Anne and Mazarin is a mystery which is not now likely to be cleared up. Were they husband and wife? There was nothing to prevent their marrying, for Mazarin, though a Cardinal, was not a priest; and all the details of domestic life in the royal family during the first eighteen years of Anne's apparent widowhood afford strong presumptive evidence that Mazarin was her husband. It is at any rate plain that he treated her as cavalierly as he did the king, and that Anne's devotion to him never slackened; indeed it is Mazarin, not Anne, who seems at the last to have wearied of whatever bond united them. "Will the woman never leave me alone!" he exclaimed during his last illness, after she had paid one of her frequent and tearful visits to his sick bed.

Be the facts what they may, Louis was powerless in the hands of his mother and the Cardinal. Uneducated, timid, shy in society, he had no course open to him but to bide his time, awaiting better days. Perhaps the only, certainly the most valuable, quality he acquired during his formative years was the ability to wear the mask as few men have ever been able to wear it; that impenetrability, that capacity for the concealment of the slightest sign of emotion, must, one thinks, have been originally adopted as a shell with which to protect himself from insults and slights which he was powerless to resent.

Emotionally as well as intellectually, Louis came slowly to maturity, and he was already in his eighteenth year when he found himself in love for the first time. The lady of his choice was Olympe Mancini,[3] the most beautiful of Mazarin's nieces, and already at

[3] SOISSONS, Olympe Mancini, Comtesse de, niece of Mazarin, second daughter of Michael Mancini, born Rome 1639; Mazarin brought her and her sisters to France, 1647; married, 20th February 1657, Eugène de Savoie, Cte. de Soissons; Superintendent of the Queen's Household, 1660; exiled 1665; suspected of having poisoned her husband, 1672; sold her post to Mme. de Montespan, 1679; implicated in the poisoning scandals, and, on a hint from Louis XIV, fled to Brussels to avoid trial, 1680; at Madrid, 1688, where she was suspected of poisoning the Queen of Spain; died Brussels, 7th October 1708.

sixteen a woman of the world; she saw at once the impossibility of marrying the king, and the prejudice to a brilliant match which any other relations with him might produce. With admirable skill she tantalized him with the prospect of delights which she had no intention of affording him, and whilst so doing rendered him the considerable service of educating him socially. The ABC of that politeness and savoir vivre for which Louis was to be so famous was learnt in Olympe's boudoir.

A year later, circumstances threw the king frequently into the society of Olympe's younger sister, Marie,[4] and for her he speedily developed the one great and pure passion of his life: a passion so strong and so innocent that he never even attempted to seduce her, but used his utmost endeavours to make her Queen of France. Few love stories have been more often told, or in greater detail: how Louis formally offered for her hand in 1659: how Mazarin sounded the queen-mother on the proposal: the hot anger with which Anne replied that if the king so disgraced himself, she would set the four corners of France in a blaze: the irresistible pressure brought to bear on Louis to force him to marry the Infanta of Spain:[5] and the final parting, at which Marie, with tears streaming down her face, said, "You are the King. You love me. And you let me go."

Still passionately attached to Marie, Louis was hustled to the Spanish frontier in 1660 to make a political marriage with the Infanta. In the circumstances a happy mating was hardly to be looked for, even had the Infanta been the type of girl who could capture and hold Louis' heart: instead of being, by upbringing and temperament, as ill-suited to him as could well be. She was the typical product of a Court and a way of life as strange and alien to Louis and his contemporaries as it is to us today; across the gulf of utterly different manners and etiquette, Paris and Madrid contem-

[4] COLONNA, Marie Mancini, La Connetable de, born Rome 1640 and came to France with her family, 1647; married, 11th April 1661, Prince Colonna; ran away from him, 1672; settled in Madrid, 1679; in 1680 a prisoner in her husband's house in Rome; husband died 1689; in 1705 she was living at Passy with her brother, the Duc de Nevers; died in Spain, 1715.

[5] MARIE THÉRÈSE, Infanta of Spain and Queen of France, daughter of Philip IV and Isabelle de Bourbon his queen, born 1637; married Louis XIV, her first cousin, 2nd June 1660, to whom she bore Louis de France, the Grand Dauphin (Monseigneur), 1st November 1661; died 1683.

plated each other with a bewilderment which usually changed into exasperation when they were brought into close contact. And this was a period at which the contrast between the two Courts was most glaring, for the French Court, let us remember, is not the Court of Versailles, but that of the Louvre. Louis had not yet imprisoned himself in the glacial etiquette of his middle years, but was the handsome young man whose ambition it was to shine as the smartest of the smart set, the man who owed his triumphs to his personal fascination. "All breathed of love," says a contemporary in describing the Louvre in the early years of the personal reign; to make love and to talk of it, to dance, sing, and act, to picnic, and to keep assignations by moonlight in the gardens, these were the occupations of Louis and his Court.

In the dark, gloomy, silent palace of Madrid, Philip and his entourage idled through the days in a routine which resembled that of a monastery rather than of a Court: insulated from Spain as Spain itself was insulated from the rest of the world, of which Spanish ignorance was as fantastic as was that of a Mandarin of old China. Charles II, Philip IV's successor, had no idea where the Spanish Netherlands were situated, and when Gramont[6] was at Madrid in 1659, a Spanish noble asked him "whether Germany was a large town, and if there were many sheep in it?" Fantastic too was the etiquette of the palace. Take for instance Marie Thérèse's daily interview with her father. Philip IV, a heavy man in his fifties who had the faculty of standing as motionless as a waxwork for any length of time, would post himself at the end of a long hall; the Infanta entered, approached a Court functionary stationed half-way up the hall, and requested the honour of an interview with "the King, my father." The functionary then marched up to Philip and transmitted the request, which was granted; the Infanta, informed of the favourable issue of her petition, approached the waxwork, which suddenly came to life, bent down, and kissed her; and the daily interview ended with the Infanta bowing herself out of the room, neither of them having spoken a word.

[6] GRAMONT, Antoine III, Maréchal and 1st Duc de, son of Antoine II, Cte. de Gramont and Louise de Roquelaure, his wife, born 1604; Marshal of France, 22nd September, 1641; died 13th July 1678.

2. LOUIS XIV

From the portrait by Mignard engraved by Nanteuil

3. MADAME DE MONTESPAN

It was on 16th October 1659 that Gramont arrived in Madrid, bearing Louis' formal request for the hand of the Infanta, and on the same day he was allowed to see his future Queen in the presence of her ladies. Gramont, who prided himself on his speeches, made as "gallant" a one as possible; after an awkward silence, the Infanta replied: "Tell my aunt (i.e. Louis XIV's mother) that I shall always submit myself to her wishes." "At my next interview," says Gramont "I tried to say in Spanish all that Gascon rhetoric could suggest to a man who was gallantizing on behalf of his master." There was the same silence, the coin dropped, and the figure spoke: "Tell my aunt that I shall always submit myself to her wishes." Gramont gave it up and withdrew, having presented Marie Thérèse with a love letter from Louis, written by Turenne[7] of all unlikely people. The ladies of the Court afterwards told him that they had never known the Infanta so talkative in company before.

What saved this ill-assorted marriage from shipwreck was the fact that the new Queen fell madly in love with her husband on her wedding night, and remained in love with him for the rest of her days: a love unshaken even by Louis' unblushing infidelities. And Louis, on the whole, treated her well, apart from insulting her with the company of his mistresses; he was invariably courteous and affable to his Queen, paid her gambling debts with little or no grumbling, and gratified her whims whenever he could do so without putting himself to any inconvenience. And, with that capacity for uncongenial toil which so distinguished him, he punctually discharged his matrimonial obligations to her throughout the whole of their married life. But he could never get any companionship from her; to sit with dignity in her arm-chair and to answer the king or the queen-mother when either spoke seemed to her an adequate discharge of the duties of private life; it was no part of the business of a Hapsburg princess to make herself entertaining. If "the King, my husband" wanted entertainment, why didn't he fill his private suite with fools, dwarves, and buffoons like "the

[7] TURENNE, Henri de La Tour d'Auvergne, Vicomte de, foremost soldier of his day, second son of the 1st Duc de Bouillon, and of his wife, Elizabeth de Nassau, born 1611. He served continuously and successfully all of his life, becoming Maréchal-General of France; killed in action at Sasbach, 27th July 1675.

King, my father?" Anne too was a Hapsburg, middle-aged and disinclined to make any social effort, whilst Louis, always difficult to amuse, shone only in public. "The King is not a person calculated to render happy even those whom he wishes to treat with the greatest kindness," said his sister-in-law, and she certainly ought to have known. They must have been deadly dull, those family gatherings, and it is small wonder that Louis looked elsewhere for distraction.

Madame,[8] sister of Charles II of England, was the first of that long procession of beautiful women who were to take his roving fancy, but she, like Olympe Mancini five years earlier, was too wise to endanger her position by surrendering to his desires, and he turned to easier game in the person of one of her Maids-of-Honour, Louise de La Vallière,[9] who became his mistress in the summer of 1661. Few royal favourites have been as sympathetically regarded as Louise, "the modest violet," who adored Louis the man, hated Louis the king as the enemy of her happiness, and never did anyone a bad turn in her life. By the callousness with which Louis discarded her, and the selfish brutality with which he treated her after she had ceased to be his mistress, she retains our pity to this day. And Louis? Surely that sublime egoist must have regretted in years to come that he had spurned the only disinterested love he was ever to know. Had she loved him less she might have held him longer; but she was too submissive, and there came a time when the king had snuffed up the incense of her disinterested worship until he had tired of its savour; the epicure needed a new sauce for his jaded palate. By the winter of 1666 it was plain to all that the star of Mme. de Montespan was rising.

Françoise Athenäis de Rochechouart-Mortemart, Mlle. de Tonnay-Charente, Marquise de Montespan, was a very different person from Louise de La Vallière; Louise was the daughter of a

[8] ORLÉANS, Henrietta Anne of England, Duchesse d' ("Madame"), fifth daughter of Charles I of England and his Queen, Henriette Marie de Bourbon, daughter of Henri IV, born Exeter, 1644; married Philippe de France, Duc d'Orleans, 1661; was the negotiator of the secret Treaty of Dover between Charles II and Louis XIV in 1670; died suddenly of duodenal ulcer in June of same year.

[9] DE LA VALLIÈRE, Louise Le Blanc La Baume, Duchesse de Vaujours, daughter of Laurent, a cavalry officer, and of his wife, Françoise Le Provost de la Coutelaye, born 1644; Louis XIV's mistress, 1661; discarded 1669; entered religion (Carmelite) 1674; died 1710.

country squire, Athenäis the descendant of one of the greatest houses of France, a house already "noble and ancient" when Amery, 1st Vicomte de Rochechouart, married Anne of Angoulême about the year 1018. Time went on, and about 1470 the senior branch of the house died out with Foucauld, 17th Vicomte de Rochechouart, who left an only daughter, Anne. Anne married about the time of her father's death and had a daughter, who in 1494 married the head of the cadet branch of her own house, Amery, 8th Seigneur de Mortemart. The Mortemart estate was raised to a Barony for their son, to a Marquisate for their grandson, and to a Duchy for their great-grandson Gabriel, who was made 1st Duc de Mortemart in 1663. Gabriel had by his wife, Diane de Grandeseigne, four daughters, of whom the third was the future Mme. de Montespan, born in 1641. She was thus three years younger than the king.

At an early age Athenäis was packed off to the convent of Ste. Marie at Saintes to pick up what education was going there: and that, we may suppose, was remarkably little, as she left it completely ignorant of spelling and grammar. In the autumn of 1660 she arrived at Court, where her striking beauty attracted considerable attention; though Louis does not seem to have noticed her, even after she had had the honour of dancing with him in the ballet *Hercule Amoureux* in the summer of 1662. On 28th January 1663 she married the Marquis de Montespan,[10] apparently in a fit of pique at her failure to attract the attention of *Monsieur*,[11] the king's brother.

The marriage was a failure almost from the outset; both fathers succeeded in swindling their children out of the bulk of their marriage portions; and Mme. de Montespan, disliking her eccentric husband more and more as time went on, settled down to the hell of keeping up appearances in the smart set at Court on an irregularly paid and inadequate allowance. Unpaid bills, reminders of overdue

[10] MONTESPAN, Louis Henri de Pardaillan de Gondrin, 3rd Marquis de, son of the 2nd Marquis d'Antin by his wife, Marie Charlotte Zamet, born 1642; by his notorious wife he had two children; died in Guienne, 1701.

[11] ORLÉANS, Duc d' Philippe de France, ("Monsieur"), younger brother of Louis XIV, born 20th September 1640; frivolous, spiteful, and a homosexual; kept in the background by the king, especially after winning the battle of Cassel, 1677; married, 30th March 1661, Henrietta of England, who died 1670; married, 16th November 1671, Elizabeth Charlotte of Bavaria, daughter of the Elector-Palatine, by whom he had a son, afterwards Regent of France; *Monsieur* died 9th June 1701.

promissory notes, money lenders' threatening letters, accumulated in the Montespan lodgings, and Athenäis became daily more desperate. Was there no way out of the dead end she had made of her life? She knew herself to be the most beautiful woman at Court, also the wittiest; and she was unhampered by scruples of any kind. She knew that if only she could capture the king's attention, she could succeed in the difficult task of keeping him amused; for she had an endless flow of clever talk, gay spirits, and mocking raillery. And she would be no La Vallière. For the reigning mistress she had a contempt too deep for words: modest little violet indeed! Stupid little fool, who, as a courtier truly said, "had never dared to ask the king for a new pin." She would order things very differently. For Athenäis was a woman greedy for life, clutching at it savagely with sharpened claws, greedy for power, money, patronage, admiration, jewelry, fine clothes, greedy even for good eating and drinking. She determined to capture Louis, and as a preliminary step installed herself in the rôle of La Vallière's confidante and dearest friend; throughout 1666 they were inseparable, and she was always running in and out of La Vallière's rooms in the palace. And, of course it was only a matter of time until Louis found her there: only a matter of a little more time until he hoped he would find her there.

Louis XIV was now twenty-eight, an age at which an ambitious young man is apt to remember on a wakeful night that middle age is fast approaching, and to ask himself what he has accomplished. It was all very well for him to say that "he was determined to let people see that there was still a king in the world," but it was high time that he passed from words to deeds. True, he had crushed the last embers of revolt in his nobility and his Parlements, he was the unchallenged master of France; but these were domestic matters and he wanted to inspire awe and admiration on the European stage. It was also true that he had made his Court the Mecca of the fashionable world: French manners, elegance, dress, and cuisine were slavishly copied wherever men strove "to live nobly;" his entertainments, ballets and fêtes were the envy of every court in Christendom. He had bullied the King of Spain, rapped the Pope sharply over the fingers, and was at the moment giving a reluctant and half-hearted aid to his allies the Dutch in their war against England, which had broken out in 1665; but to find himself involved, as he had been since January, in a war with Charles II, was merely an exasperating setback to his long-term plans, which necessitated the enlistment of England as a permanent ally. He was deriving no satisfaction from the successes of his contingent in Holland, for, as he tells us himself, he always felt that where his troops distinguished themselves in his absence, it detracted from rather than augmented his own glory. And even at home he was beginning to have a suspicion that all was not as it should be. Louis is far too often represented as Jupiter reclining on Olympus, serenely indifferent to the doings of mortals, but as a matter of fact he kept his ear very close to the ground. "Kings must satisfy the public," he often said: but was he doing it? He may have been given a hint by some exceptionally audacious courtier that he was beginning to be known in Paris as "The Ballet King," and some blunt soldier may have told him that he had been referred to in army mess-rooms as the "Marquis de Parade." There was much in his reflections to make him restless, uneasy, and eager for distraction: and here was Mme. de Montespan only too willing to distract him.

Athenäis at twenty-five was even more beautiful than she had been at nineteen; a woman of middle height, with an exquisite figure, the much admired roses and cream complexion, heavy masses of chestnut hair, and large blue eyes which could languish or sparkle as the occasion demanded. Far cleverer than Louis, she had the knack of adapting her conversation to his every mood, and keeping it on a level which never bored him. "She was," says a contemporary, "not only witty herself, but managed to give those with whom she conversed the illusion that they too were witty." St. Simon, writing at the time of her death in 1707, says,

> "She was the best company in the world. . . . There never was anything like her conversation; it was an incomparable blend of wit, eloquence, and the most delicate politeness. She had such an odd way of putting things, and such a natural genius for hitting off the right expression that she seemed to have a language peculiar to herself. This language was quite delightful. . . . It was the language natural to her family."

Of her beauty and her wit there can be no doubt, and yet somehow she fails to charm us; for the more we know of her, the less of human worth there seems to be under that dazzling exterior. And wit is not a quality which wins our affections, especially the famous wit of the Mortemarts; our laughter at its sallies is instantly checked by the realization of its brutality. One illustration will suffice to make the point clear. Mme. de Montespan's brother, the Duc de Vivonne, lived on bad terms with his wife,[12] and on still worse terms with his son, the Duc de Mortemart;[13] and it was only with extreme difficulty that he was persuaded to visit the latter when he was dying. The deathchamber, after the fashion of the time, was of course packed with visitors of the first quality, all touching their eyelids at decorous intervals with their lace-fringed handkerchiefs, and amongst them Vivonne noticed his wife; Vivonne leant against a table and stared at the sick man; then said, "Ah, poor fellow, he won't get over it. I saw his poor father die in exactly the same way." And, with a bow to his Duchess and the assembled company, he left the room.

I think the secret of Athenäis' failure lies in that word "brilliance" which is over and over again applied to her; it is the heartless brilliance of a character in a Restoration comedy, the metallic sheen of some perfectly fashioned toy, or at best the sinister and challenging beauty of some vivid tropical flower. And one is often conscious in her presence of a faint odour of decay, as of a very old tree still making a brave show externally, but rotten at the core. The Mortemarts were too old, the curse of insanity had crept into their blood, they were ripe for the axe. Ambition they still had, and in none did it burn more fiercely than in Athenäis: an ambition which must be satisfied, if not by God then by the Devil; and, little though it was yet suspected, she was already treading in forbidden paths. The whole story of Louis XIV's France is not written in a great

[12] VIVONNE, Antoinette Louise de Mesmes, Duchesse de, elder daughter of Henri de Mesmes and of his wife, Marie de La Vallée-Fossez, born 1641; "the King could not do without her company, but he was very far from having it whenever he liked;" she died in 1709.

[13] MORTEMART, Louis de Rochechouart-Mortemart, 3rd Duc de, son of the Duc de Vivonne(?) and of Antoinette Louise de Mesmes, born c. 1659; married Anne Marie Colbert, worth "several millions" 1679; died 1688; "highly spoken of."

literature, the magnificence of Versailles, and in that splendour which a blinded Europe did its best to emulate. To the king and his contemporaries the Devil was very real and very close, and Athenäis was already his suppliant; already she knew too well the miry lanes under the Paris ramparts where the sinister little houses, which stood shuttered and silent in the sunlight, awoke after dark when masked great ladies knocked in a peculiar manner on their doors and were instantly admitted; great ladies who fondly imagined that because they were dressed as kitchen maids their identity was hidden from the unholy crew of illegal midwives, abortionists, soothsayers, witches, and poisoners watching the callers from their respective peep-holes. But, as I say, not even her intimates had at this time any suspicion of this side of Mme. de Montespan's life.

She had her good qualities, but her apologists seem to me to have over-stated her case; that she was generous to the poor and a lavish patron of struggling men of letters is undoubtedly true. But I can find little evidence in support of the contention that she was a good mother; in point of fact she seems to have been the worst type of mother, the woman who sees her children but rarely, overwhelms them with gifts and caresses on one visit, and on the next raves and storms at them for no reason at all. We are told of her that at a time when displays of rage at the card table were common in good society, no losses could affect her temper; and it would have been very much to her discredit if they had. I too would sit in at a game of poker with the most admirable good humour if I had, like her, the assurance that my winnings were to be my own and my losses were to be paid by the Treasury.

By the end of the winter of 1666 no one at Court, except of course the Queen, was in any doubt that Louis was about to abandon Louise de La Vallière for Athenäis de Mortemart; even poor Louise saw it, though she still hoped against hope that her dear friend could not be contemplating such abominable treachery. But in the spring of 1667 Louise received a stunning blow. On 24th May Louis left for the front to command against Spain in the War of Devolution, and the queen, with her ladies, was ordered to proceed to Avesnes in the back area, there to await Louis' return from the battle zone:

and Louise was not "commanded" for the journey. This was more than even the timid La Vallière was prepared to stand; she set out for the front unbidden and arrived at La Fère on the 20th of June, where she met the queen, who was transported with rage at her impudence; but in spite of the nature of her reception she declined to leave the travelling Court. Mme. de Montespan's comment on the incident has been preserved for us: "Heaven preserve me from being the King's mistress, but if I was, I should be ashamed of showing myself before the Queen:" a remark which won an approving smile from poor blind Marie Thérèse. But the wretched La Vallière gained nothing by her audacity; Louis treated her with marked coldness, whilst insisting that she should be received by his Court with the honours due to a Duchess of France, and even Louise realized that she had lost the last remnants of Louis' love. The Court stopped at Avesnes from the 9th to the 14th of July, and it was during those five days that Athenäis decided the psychological moment had come for granting Louis' desires. *Mademoiselle*[14] tells the story of the coming together of the lovers with her customary discretion:

"Mme. de Montespan . . . was lodging with Mme. de Montausier[15] in one of her rooms, which was next to the King's apartment; and it was remarked that there *had* been a sentry on a step which was between the two, but that he had been removed. The King often stayed quite alone in his room, and Mme. de Montespan did not appear in the Queen's suite."

By February 1668 it was beginning to be whispered in the inner ring that Athenäis was the king's mistress.

But what, the reader may ask, was Louis XIV doing at the front? What front? Who was he fighting, and why? He was taking the first step on a path which over forty years later was to lead him to the edge of the precipice.

[14] MONTPENSIER, Anne Marie Louise de Bourbon, Duchesse de ("Mademoiselle"), born 1627, only child of Gaston de France, Duc d'Orléans, by his first wife, Marie de Bourbon, Dchesse. de Montpensier; richest heiress in France; married (secretly) Antonin Nompar de Caumont, Cte., and afterwards 1st Duc de Lauzun, about 1671; died 1693.

[15] MONTAUSIER, Julie Lucie d'Angennes, Duchesse de, fourth daughter of 1st Marquis de Rambouillet, by his wife, Catherine de Vivonne (the "salon" Mme. de Rambouillet); born 1607; Governess to the Children of France, 1661; died, November 1671.

Louis initiated nothing in French foreign policy; he merely quickened the tempo and enlarged the plan of its traditional aim, the crushing of the power of the House of Austria. And, for the next twenty years, his personal diplomacy was to be brilliantly successful: so successful indeed that he was to be lured after that perilous will-o'-the wisp "The Universal Monarchy." The dream or rather the nightmare is still with us, though we no longer use the same name, and Louis' imagination followed a familiar pattern: France, permanently mobilized, its frontier the Rhine; a ring of vassal states surrounding France, and out beyond the vassals, a Europe in which French influence was paramount. From North Africa to Stockholm and Warsaw, from Lisbon to the plains of Hungary, no one was to blink an eyelid without the permission of Louis XIV. It was a lovely dream, and we shall see what came of it.

On 24th May 1667 Europe got a foretaste of what was in store for it. Louis, with Turenne and 35,000 picked troops, suddenly invaded the Spanish Netherlands "to enforce his wife's just claims"; claims which were in fact as flimsy as they could well be. Spain, said Louis, had never paid his wife's dowry: her renunciation of any share in the Spanish inheritance was contingent on that payment being made: but, to save trouble all round, he, Louis, would advise his wife to content herself with such property as was hers under the Netherlands *Jus Devolutionis*: he deprecated the idea of calling this a war: he and his wife were merely making a trip with a military escort to receive their new estates from the caretakers. Europe was stunned at the monstrous impudence of an annexation of a large part of the Spanish Empire under cover of a law governing private inheritance in a small portion of the country annexed, and the Dutch, who had Louis as their neighbour on his new frontiers, were very frightened; Spain published a manifesto which was a dialectical victory; Louis' case was torn to shreds; but the manifesto did nothing to rebut the 35,000 arguments which Louis advanced on his side. The "war" was a farce, and within two months it was all over. Louis the conqueror returned to Paris, where, after receiving an hysterical ovation, he set to work feverishly on further mischief. On 19th January 1668 he signed a secret treaty with the Emperor to divide the Spanish Empire between them on the death of Charles II, and in February he suddenly fell upon another outlying Spanish possession, the Franche Comté on the Burgundian border. But Europe was now awake to what was happening, and in April the first of a long series of attempts was made to put the brake on Louis' activities; England, Holland and Sweden signed the Triple Alliance, whose avowed object was to resist French aggression; a league which was so far successful as to force Louis to sign the Treaty of Aix-la-Chapelle on 2nd May. The French king, the adroitest politician of the day, had the good sense to make a virtue of necessity; he saw he could easily retake his present conquests when Europe had gone to sleep again; he saw that a show of moderation would be the best lullaby if he could sing it; and in the meantime he would set to work to isolate the Dutch, the leading spirits in the League against him. And with his secret Partition Treaty in his pocket he could very well afford a little temporary territorial loss. He renounced the bulk of his conquests, to the great annoyance of the French people, retaining only such frontier fortresses as would serve for a jumping-off place for further aggression. But he was none the less exceedingly angry at the interference with his schemes, and he never forgave the Dutch. He began to lay his plans for swallowing both them and the abandoned portion of the Spanish Netherlands at one mouthful.

2. *To the King, a Son*

ABOUT two o'clock on the morning of the 1st of April 1670, the gate leading from the small park of St. Germain into the highway opened cautiously, and there emerged a richly-dressed gentleman, muffled in a cloak, carrying a new-born child, and in mortal fear lest it should begin to cry. He entered a waiting carriage which immediately drove off into the darkness.

It reads like the opening paragraph of a novel by Dumas; but in fact it is the Cte. de Lauzun's[1] own description of the scene, and the child whom he was carrying, wrapped in a napkin (for there had been no time to clothe him) was the future Duc du Maine, the subject of this biography; born at midnight, the child of the king and Mme. de Montespan.

There were several reasons for the elaborate precautions which were taken to keep the birth of the child secret: first and foremost, the character and behaviour of the injured husband, M. de Montespan. He was incapable of appreciating the honour which Louis had done him, he was very angry, and worst of all, no one knew when or where he was going to break out next; as early as September 1666 he had delivered a stern public sermon to the king, in his own palace, fortified by many Biblical quotations in which he compared him–unfavourably–with King David. In this year he had suddenly burst in upon the Court at St. Germain and had attacked the Duchesse de Montausier as being a go-between in the king's seduction of his wife; or at least that is a bowdlerized version of what he said. His address left the lady extended on her bed, where she was found by *Mademoiselle*, who reported that the bed itself was shaking with rage and fright. The king was told; Montespan's arrest was

[1] LAUZUN, Antonin Nompar de Caumont, 6th Cte. and 1st Duc de; born 1633; disgraced 1671 for marrying *Mademoiselle* in defiance of the king; imprisoned, 1671–81; died 19th November 1723.

ordered; but the Marquis had already vanished. His latest exploit had caused immense amusement to all France excepting only the king and his mistress. Montespan had solemnly announced the death of his wife, a pompous funeral had been conducted with all the appropriate ritual, and his household had been put into full mourning. What was even a Louis XIV to do with such a man? His helplessness in the Montespan affair is an illuminating commentary on that absolutism of his, of which we are told so often; here we have the all-powerful king powerless in the hands of an insignificant noble who was causing him acute annoyance. And, what is more, a noble who had no backing except for a small section of public opinion. For his family gave him no support; its most powerful member, Montespan's uncle the Archbishop of Sens,[2] had only one anxiety, namely to keep his eyes shut to what was going on; and as for Montespan's father,[3] when the Marquis told him of the dishonour which had fallen upon their House, the old gentleman's face lit up and he exclaimed, "God be praised! Here is Fortune knocking at our door at last!"

And now further trouble was brewing for Louis. Careful though the king and Mme. de Montespan had been, it was not possible to prevent a hint of the latter's condition from reaching her husband, and M. de Montespan's capacity for objectionable practical jokes was apparently inexhaustible. There was a rumour that he was prepared to state on oath that he was the father of the Marquise's child and subsequent children, and to claim their custody from the Courts. Which would put Louis in a pretty dilemma; the assertion of the Marquis could of course easily be disproved, but this would produce a scandal of European dimensions. In fact it was simply impossible that the King of France should be involved in such a case. Louis thought of the ballad-mongers of his good town of Paris, and writhed helplessly.

Then there was the Church to be considered, to say nothing of public opinion, sections of which differentiated sharply between the

[2] Sens, Louis Henri de Pardaillan de Gondrin, Archbishop of, fourth son of the 1st Marquis d'Antin; born 1620; died 1674; "a worldly prelate, whose disorderly life caused considerable scandal."

[3] Antin, Roger Hector de Pardaillan de Gondrin, elder brother of the foregoing.

king's relations with La Vallière and his liaison with Mme. de Montespan. That the handsomest young man in France should be debarred by his Crown from seducing a pretty maid-of-honour was to deny the king an adventure which was open to the most obscure gentleman in his realm; and if children had come of it, well, we all know that omelettes entail broken eggs. But, apart from the fact that Louis was now over thirty, people who had smiled sympathetically at the story of La Vallière, took a rather different view of the seduction of a married woman by a married king, and the appearance of a bastard family, the fruit of a double adultery. Those who took this view were doubtless a minority, but an influential one.

So on all accounts, it would be just as well if the existence of this new left-hand family was known to as few people as possible.

Louis' scheme for the concealment of his new liaison was one of which only a man of his sublime selfishness could have been capable; Louise and Athenäis were to remain the dearest friends, sharing apartments in the palace: and whilst the former continued to receive the public honours of royal mistress, Athenäis was to receive everything else. The king was perfectly well aware that Louise was still deeply in love with him, and he knew the agony which he was inflicting upon her, but his serene tranquillity remained unaltered; with a polite bow to his cast-off mistress, he would pass through her room into Athenäis' bedroom, leaving Louise alone with her memories, separated by a door from the lover whom she could picture only too vividly in the arms of another woman. One can find no excuse for Louis, and it is difficult to decide which disgusts us most, his brutality or his coarseness. At last even Louise could endure no longer, and at dawn on the day before Ash Wednesday 1671 she fled alone to Chaillot to beg admission to the Convent of Ste. Marie. And now at last Louis was seriously upset; Lauzun, Bellefonds,[4] and Colbert[5] were successively despatched to Chaillot

[4] BELLEFONDS, Bernardin Gigault, 1st Marquis and Maréchal de, only son of Henri Robert, 5th Seigneur de Bellefonds, by his wife Marie d'Avoines, born 1630; made his fortune by having shown attentions and deference to Louis XIV in the days when he was a puppet in Mazarin's hands; the king remained his friend all his life; died 1694.

[5] COLBERT, Jean Baptiste, son of a Reims linen merchant, one of the three great Ministers of the reign, born August 29th 1619; overthrew and succeeded Fouquet,

to persuade her to return to Court, and Louise, with a weakness which she herself was the first to condemn, yielded to Louis' prayers; on her arrival at the palace, Louis, in tears, took her in his arms and kissed her. But it was a kiss of pardon not of love; and in forgiving her the trouble she had caused him, he no doubt promised himself that all should not only be forgiven but forgotten. But the latter he could not manage to do for some time, and indeed a day or two later we find him bursting into tears in his coach at the recollection of Louise's selfishness and ingratitude. The poor woman's sufferings were to endure for another three years, until 1674, when the king's recognition of Athenäis as his mistress made Louise's presence at Court no longer necessary to him; on 19th April 1674 she entered the Paris Carmelites as Soeur Louise de la Miséricorde, and there she died in 1710. To the last, she was not infrequently visited by the ladies of the royal family and of the Court; and it is entirely characteristic of Louis that though, so far as we know, he never sent her any message or even enquired how she fared, he never failed to warn princesses about to pay her a visit to remember that the Carmelite nun was also a Duchess of France, and must be made to seat herself in their presence.

The birth of the future Duc du Maine in 1670 introduced a further difficulty into an already complicated situation. What was to be done with the child? Children perhaps, for efficient contraceptives were as yet unknown. Louis was fond of children, and was, after his own fashion, a Christian; he recognized his responsibilities towards the infant whom his sin had brought into the world, and had no intention of evading his duty towards it. Long, anxious, and embarrassed must have been the conferences between the father and mother. And then suddenly–we do not know the exact date–Athenäis' despondent face lit up–"I have it, Sire," she cried, "the widow Scarron." "The widow Scarron–ah–um," Louis would reply.

His Majesty did not like his mistress's old friend the widow

1662; his wife, Marie Charron, whom he married 1648, brought up the king's bastards by La Vallière; first man to make "the Budget a balance sheet, not a statistical anthology;" extirpation of the Huguenots, 1686, ruined his vast plans for French commercial expansion; died September 1683.

Scarron; that she was noble, devout, poor, and of irreproachable character he would readily have admitted. Nay, more, that she would probably carry out her duties as governess as well as any woman in France he was prepared to concede. But she had a reputation for wit: "your blue stocking," the king called her slightingly in speaking of her to Mme. de Montespan. She was the widow of that rackety comic poet whose circle had, in his mother's time, been one of the most brilliant in Paris; she was a well-known figure at the Hôtels de Richelieu and d'Albert; she was the sort of woman who read poetry, and the king, darkly but unjustly, suspected her of writing it. On the whole, he thought the widow Scarron would not do.

That he should dread to be brought into contact with another female wit is understandable enough. The wit of the Mortemarts was as unmistakable a family heritage as the greed of the Condés, the surliness of the Rochefoucaulds, or the affability of the Guises. Louis had now lived in the closest intimacy with Françoise de Mortemart for a couple of years, and though the period of constant storms had not yet set in, he was becoming conscious that what is wit in public is apt to become shrewishness in private. To see his lovely, jewelled, flashing mistress's triumphant rapier play in the salons of the Louvre was one thing: to encounter the rapier oneself in one's inner penetralia, where one was no longer the Sun-King, but must stand or fall as Louis de Bourbon, was quite another. He had every intention of being a good father to his Montespan's children, and must necessarily therefore see a good deal of their governess; and it seemed to him that one professed wit, an angry and neglected queen, and a sorrowful discarded mistress was as much femininity as he was likely to be able to handle, without adding another wit to the ménage. But he allowed himself to be talked over.

As a matter of fact the king was both right and wrong about the widow Scarron; though she had lived much among the wits, she was not in the least the sort of woman Louis imagined. She is one of the most complex and enigmatical figures of the century, and as she was to exercise an immense influence on the Duc du Maine for the rest of her life, we must try to get some clear picture of her.

Her early life provides a ready-made plot for a picaresque novel. Demoiselle Françoise d'Aubigné was born in 1633 in the prison of Niort, in which her worthless father[6] was incarcerated: what for we do not know, nor how he extricated himself. But in 1639 he sailed for the West Indies, where he had obtained a government employment, a post from which he was soon dismissed for misconduct, and died in 1647 having spent his last years as a beachcomber in Martinique. He left a destitute widow, and two small children. Somehow the unhappy family managed to secure a passage to France, where the mother maintained them by the work of her hands, until little Françoise was taken into the keeping of a Calvinist aunt who converted her to the Reformed Church. Her more distinguished aunt, Mme. de Neuillant, who seems to have ignored the connection until this time, was roused to indignation by the story of her conversion, and intervened with a lettre de cachet to get the child into a Paris convent, where needless to say she was soon re-converted to Roman Catholicism. Françoise, though penniless, was a lady, and on her emergence from the convent her singularly disagreeable aunt grudgingly admitted the necessity of presenting her in such society as was open to them. "The pretty Indian," as Mlle. d'Aubigné was called, had wit, charm, and beauty; she was lucky in that her début was made at a period when these qualities, unaided by wealth or position, were a passport to the best society in France. The Chevalier de Méré[7] took her up: the Duchesse de Lesdiguières interested herself in her: admission to the Hôtels d'Albret and Richelieu was obtained: and when in 1652 Françoise married the playwright Scarron,[8] she already had a position of her own in literary and artistic society. In 1660 her husband died, leaving her little or nothing, and poverty or worse seemed to be the destiny of the beautiful twenty-five-year-old widow. However, a pension from the queen-mother was procured by the intercession of her fashionable friends, and the danger was temporarily averted. But in

[6] AUBIGNÉ, Constant, Baron de Surineau, 1585–1647.
[7] MÉRÉ, Chevalier de, 1620–85, wit and critic, whose writings are said to have influenced Pascal.
[8] SCARRON, Paul, 1610–60, playright and poet; his best work, *Le roman comique*, published 1649.

1666 the queen-mother died, and with her died the modest pension. The widow was once more reduced to poverty, and many offers of a home were made to her, but she somehow contrived to make ends meet for a time in her little lodging in the Rue. St. Jacques; but she was gradually sinking, and was ultimately reduced to soliciting any honourable employment. She was on the point of going to Lisbon as waiting-woman to Marie de Nemours,[9] the new Queen of Portugal, when she had the good fortune to meet Mme. de Montespan. The favourite took a liking to her at sight, and Mme. Scarron explained her troubles, and the absolute need in which she stood. Mme. de Montespan, who could at times do a good-natured act, bestirred herself in the matter, and on 23rd February 1666 the widow received the precious royal warrant that established her in the enjoyment of a pension of 2,700 livres, or say £135 a year of our money.

All the world knows the rest of the story; how she became governess to the king's bastards; the Trollopian leisureliness of the king's courtship; and how the girl, born in a prison, thankful to range the common barefoot in charge of her aunt's geese, the woman who had thanked God for the chance to be a servant of a Queen of Portugal, became the wife of a King of France.

She has not had a fair trial in the court of posterity. Charming she was, by testimony which cannot be doubted or ignored, but charm is a volatile and evanescent quality, and she herself, unlike Mme. de Sévigné,[10] has done little to preserve it for us in her writings. Virtue was her idol: to charm and to be virtuous, her twin ambitions. In her first object she succeeded, and the weight of evidence is in favour of her having also done so in her second; but at the price of a constant wariness, a discretion, a reserve, which early became second nature to her. A penniless, unprotected, and beautiful woman was fair game for the first comer, but it was her

[9] PORTUGAL, Queen of, Marie Françoise Elizabeth de Savoie, 1643?–83, daughter of 5th Duc de Nemours, married 1666 Alphonso VI of Portugal; preferred his brother, Pedro; staged the revolution which put Pedro on the throne, 1668; the Pope annulled her marriage to Alphonso, 24th March 1668, and she married the new king, 28th March.

[10] SÉVIGNÉ, Marie de Rabutin-Chantal, Marquise de, 1627–96, famous for her letters; left a widow, 1650.

glory that no man had ever insulted her, and in old age she could boast truly that,

"In the fine world I was sought after and esteemed. The women loved me because I was meek in society. The men followed me because I had the graces and beauty of youth. I have seen something of everything, but always in such a way as to gain a blameless reputation. The liking I inspired was rather a general friendship than love. I did not desire to be loved in particular by anybody. I wished my name to be uttered with admiration and respect, I wished to play a fine part, and above all to win the approbation of good people: that was my idol."

Already we have a sense of a woman very much on her guard against a world which she had found no reason to trust; we feel that each word has been weighed, selected, considered in its relation to the sense of every other word before it it allowed to escape on paper; there is a dryness, a lack of colour in much that she writes, which suggests an earlier draft, from which has been excised everything that could give more than the absolute minimum of fact and opinion which the situation calls for. She has a wonderful power of not giving herself away. Reserve, however valuable a quality it may be to its possessor, is not an attractive one to those brought in contact with and foiled by it: and therein evidently lies the explanation of that something faintly repellent which we find in Mme. Scarron. "I have," says Mme. du Deffand, "a high opinion of her intelligence, little esteem for her heart, and no liking for her person." And even Ste. Beuve, though he is appearing as counsel for the defence, cannot disguise the precarious hold which her charm has upon us:

"She may be abused at a distance, but one cannot attack her with impunity at close quarters. She impresses by a tone of noble simplicity and discreet dignity: she pleases by the perfect and piquant expression she is able to give to what is right and just: there are times even when we might say she charms: but, as soon as we quit her, this charm is no longer able to hold us, and our prejudice against her personality regains the upper hand."

I have said that she has not had a fair trial, and this is chiefly due to the formidable quality of her enemies, particularly of St. Simon.[11]

[11] St. Simon, Louis de Rouvroy, 2nd Duc de, 1675–1755, author of the famous memoirs. Only son of Claude, 1st Duc de St. Simon, by his second wife, Charlotte de l'Aubéspine.

To the general reader the seventeenth century means the memoirs of St. Simon; this incomparable and exasperating writer towers head and shoulders above the whole of Versailles, and we never forget his portraits, his vivid thumbnail sketches, the dramatic scenes which spring to life beneath his magic touch. How exquisitely drawn, how they glow with colour, and how valuable they would be to the historian, if only they happened to be true! Now who is this wonderful St. Simon, this man from whom no secrets are hid, who lays bare the hearts and brains of all his contemporaries from the king in his innermost privacies to the footman in the antechamber? St. Simon arrived at Court in 1691 at the age of sixteen, when Mme. de Maintenon was fifty-six and the king fifty-three. On his own showing, he made few friends, and none at all of his own age; he attached himself to a little group of elderly people, who yielded, as old people will, to the flattery of a young man's admiration. All were people of position, some had influence, two were cabinet ministers. But does it follow that they bared their hearts to St. Simon? Louis did not encourage ministers who babbled, and yet we are asked to believe that they let the idle inquisitive little duke into all their secrets. St. Simon's inaccuracies, indeed often fictions, have been exposed again and again, and this is not the place to do it once more. Until the king's death he was as complete a nullity as it was possible for a man of his rank to be; you may turn over page after page of contemporary letters and memoirs without his name catching your eye. And when it does, like as not it will be a reference to the verses on him which amused all Paris, in which he is shown on his arrival in Heaven, complaining bitterly that his hassock is not of the privileged dimensions reserved for the exclusive use of a duke and peer of France. Spanheim, the Brandenburg resident at Paris, in a very full dossier compiled for the use of the elector's secret service, gives an an analysis of the character and position of everyone at the French Court; to St. Simon he accords just under three lines, and here they are: "Peer of France, Governor of Blaye, Governor of Senlis, Captain of Pont Ste. Maxence, Colonel of Cavalry–to whom no one pays any attention."

On the evidence of his own memoirs, St. Simon does not seem

to have spoken to Mme. de Maintenon half a dozen times in his life, and then only on formal visits of compliment. His detestation of her rests on her affection for the Duc du Maine, and on her blindness, shared by most of her contemporaries, to the merit of the Duc de St. Simon. Yet such is St. Simon's genius that in 1742 – twenty-three years after the death of the woman whom he had hardly spoken to – he sits down to draw that famous portrait which still passes for Mme. de Maintenon; the old sorceress, concealed behind, and working the king as a showman does a puppet, the Tartuffe in petticoats, redeeming a youth of debauchery by a malevolent prudery and sham devotion, the evil genius of France.

The Duchesse d'Orléans,[12] Louis' sturdy German sister-in-law, is a franker enemy, and one whose mud is more apt to stick, because we like her and we like her letters. She comes as a breath of mountain air blowing through the overscented rooms of Versailles, with her country walks, her picnics, her open bedroom windows, and her horror of fleas and foul linen under pearls and diamonds. And further, she had some reason for hating Mme. de Maintenon whom she quite rightly considered to be the enemy of her son. But *Madame*, as she was called at Court, is an uncommonly good hater, prepared to believe literally anything against those whom she hates, and her tirades against "the old excrement," as she usually calls Mme. de Maintenon, are not to be accepted as evidence.

The third contributor to the Maintenon of popular fancy was not, like the other two, her enemy, but merely a Franco-Danish freelance journalist and author, one La Beaumelle, whose life would be well worth writing. At the age of twenty-two, already with many adventures to his credit, he had in 1748 persuaded the King of Denmark to endow a Chair of French Belles Lettres at Copenhagen University and to make him the Professor. In 1750 he came on a visit to Paris, where he fell in with Racine, a son of the poet, who was known to have a collection of one hundred and sixty-three letters written by Mme. de Maintenon. What then took place is

[12] ORLÉANS, Elizabeth Charlotte of Bavaria, 1652–1722, daughter of the Elector Palatine; became second wife of Louis XIV's brother, *Monsieur*, 1671; bore three children, two surviving infancy, 1st, Philippe, afterwards Regent, 1673, 2nd, Charlotte Elizabeth, afterwards Duchesse de Lorraine, 1676; widow, 1701.

obscure. Racine himself says that he lent his collection to La Beaumelle to read, as a preliminary to their collaborating in an edition of them. Beaumelle says that he bought them unconditionally from Racine for 200 louis. And Voltaire says that La Beaumelle stole them off his host's mantelpiece while his back was turned. However that may be, Racine heard nothing more of his letters until 1752, when to his astonishment he one day found at his bookseller's a brand new *Life and Letters of Mme. de Maintenon* by the Sieur de La Beaumelle. His astonishment was still greater when, on getting the book home, he found that his hundred and sixty-three letters had grown to two hundred and ninety-eight, and that the additional letters formed by far the most interesting part of the collection. La Beaumelle had in 1750 expressed his disappointment that none of the letters dealt with Mme. de Maintenon's early years, or shed any light on her relations with the king; he never offered any explanation of where he got the additional letters from; and in fact could not, for he had manufactured them himself. So neatly did he do his unscrupulous work that, in spite of the fact that we possess Racine's copy of Beaumelle's book, with his own marginal notes distinguishing the true letters from the fabricated ones, the latter have continued to circulate ever since, with incalculable damage to Mme. de Maintenon's reputation; for the forgeries round her off so nicely, they answer so piquantly those questions about her early years and her later relations with Louis, they fill in all the tiresome gaps in the story. But their falsity would be demonstrable without Racine's written evidence; in nearly all cases the dates are not only wrong but impossible and the most intriguing passages, those in which she describes the successive stages of her capture of the king, are addressed to Mme. de St. Géran.[13] Now is it conceivable that Mme. de Maintenon, who never gave herself away in her life, should have done so on sheet after sheet of paper to a feather-brained woman of doubtful reputation, and one who at the time the supposed letters were written, was living under the same roof as herself? The evidence of the La Beaumelle letters would not hang a dog; we may dismiss from our minds the infamous one to an admirer in which she is

[13] St. Géran, Françoise Madeleine Claude de Warignies, Comtesse de, 1655–1733.

made to say that she hates poverty more than she loves virtue: or those in which she sniggeringly confides to her dear St. Géran that she sends the king away "always rebuffed, but never despairing;" and, too, her cynical letter on the forcible conversion of the Huguenots after the Revocation of the Edict of Nantes.

Much, indeed most, of the evidence for the defence has been destroyed, and it is the more irritating in that we have watched its destruction; towards the end of her life, Mlle. d'Aumale, her secretary, found her one day preparing to burn her vast accumulation of private papers, and pleaded for the retention of at least a selection of it. But it all went to the flames. "I wish to be an enigma to posterity," said Mme. de Maintenon as she supervised the bonfire. Was it all evidence for the defence, one wonders? Or did it include faded letters from the long dead Villarceaux,[14] assignations, borrowings of Ninon de l'Enclos'[15] too famous yellow room, proof of any or all the charges upon which we stumble in the dark and dirty labyrinth of *La France Galante* and *L'Histoire Amoureuse des Gaules?* We shall never know. To those who endeavour to explore the lumber rooms of history, she can be as exasperating as a living person; how many clues lead one to that locked door, in front of which stands the reserved beautiful woman with the faint unfathomed smile, who remains, as she wished to be, an enigma to posterity.

It turned out to be unexpectedly difficult to get Mme. Scarron to undertake the duties designed for her; there was much coming and going of mysterious ambassadors, many doubts and hesitations. But from the outset, Mme. Scarron did not waver: if the child were that of a subject, then she would not take charge of it: if the king ordered her to take charge of his children, she would obey him. The distinction may seem to us somewhat pettifogging; but we must remember that the secret was a jealously guarded one, that Mme. Scarron lived obscurely and remote from Court intrigue, and that it was generally supposed by outsiders that Mme. de Montespan

[14] VILLARCEAUX, Louis de Mornay, 1st Marquis de, ob. 1691, witty libertine, seduced his *fiancée* at age of twenty; lived with Ninon de L'Enclos, 1652–5; sent to the Bastille, 1660; severely snubbed by Louis XIV, 1671, for offering to procure his own niece for his use.

[15] L'ENCLOS, NINON DE, 1620–1705, most famous courtesan of her day, but also the friend of everyone worth knowing in France.

had deserted her husband for de Lauzun, who, as we have seen, was in fact the king's confidant in his intrigue. In the finish, Louis was forced to see Mme. Scarron himself and give her an order to take charge of the child; and here we get our first glimpse of Mme. Scarron's deferential inflexibility. Not a move from her so long as there was any doubt of the paternity of the child, and the king manoeuvred into a position in which he had virtually to admit to her with his own lips that he was the father. When details of the transaction became public, society applauded the nicety of Mme. Scarron's tact and virtue in a difficult situation, odd though it seems to us today; to have taken charge of the bastards of a courtier would have been to degrade her own nobility, and might even have been inferentially damaging to her dearly prized reputation. But to be Governess of the Bastards of France was quite another matter; it was, to be sure, regrettable that their mother was a married woman. But, after all, the king was the king, holding an intermediate rank between God and man, and was accountable to God alone. The holder of an appointment in the entourage of a Bastard of France aroused no other emotion at Court than that of envy.

And so Mme. Scarron was installed as governess of the secret nurseries, to which came a little girl in 1669, followed by the Duc du Maine in 1670, the Cte. de Vexin in 1672,[16] Mlle. de Nantes in 1673[17] and Mlle. de Tours in 1674.[18]

The most superficial dabbler in the seventeenth century cannot fail to grasp as one of its obvious features, the amazing physical energy of its inhabitants. Pepys is the English exemplar who comes most readily to mind, but between 1670 and 1674 Mme. Scarron led a life from which even Pepys might have recoiled. Her duties would have been sufficiently exhausting had the children been all in one house, but as an additional precaution for securing secrecy

[16] Vexin, Louis César de Bourbon, Cte de, 1672–1683.

[17] *Duchesse, Mme. La*, Louise Françoise de Bourbon, Duchesse de Bourbon, 1673-1743. Married the Duc de Bourbon, known at Court as *M. le Duc*, 1685; was the liveliest of the family, and in frequent disgrace with the king; by 1697 was the mistress of Prince de Conti; king paid her debts in 1699, and again in 1700; intimate friend of *Monseigneur* (The Dauphin); in love with Marquis de Lassay, 1711; favourite sister of the Duc du Maine; on more familiar terms with the king than any of his other children.

[18] Tours, Louise Marie Anne de Bourbon, Mlle. de, 1674–81.

each child had a house of its own, and these houses were scattered round the suburbs, with the unfortunate governess in control of all. As soon as Mme. de Montespan was about to give birth to a child, Mme. Scarron would be sent for, the infant would be handed over to her, hidden in a shawl, and the masked governess would return to Paris in a hackney cab, in terror of discovery. But her troubles were then only beginning:

"Often she would be up fourteen or fifteen times in a night; she would watch, to let the nurses sleep . . . and in order that her friends might suspect nothing, it was necessary for her to see them as usual: having run about all night from house to house, she would appear in the morning as after a good night's rest (Mlle. d'Aumale)."

But strive as she would, there were suspicions, and as early as the winter of 1672 her sharp-witted friend Mme. de Sévigné had her doubts–"Mme. Scarron's life is an astonishing one," she cries, "no mortal, without exception, has any intercourse with her. I have had a letter from her, but I take good care to say nothing about it, for fear of the innumerable questions I should be asked."

Even manual labour was not spared her in the effort to preserve the secret; listen to her own account of these early days:

"This singular honour cost me infinite pains and trouble. I had to climb ladders and do the work of upholsterers and other tradespeople, whom I was not allowed to let into the house. I did everything, the nurses refusing to turn their hands to anything in case they should tire themselves and spoil their milk. I often had to go on foot, and in disguise, from nurse to nurse, carrying clean linen and food. I sometimes was up all night with one of the children who was ill; then in the morning, I would slip into my own house by the back door, dress, enter my carriage, and be driven to the Hôtel d'Albret or the Hôtel de Richelieu, so that no one would even suspect that I had a secret to keep. People wondered why I was growing thin."

It was not until 1673 that this extraordinary life ceased; by then the secret was, to the initiated, a secret no longer, and the whole family was transferred with Mme. Scarron to a house at the end of the Rue Vaugirard, which then stood practically in the open country. But Mme. Scarron's troubles were by no means over; there was constant sickness in the royal nursery, and the sufferers were lovingly tended by the governess; in 1672 the first little girl died, and

Mme. Scarron, says her niece, "felt it like a mother, and much more than the real mother." Did the real mother, one wonders, feel a chill of apprehension when the king returned from seeing the depth of the governess's sorrow at the death of his child? "She knows how to love," said Louis to his mistress, "there would be great pleasure in being loved by her."

But from this grief Mme. Scarron soon recovered; little girls of three, even when they were bar-sinister royalties, were not very important in seventeenth-century France, and already her favourite was the Duc du Maine, whom she really loved as a mother, and whom she continued to love all her life. In this year, at the mature age of two and a half, the Duc du Maine makes his first public appearance; it must have been an exciting day in the Rue Vaugirard, for Maine's sister, Mlle. de Nantes, was the other participant in the day's ceremony, namely her christening, with her brother as godfather. How the two children behaved on that 18th of December at the church of St. Sulpice we do not know, but Maine's part was evidently purely formal, for we note that he had as proxy "messire Dandin, priest."

To christen Mlle. de Nantes was a simple enough matter: the trouble came later, when the baptismal certificate had to be filled in. Whose child was Mlle. de Nantes? What was the name of the godfather? In point of fact these questions proved unanswerable, and remained unanswered; the certificate still exists, and on it we read that Mlle. de Nantes, christened Louise Françoise, is born of "blank," and that Louis Auguste "blank" is the godfather. Indeed, legally speaking, two more days were to pass before Mme. Scarron's charges can be said to have been born; it was not until the 20th of December that the Parlement registered Letters of Legitimization in which the titles by which they are known to history were conferred upon them, and in which the difficulty about Mme. de Montespan was simply evaded by not mentioning her at all–"The natural love which we bear our children, and many other reasons . . . obliges us to recognize . . ." So runs the preamble.

With their legitimization came some relaxation of the secrecy which had surrounded their existence; in this same month of

December we find Mme. Scarron one of a supper party, which included Mme. de Sévigné, who remarks what fun she had in taking the governess home to the Rue Vaugirard,

"a large and beautiful house, in the open country: no one allowed into it: there is a big garden, handsome, large rooms: she keeps a carriage and pair: dresses modestly and magnificently, like a woman who lives among people of quality."

Before the end of the month the Duc du Maine had what we may call a dress rehearsal for his presentation to the great world. "No one," says Mme. de Sévigné, "has yet seen the little princes, but the eldest has spent three days with his father and mother; they say he is a pretty child, but no one has seen him." We can imagine from personal recollection the sort of trouble that Mme. Scarron must have taken to ensure that her favourite made a good impression at Court–the innumerable "don'ts," the dressing in his very best, the curling, combing, perhaps even washing; for washing was coming into favour, and the king his father washed his hands every morning and occasionally his face. At any rate the visit was such a success that Louis decided to close the establishment in the Rue Vaugirard, and before the summer of 1674 the duke, his governess, and his sisters were installed in Mme. de Montespan's suite at Court. The mother, whose interest in her family was both intermittent and capricious, seems to have troubled herself very little about the move, and it fell to the lot of the devoted Mme. Scarron to wind up the old establishment, and to keep an eye on the former servants. A letter to her confessor, doubtless only one of many on this subject, survives;

"You will remember that when Mme. Barri, the nurse, left us, you and I asked her what she wanted, and she got 3,000 francs, with which she was going to do marvels; this of course has all gone, and she has since had 200 francs a year and frequent other help. But she is again dying of hunger, and to get rid of her continual importunities, here are 200 pistoles[19] for her; but as this is positively the last time, see if you cannot find some means to lay out the money usefully."

But the trials of closing down the Rue Vaugirard house were trifles compared with the grief and anxiety which came upon her

[19] Spanish gold coin worth about 16s., and accepted as legal tender in France.

with the disastrous illness of "my little prince" in this year; an illness, painful in itself, ultimately found to be incurable, which was to have a profound psychological effect on Maine for the rest of his life. Whether the contemporary account can be accepted by the modern physician I do not know, but the result of the complaint was that the boy entered on his fourth year permanently lame;

"M. le Duc du Maine was born straight and well made, and remained so until he was three years old, when in getting his back teeth he fell into such terrible convulsions that one of his legs grew much shorter than the other."

All that money could do was of course done, but the Paris Faculty had to admit itself baffled, and as a last resort the duke was sent under Mme. Scarron's care in the spring of 1674 to consult a famous quack at Antwerp. It is pleasant to know that the child was well enough to enjoy the journey, as indeed what child would not? To travel day after day in a coach, catching a first glimpse of the world outside his nursery, the highways with his father's marching soldiers, the inn or country house at nightfall, the corn-laden lands a green sea in the spring sunlight, the great and famous cities of Flanders. For the first and last time in his life he travelled as a private individual; the king had decided that the incognito was to be preserved outside his own frontiers, and Mme. Scarron had become for the occasion the Marquise de Surgères from Poitou, travelling with her invalid son. If there was in this masquerade a liberty keenly enjoyed by both child and governess, there would also be drawbacks; true, there would be no tedious receptions and visits of compliment to the tired travellers in the evenings, but on the other hand there would be no carefully prepared lodgings awaiting them at the day's end. And taking pot luck with a country noble for the night was a venturesome experiment; certainly all along the roads of Europe, one gentleman's house was as freely open to another as was an inn, but the country gentleman was, generally speaking, not rich, and the spirit of hospitality would often be more evident than its substance.

The visit to Antwerp was a failure, accomplishing nothing but a considerable amount of suffering for the unlucky child, and sending him home to France as crippled as when he set out. Few records of the journey remain, once we have deducted the letter supplied by the ingenious La Beaumelle, but there is one significant glimpse of the care and love which protected the little Louis Auguste; Mme. de Scarron herself was fond of telling in after years how the Antwerp quack, when asked for the names of the mysterious foreigners, replied that he could not say anything about them except that it was obvious that the woman with the young nobleman was really his mother. By the beginning of the summer they were back at Court, where Maine's health was a source of constant anxiety; and Mme. Scarron, in the midst of her trouble, finds time to laugh at herself for giving so much love to a child who is not her own, and whom she will never have to settle in life. But if his health was unsatisfactory, the duke was rapidly progressing in mind; he was, as he could hardly help being, beautiful and precocious, and he already showed signs of having inherited something of his father's conversational charm and quickness. The king adored him, and it was said on all sides that the pupil of Mme. Scarron showed much more promise than the pupil of Bossuet, the thirteen-year-old Dauphin;[20] it was a point on which king and governess saw eye to eye, and it was in their tête-à-tête admiration of their beloved Duc du Maine that Louis finally disabused his mind of the unflattering idea which he had entertained of Mme. Scarron. In September 1674 they are both overjoyed to find that he is a little better, and by the end of the month they are persuading each other that he is in perfect health.

Already his education was engaging their serious attention, both somewhat hampered by the butterfly Mme. de Montespan, who, normally not concerning herself with the matter at all, would occasionally intervene to upset their plans, and was particularly anxious that all expense should be avoided; one suspects that jealousy of the governess rather than interest in her children prompted her random incursions into the educational sphere. "One rails at the friend," writes Mme. de Sévigné in 1675, "for having too much friendship for the governess . . . this secret rolls underground for

[20] Dauphin, Louis de France, known at Court as *Monseigneur*, 1661–1711; was completely effaced by his father and played a secondary rôle all his life.

the last six months." What picture can we recapture now of nursery life in the France of the seventeenth century? No world changes less in externals than that of the nursery, and toys at least seem to have been much the same since the earliest days. We have a list of those belonging to the Dauphin, afterwards Louis XIII, in the first decade of the century, and those of the Duc du Maine must have been very similar–a complete suit of toy armour, bows and arrows, a small arquebus for shooting sparrows, cannon made of cardboard or silver, soldiers of lead, wood, and earthenware: a black horse with a soldier upon it: a Turkish trumpeter, mounted: and a model house furnishing. Doll's houses were in good demand, and at least one survives, which, with its vast kitchen and heavily worked furniture in the salon, looks very realistic. In the garden there would be swings and see-saws to say nothing of outdoor games; and, if you were a Duc du Maine, you would no doubt be able to borrow the services of a sergeant of the Guards to help you construct a model fortified city which you could attack or defend, as had been the favourite outdoor play of the child Louis XIV. In the winter evenings the children and grown-ups would join in playing blind man's buff, then a favourite adult game, often played at Court in Louis' younger days. Tips, I imagine, would be plentiful from papa, who was always a generous man in that sort of way, and probably there would be further money presents from courtiers anxious to salute the rising sun; and money would come in very handy in days when, by our standards, the price of toys seems to have been exorbitant. Naturally we do not often come across figures, but we know that Condé,[21] at a time when his finances were in great disorder, gave two thousand crowns–say five hundred pounds–for a doll's house for his daughter.[22] It is to be hoped for Maine's sake that soldiers were cheaper than doll's houses, or alternatively that he did not have to buy his own. Illness and lessons, those twin bugbears of childhood, the boy had in full measure; but he was extraordinarily quick-witted, and his lessons do not seem to have troubled him overmuch: he being lucky in that in his early years they were given

[21] Condé, Louis II de Bourbon, 4th Prince de, 1621–86, known at Court as *M. Le Prince*, and popularly as *M. Le Heros*; next to Turenne, the foremost soldier of his day.
[22] Bourbon, Mlle. de, 1656–60.

him by Mme. de Maintenon,[23] according to a modern critic "the greatest nursery governess the world has ever seen." From his earliest youth he was brought up on the fundamental rules which were later to make the name of St. Cyr, first that you must speak to a child as reasonably as you would to an adult, and secondly, that while you must enter whole-heartedly into its amusements, there must be no assumption of baby talk or manners: on the contrary, the child must always be brought up to the adult level by addressing it as a reasonable being. To this rule we may no doubt attribute Maine's precocity, which so delighted the Court. At about this time, his father desired to see him quite alone, without his usual retinue of nurses, or even his governess; the duke did not cry, and without any signs of fright spoke so apropos on all sorts of subjects that Louis was delighted. "How could I not be reasonable when Mme. de Maintenon is reason itself?" said the little duke in answer to his father's congratulations. And if the king improved the reply in telling the story, which sounds suspiciously likely, there still remains a picture of a remarkably self-possessed little boy.

But overshadowing everything else was the constant anxiety of the father and the governess about the duke's health. In November 1674 a new English doctor was called in, of whom much was hoped, but in the following month the child was a pitiable object, having a quartan ague, a bad cold, and an open abscess. By the end of the month he was worse, and Mme. de Maintenon writes to M. Le Ragois, his newly-appointed tutor, to say that all projects for his education must for the time being be abandoned. There was no improvement during the rest of the winter, and in the spring of 1675 it was decided that he should be taken by Mme. de Maintenon to the waters of Barèges, a little town in the extreme south of France, in sight of the Pyrenees. She set out with her charge on 28th April, and on 8th May she writes from Mantelan,

"We travelled until yesterday without any bother, at least so far as I was concerned. M. le Duc du Maine had one of his feverish turns, but today

[23] MAINTENON, Marquise de; in 1674 Louis XIV expressed his gratitude to Mme. Scarron for her care of his bastards by giving her the money with which to purchase the Marquisate of Maintenon. Henceforward, Mme. Scarron is the Marquise de Maintenon, and will be so referred to from now onwards.

he is perfectly well again. . . . M. le Duc du Maine is delightful company; he needs continual care, and my tenderness for him makes this very pleasant to me. The Almoner does not see me often, as he travels in the second carriage: all the better, and I have more pleasure in seeing his expression, according to the goodness or badness of the inns, than I would have in listening to his grievances. He piques himself in not succumbing under the fatigue of a journey made in the depths of a carriage, doing three hours in the morning, and the same after dinner, finding meals ready for him everywhere. I hear Mass before we start, so as to facilitate his breakfast arrangements, for he complains of the heat of his blood, and the devouring nature of his stomach. I do not know what his stomach does, but I do know that he devours his food. His nose began to bleed the other day . . . which gave him a great fright."

By the 20th she has got her convoy as far as Pons, and is in a depressed mood; the servants are sick, the Almoner thinks he is going to be sick, and she cannot get half-an-hour to herself. But by the 28th, when they are south of Bordeaux, she writes in better spirits:

"The weather is lovely, we have everything we want, and if nothing unexpected happens, I shall regard this as a less tiring journey than that from Paris to Versailles. We are received everywhere as if we were the King himself, and I must admit that Guyenne could not have surpassed itself in its demonstrations of joy . . . we were nearly stifled with caresses at Poictiers. M. le Duc de St. Simon entertained us magnificently at Blaye[24], and the magistrates of Bordeaux came to fetch us in a gorgeous boat; one of our train was drowned whilst we were embarking, and the Almoner thought it a flying in the face of providence not to take warning by this example. We travelled very pleasantly with forty rowers, and when we came in sight of the city, more boats came out to meet us, some full of violins, the others of trumpets; as we got closer in, nothing could be more beautiful than all the cannon of the Château Trompette and those of the ships which followed us, and the shouts of *Vive le Roi* from the infinite crowds of people on the river bank. M. le Maréchal d'Albret,[25] who came to meet us at Pons, conducted our prince, who was received by M. de Montégu and all the magistrates, who made him a complimentary speech. Then we got into a carriage, with a hundred others following us; we were more than an hour in going from the bridge to the house. . . ."

The mask is off with a vengeance now. Consider the contrast with the journey of the pretended Marquise de Surgères and her son to

[24] St. Simon, Claude de Rouvroy, 1st Duc de, 1606–93; father of the famous author of the memoirs.

[25] Albret, César Phoebus de Pons, Maréchal d', 1614–76.

Antwerp in the previous year: as Mme. de Maintenon says with perfect truth, if it had been Louis XIV himself, the reception could not have been more pompous, more enthusiastic. It sounds odd to modern ears, this reception of the bastard child of an unacknowledged mother, but there can be no doubt of its spontaneity. This was how the people felt; he was the son of their adored king, this handsome, polite little boy had in his veins the sacred blood of France, and the nation at large made very little distinction between a legitimate and an illegitimate prince. It is the fashion to hold up one's hands these days at the Asiatic arrogance with which Louis XIV imposed his bastards on France. Louis, we are told, fashioned France to his liking; but the more we look into the matter, the clearer it becomes that France fashioned Louis just as much as Louis fashioned France. We have seen his efforts to keep the existence of his bastards a family secret; so far from being anxious to elevate them, he was at first reluctant to do so, and subsequently never promoted them a step in advance of what public opinion would stand. Had not the reception of the Duc du Maine throughout France in 1675 encouraged him to proceed, it is very unlikely that any of these children would ever have emerged from a position of privileged obscurity.

On 20th June the travellers reached Barèges, their destination, after eight weeks on the road. "It did not take me so long to go to America," says Mme. de Maintenon, who goes on to remark, "We have begun to bathe our prince, who so far is neither the better nor the worse for it; it is too early to judge. I have seen (various people) but everywhere was so overwhelmed with honours paid to M. le Duc du Maine that I had no strength left to talk to people whom I could treat without ceremony." On 8th July she is having trouble with the servants: "All the girls are always sick; they are real cockneys, who begin to find the world altogether too big a a place once they are past Étampes." By the time the treatment is finished, her anxious love for her pupil has persuaded her that he is much better, and soon she is on her way northwards again. On 16th October, whilst passing through her native province, she writes to her brother that everywhere she hears around her the accent of Poitou, which makes all company good company, and that, to crown everything, the prince is better:

"M. le Duc du Maine can walk, and though not very vigorously, there is reason to hope that he will walk as well as anyone else. You cannot know all the affection I feel for him, but you can understand it sufficiently to know how happy I am that the trip has been such a success."

By the 28th the travellers had arrived at Richelieu, and Versailles was reached on 5th November–"No surprise could have been more agreeable to the king," says Mme. de Sévigné; "he did not expect M. le Duc du Maine until the following day, and when he saw him come into his room, led by the hand by Mme. de Maintenon, he was in a transport of joy."

3. *The Infant Phenomenon*

THE Duc du Maine was delighted to be home again; he was tired of the interminable roads, receptions, harangues from groups of solemn old men, baths, a little tired perhaps even of the loving vigilance of his governess; eager for the company of his father and the flattery of the Court. He was in high spirits, and the general verdict of society was that he had come home more of a prodigy than ever; he was even something of a hero, for in those days not one person in ten knew where Barèges was, and those who did, understood that it was in sight of mountains—regarded in the seventeenth century as objects of horror—and approached by "dreadful footpaths." Maine had made a new watering place the fashion.

Such an acute little boy must speedily have discovered that the home to which he had returned was not that which he had left; on the surface, things were much the same, but the atmosphere had changed. Sharp grown-up voices would darken his play, the sun would go in, and a chill breeze blow through the nursery; he would be roughly spoken to for no apparent reason; there would be a lurking insecurity and discomfort in his daily life, of which he would be intermittently but acutely aware. In short, his father and mother did not stand in the same relation to each other as they had done.

The trouble had begun in Holy Week, which in 1675 fell in mid-April. Mme. de Montespan was a Christian, even a devout one, of a rather odd kind. She had failed to kill a most inconvenient conscience and she had viewed the approach of Easter with profound misgivings; she wanted, in her own words, "a broad-minded confessor." In fact, like so many of us, she wanted an impossibility; she wanted to continue to live in mortal sin, and she wanted to receive absolution for so doing. She probably would not have got absolution, even from a Court confessor, but she made the mistake, surprising for so clever a woman, of thinking that a village curé, dazzled by her position, would make no difficulties. Her chambermaid praised the "broad mindedness" of one Lecuyer–all honour to his name, let us preserve it–who was the priest of the village church at Versailles. But the result was both unexpected and humiliating; on learning the name of his penitent, the priest asked her angrily if she was that Mme. de Montespan who was scandalizing all France: and bade her go away and repent of her sins before throwing herself at the feet of Christ's minister. Mme. de Montespan went away, but it was at the king's feet that she threw herself in an agony of rage, humiliation, and furious prayers for vengeance. This was a second and worse mistake; she ought to have known her lover better, to have realized that the man who had allowed Mascaron to preach a devastating sermon on the sin of adultery before him and his whole Court a few years earlier, was not in the least likely to resort to an exercise of unjust and arbitrary power in such a case as this; indeed, had she not been so blinded with rage, she might have paused to appreciate the significance of the fact that this same Mascaron[1] stood unrebuked for a sermon preached at Versailles only a month earlier, in which he had told the king, flushed with his easy victory over the Dutch, that a hero was a robber who did at the head of an army that which an ordinary robber does single-handed. All that Louis could be got to promise was that he would consult Bossuet.[2] Bossuet not only supported the parish priest, but very bluntly gave the king to understand that the case involved not one, but two mortal sinners and that so far as he, Bossuet, was concerned, a separation was the absolutely indispensable preliminary to either of them being allowed to receive the Sacrament. Louis had many faults, but an indifference to the distinction between right and wrong was not one of them. That he was a sinner, and a sinner whose example had already done infinite harm, he was well aware;

[1] MASCARON, Jules, 1634–1703; born at Marseilles, Oratorian and popular Parisian preacher by 1671; much a favourite of Louis XIV; Bishop of Agen, 1679.

[2] BOSSUET, Jacques Bénigne, 1627–1704; famous preacher and ecclesiastical writer, theologian, leader of the Gallican party; ordained 1653; Bishop of Condom, 1669; tutor to *Monseigneur,* 1670; Bishop of Meaux, 1681.

his mother had instilled into him, if not exactly a love of God, at least a very real fear of the Devil, which he never lost, and the great festivals of the Church found him remorseful, troubled at the prospect of not making his devotions at all, or of making them in a very unsatisfactory state. After a few days of reflection Louis commissioned Bossuet to tell Mme. de Montespan that they must part; he communicated on Easter Day, 14th April 1675; Mme. de Montespan too, made her Easter communion and then retired to her suburban house, Clagny; Louis left for the front on 10th May; and on the 28th Mme. de Maintenon left for Barèges with the Duc du Maine.

But, alas for good resolutions. As the dull weeks wore on, Mme. de Montespan grew more and more conscious of all that she had lost, more and more indifferent to her eternal gains. She had ascertained that Harlay,[3] the Archbishop of Paris, who was indeed not in a position to throw stones, was prepared to take what we now call a "realist" view of the situation, and that Father La Chaise,[4] the king's confessor, might be trusted to carry out his spiritual duties with a measure of discretion. In fact, if she could recover her position at Versailles, it seemed possible that she might still reign there, and with a conscience at rest. There was no doubt that Louis still desired her, and he was at headquarters in the field, far removed from the formidable influence of Bossuet. What letters or intermediaries passed between the two, we do not know, but the king's return from the front in the latter part of the summer was preceded by orders from him that Mme. de Montespan was to be at Versailles on his arrival. Bossuet made a last effort; he met the king on the road, eight leagues from Versailles, "with a religious sadness on his countenance." But he was not even allowed to expostulate by Louis, who was in his most arrogant mood—"Monsieur, words are wasted. I have given my orders, and they will be carried out."

In the newly completed château of Versailles, the king himself

[3] Harlay, François de Chanvallon, 1625–95.

[4] La Chaise, François d'Aix, Father, S.J., 1624–1709, son of an army officer, became confessor to Louis XIV, c. 1677; the king was first attracted to him by their both being medal collectors; married Louis and Mme. de Maintenon, 1684.

allotted the accommodation; Mme. de Montespan received twenty rooms on the first floor, and the king's wife sixteen on the second.

But we must be charitable enough to remember that in Louis' case at any rate the new arrangement was intended to be very different from the old one. There were to be no sexual relations between him and Mme. de Montespan; he was never going to see his former mistress alone in any circumstances, but always in a room full of people. He had remembered that Mme. de Montespan was the holder of a Court appointment, and to banish her from a salaried post because she had fallen in love with him would be an act of gross injustice. Moderation in all things. Why should she not live at Court, asked the needy Mortemart relations; her birth entitles her to live there, and she can live as Christian a life at Versailles as anywhere else.

And so the new arrangement came into force, inaugurated with much solemn publicity; a day was appointed for the king to visit Mme. de Montespan in her apartments; and, in order that slander should not have the slightest material to feed on, it was agreed that the gravest and most respectable matrons of the Court should be witnesses of the interview. The king arrived, there was a little general conversation; then he started to chat with Mme. de Montespan, whom, as it were insensibly, he drew into the window; the two spoke in low voices for a time, and were observed to shed tears; and after a few minutes, Louis bowed to the ladies, Mme. de Montespan dropped a curtsey, and the pair withdrew into Mme. de Montespan's bedroom. "The result," says Mme. de Caylus[5] airily, "of this famous meeting was the Duchesse d'Orléans[6] and later on the Cte. de Toulouse."[7]

So the new scheme turned out to be the old scheme after all, but the old scheme with a difference. Things could never be as they had been before that meddlesome Bossuet with his tiresome, nay terrible talent for unforgettable speech, had intervened at Easter. Each now

[5] Caylus, Marthe Marguerite Le Valois, daughter of Philippe Le Valois and Marie Anne Hyppolite de Châteauneuf, 1673–1765; distant relation of Mme. de Maintenon, by whom she was brought up.

[6] Orléans, Louise Françoise de Bourbon, Duchesse d', 1677–1743.

[7] Toulouse, Louis Alexandre de Bourbon, Cte. de, 1678–1737.

saw daily in the other, sin wilfully persisted in; "It is not so much my fault as yours," must have been in each heart. The quarrels were more frequent, the reconciliations more perfunctory and less enduring. The significant blindness of the royal confessor was apparently not all that was necessary for a quiet conscience, though Mme. de Montespan nicknamed him *La Chaise de Commodité* and all France laughed. But the laughter brought no ease to the king's soul.

Louis' preoccupations, however, were by no means entirely domestic during these years, for as we see, he is at war again, this time against the Dutch. The Franco-Dutch War of 1672–78 is usually described as one of wanton aggression on the part of Louis XIV, and so it certainly was, but it was not a case in which he acted in opposition to public opinion; on the contrary, the whole country was enthusiastically behind him in his onslaught on that republic. For a variety of reasons: to begin with, society in general had never forgiven Holland, then its ally, for making a separate peace with the Hapsburgs in 1648, leaving France to fight single-handed against the common foe for another eleven years; and to this grievance had been added that of the Dutch interference with Louis' expansionist schemes in the Devolution War. Colbert, with his influential and rapidly expanding Civil Service, was engaged in a losing trade war with Holland all over the world; and if the Dutch won it, what became of the Colbert creed that a planned economy, by its superior efficiency, would always undersell free enterprise? To abandon his theories or to see them proved erroneous was impossible: he voted for the only way out of the difficulty, the military destruction of free enterprise. The Home Office disliked the Dutch because they had a free press, given to pungent criticism of France and the French: the Church disliked them because of the support and refuge they gave to French Protestants: and every Frenchman disliked them because they were the wealthiest nation in Europe, with a standard of living incomparably higher than that of their neighbours. Finally, the nobility, living in enforced idleness, joyously welcomed the prospect of any war with anybody.

On 23rd April 1672 Louis and Turenne launched their magnificent army of 120,000 men against Holland, which had, to oppose the torrent, 25,000 ill-paid, ill-trained, ill-led troops. And at first all went well for Louis; he forced the Rhine crossings without difficulty and spread over Holland, which, to save Amsterdam itself, had to play its traditional last card. The country was flooded, and the French advance checked; but by July, Louis was master of three of the seven provinces of the republic. However, when the king took the field in 1673, he was confronted with the problem of accelerating the tempo of a blitzkrieg which had already lost its initial momentum, and this turned out to be impossible; not only owing to the state of the ground, but because Europe was at last awake to its danger, and the Empire, Spain, Denmark and Lorraine were marching to the support of Holland. Politically, too, the tide had turned, for one result of Louis' aggression had been the downfall of de Witt and his replacement by William of Orange, the implacable enemy of the French king. Even so, the allies barely held their own against the might of France, and, though Louis failed in his attempt to make Holland a vassal state he and his country emerged from the war with an increased prestige and substantial gains; by the Peace of Nimeguen in 1678 Holland indeed got off lightly, but Louis secured a line of fortresses running from Dunkirk to the Meuse, the Spanish province of Franche Comté (for the second time), and a spring-board on the Rhine at Brisach, handy for invading the Empire when the fancy took him.

But let us leave these high matters and return to the château of St. Germain in the summer of 1676, from where Mme. de Maintenon is hinting in her tight-lipped way that the little Duc du Maine is becoming something of a handful.

"I had hoped that being here without Mme. de Montespan, I should have got some rest; but I am having almost as much trouble as if she were here. We shall soon have M. le Ragois, which will be a relief to me."

M. le Ragois, we may remember, is the duke's tutor, and it looks as if, owing to Maine's health, he had not yet taken up his duties. And indeed it seems as if the tutor was successfully evaded for the rest of the year, for while his arrival is often looked for, he never seems to materialize. By July the Court had reassembled at Versailles, the king back from the front, Mme. de Montespan home from the waters of Bourbon, "astonishingly beautiful," but complaining that her cure, instead of curing one sore knee, had given her two; and of course Maine and Mme. de Maintenon were back from St. Germain. The boy was much in the limelight in that summer—"incomparable"—"astonishing wit"—"you cannot imagine the things he says"—thus runs the breathless chatter of the ladies. So women have always talked about children, and so they always will, but in fact we have no trouble in imagining the flushed, excited, happy child, with his shrill voice, showing off to his heart's content in the middle of a circle of admiring women. The weather was glorious, and there were lots of exciting things to do, as for instance to attend a supper served on board gondolas in the canal on an August evening when the boy was in the highest spirits. Papa still keeps up some faint show of mystification about Maine's history: "he is discouraged from addressing the King as papa." One can see the half smiling frown with which this mode of address is discouraged in the royal gondola: whereupon the prince fills his glass, and, laughing wildly, drains it to "the health of the King, my father," then buries himself in Mme. de Maintenon's arms.

We hear nothing of the duke's doings again until May 1677, when he and his mother are the guests of his governess at Maintenon, where Mme. de Montespan had gone in great secrecy to give birth to the future Duchesse d'Orléans; it is worth noting in passing, as an illustration of how Mme. de Maintenon's credit had grown in the last seven years, that she flatly refused to take charge of Louis' post-reconciliation family, which was brought up with all the old secrecy in the Rue Vaugirard by Mme. de Louvois.[8]

Throughout May, Mmes. de Montespan and Maintenon were engaged in a duel of wits at Maintenon; the duke was to go to the Pyrenees again this summer, and Mme. de Montespan, whose jealousy of the governess was increasing, was anxious that they should start before the king's return from the front. But it was Mme. de Maintenon who won the battle, and when the king

[8] Louvois, Anne de Souvré, Marquise de, 1646–1715, daughter of Charles, 5th Marquis de Souvré, married the Marquis de Louvois, 1662.

returned on 1st May, his son was at Court to welcome him. But his holiday with "mon papa" was a short one, for on 8th June, with all the usual retinue, he and Mme. de Maintenon set out once more on the long road to Barèges. On the 12th they were lodged at Fontevrault with the abbess, Mme. de Montespan's sister,[9] lovely and learned, whose favourite reading was Homer, and who was engaged in the translation of Plato from the original Greek. Coignac, of which town Mme. de Maintenon's brother, the Cte. d'Aubigné,[10] was governor, is on their itinerary, and from Fontevrault she writes to concert with him how they are to manage about the hospitality which he must offer them:

"Let me know in advance how you want to receive us . . . we have a lot of servants who are difficult to please. Do you count on us stopping in the château, I mean the prince and myself? Is there handy hotel accommodation for all the train? Would it be better if we all put up at an hotel, and you just gave us dinner on the day we intend to be there? Do not fail to come out a league or two from Coignac to meet the prince. He and I have our beds with us, so you do not need to bother about furniture. He has with him M. Fagon,[11] M. le Ragois, his tutor, an almoner, six valets de chambre, and all sorts of people. I have three women . . . the prince and I sleep in the same room."

We do not know how the reception at Coignac went off, but we do know our M. d'Aubigné, and we may feel tolerably certain that either his sister or the king ultimately paid liberally for any expense to which he had been put in the matter. By 30th July the prince has reached Barèges again, and Mme. de Maintenon is able to take stock of the tutor, who has at last entered upon his duties; and is relieved to find him one of the best of men, very honest, and a man whose good and upright maxims will be valuable to his pupil. It was time for a tutor to take a hand in Maine's improvement, for clearly Mme. de Maintenon is discovering that the boy is getting beyond feminine

[9] FONTEVRAULT, Marie Madeleine Gabrielle de Rochechouart-Mortemart, Abbesse de, 1645–1704, fourth daughter of the 1st Duc de Mortemart; entered religion (Benedictine), 1671; abbess of Fontevrault, 1671.

[10] AUBIGNÉ, Charles, Cte. d', 1634–1703, Mme. de Maintenon's brother, and, like her, born in Niort gaol; very unsatisfactory officer, and a spendthrift; through his sister's influence, held several minor posts and was granted sundry pensions.

[11] FAGON, Guy Crescent, 1638–1718. Paris lawyer's son; doctor of medicine, 1664; Physician to the Bastards of France, 1677; First Physician to Dauphine, 1680; First Physician to Louis XIV, 1693.

control; the flattery of the Court is beginning to do its work, and she is having to scold the duke for his pride and arrogance. "Look at the king," she says, "there is no politer man at Court: he is not touchy like you." "Yes," was the reply, "but then he is sure of his rank, and I am not sure of mine." Could a seven-year-old child have made this retort? Could he have understood the difficult rank which he held? To us it seems very improbable, but we cannot dismiss the story as invented; the century was an amazingly precocious one, and the evidence of its precocity is not confined to a few tales like this, it meets us at every turn. Bignon,[12] a barrister, published a description of the Holy Land at the age of ten, and *Observations on Roman Antiquities* when he was thirteen; Châteaumorand was nine years old when he fought at the Battle of Southwold Bay in 1672; Torcy,[13] Foreign Secretary to Louis XIV in the closing period of the reign, wrote his private letters in Latin in preference to French when he was eight years old. One could go on multiplying such examples, but they may be generalized into the statement that at an age when the English youth of today is hoping for a place in the school eleven, the French youth under Louis XIV knew that if he was not then amongst the probables for the command of a ship or a regiment, he most likely never would be.

By 22nd August Barèges has been abandoned for Bagnières in the same province, the prince has taken more than half the prescribed course of treatment, and there are the usual hopes of his cure. But his health was still in fact very uncertain; he had been ill on the journey down, at Amboise, and again at Barèges, where he had had fourteen fits of quartan ague, which, "joined to the boredom of the place," had produced a bad effect. Nor was Bagnières doing for him what his advisers hoped. When the fever left him, the old abscess had broken out again, and Mme. de Maintenon was wondering if it would be possible to keep him alive—"and to crown my despair, he is the prettiest creature in the world, whose wit surprises me twenty times a day."

[12] BIGNON, Hiérome I, 1590–1656; "the Cato of France."
[13] TORCY, Jean Baptiste Colbert, Marquis de, 1665–1746; "his usual reading was the Bible, and he knew all the Psalms by heart."

To this year belong the first of his surviving letters, addressed to his mother:

"I was very relieved, beautiful lady, when I saw that you had not forgotten your *mignon*. You know how I like getting letters, and I was delighted to get one from your pretty hand, all full of love. I am going to write to the little Rochefort, but I begin with you, for my heart speaks to me much of you. I beg you, madame, not to let the king forget the *mignon*."

And to the king:

"I was jealous, Sire, of the letter with which you honoured Mme. de Maintenon, for I am so sensitive to the marks of your friendship that I cannot bear that you should bestow it on others. The news I have from the beautiful lady will rouse me to sustain the reputation which I flatter myself I have, there being nothing in the world to me more precious than to be pleasing to your majesty."

As with his *mots*, so with his letters, the suspicion arises, are they his own? Those of us who were lucky enough to begin our education under a governess will look back to letters we wrote in those days to our parents. There was the letter which was frankly a copy of the governess's draft, but there were also those later letters which only a casuist and a literary critic could fairly assign to their real author: letters strongly in the style of the governess, but with a good deal of oneself in them. I think we may safely put these down as "suggested" or "inspired" letters. The next sounds more like a real child's letter, and is addressed to his mother:

"I love you dearly. I am going to tell you the news of the house. I am very contented with Ferrarois, and the same with M. le Ragois: and superlatively with Mme. de Maintenon."

The next, though a genuine letter in the textual sense, suggests Mme. de Maintenon's response to one from Mme. de Montespan, in which the mother had congratulated the prince on his last effort, and had asked for a fuller account of his daily life.

"I am going to tell you all the news of our lodgings to amuse you, and I will write much better when I think it is for you. Mme. de Maintenon sews all day, and, if one would let her do it, would write all night. She works every day at improving me, she hopes to succeed, and so does *le mignon*, who will do what he can to be a sensible man, as he is dying with anxiety to please the king and you. On the journey I read the life of

Caesar, that of Alexander, since I came here, and yesterday I started Pompey. Mme. de Maintenon had the vapours yesterday and only got up for Mass. M. le Ragois is taking the waters . . . M. Fagon gave me the little bath yesterday. I hope he will be more moderate another time, and that I shall not cry so. I bathe in the bath on cool days, and in my room if it is hot. The Almoner continues to be a Tartuffe . . . Lutin is very lazy, and on bad terms with Mme. de Maintenon . . . Hénault is indulgent in all things I need. La Couture does not like lending me Mme. de Maintenon's clothes when I want to dress up as a girl."

The last touch is delightful, whether supplied by Mme. de Maintenon or the writer. Is the Almoner our old friend of 1675 one wonders, or have we got a new one? The public baths appear to have been in the open air, hence his not bathing in them in hot weather. It is a little surprising that he should have enjoyed dressing up as a girl, for he was still in petticoats at the time, as we discover from another letter to his mother, in which he petitions to be breeched, on the ground that petticoats impede his walking. We might have thought that a decision on this last point could have been reached by the governess on the spot, and not by the mother many hundreds of miles away. But that is not how things were done in old France, and we may be sure that the Duc du Maine's request was transmitted through the proper channels to the king himself; at least I think the inference may fairly be drawn from the fact that there still survives a minute from the great king to the great minister, Colbert, conveying the momentous decision–"My daughter of Blois has asked permission to give up wearing her bib. I consent. Signed, LOUIS."

On the 12th September Mme. de Maintenon writes to her brother to say that they are starting on the homeward journey, and will again be passing through Coignac, which they will reach on the 24th, and where they will stay over the 25th: both fast days as she points out propitiatingly. But, she adds, it will be necessary that the prince has meat at his own little table all by himself.

We should like to know more of the duke's doings at Coignac, where he seems to have considered it due to his position as a courtier to fall in love with the ten-year-old Mlle. de Villette-Murçay, his governess's niece; in so doing he showed that his good taste was as precocious as his wit, for the little girl turned into that delightful Comtesse de Caylus, whose *Souvenirs* are amongst the most charming memoirs of the period. He writes to her on the day of their departure, promising to send her his portrait from Paris, so that she may always have her lover before her eyes; and though he never was to be her lover, the two remained friends for the next fifty years.

The change of air and the journey apparently did the duke good, even if the lameness remained, for the early winter brings no bad news of his health: and indeed we hear of him once only again before Christmas, when Mme. de Maintenon writes to her confessor to say that a present to the duke would be favourably received, but advises him to send something other than money, which at Versailles, will simply be thrown away. His Versailles festivities seem to have been too much for Maine, for in January he has been moved to the comparative peace of St. Germain, suffering from intermittent fever and a fistula, but struggling against his troubles with admirable courage. Louis XIV left for the front on 7th February 1678, taking Mme. de Montespan with him, and Maine writes to say how distressed he was at seeing her departure; but adding the great news that the king nodded to him as he was coming out of chapel, and expressing his delight at the honour. In his next letter he promises his mother not to forget to look after her cows while she is away, and we gather that the cows lived at Maintenon, for in the same letter he says that he is looking forward to going there, though he is already a sufficiently accomplished flatterer to hint that when one cannot be with the king, it does not much matter where one is. In writing to the king, we notice with some disgust how completely the boy of eight has already caught the tone of adulation which was now de rigueur; as for instance in his letter of 13th March:

"Sire, if Your Majesty continues to capture towns, I shall grow up very ignorant; for M. le Ragois and I always stop work when the news of a victory arrives, and I only leave off this letter to you in order to make a *feu de joie*."

But throughout the spring, the duke and his governess were engaged on a more important business than the mere routine correspondence of a man of fashion. A great surprise was preparing for his father and mother when they came home from the wars; Maine was correcting and revising his literary compositions for the press. And in due course there appeared an indubitable, real, printed book, bearing the title *Oeuvres d'un auteur de sept ans*. How one envies him. How he must have looked back in later troubled years to those summer months of literary fame. We cannot think of it without a pang, we commoners of a less favoured age, whose juvenile productions circulated in blotched manuscript, with no nearer approach to the dignity of print than a wavering block letter title page in a school exercise book. But Maine, lucky child, appeared in full calf and gilt, doubtless with the Chancellor's licence, the *cum privilegio regis*, and all the rest of it. Eight copies only were printed, of which four were known to exist in 1865, one being in the possession of the Duc de Noailles: doubtless the copy which the author presented to Mme. de Maintenon. The book is something more than a child's plaything, it is a little bit of the history of the grand siècle; Racine wrote the dedicatory epistle, M. le Ragois the preface. Then follow four or five madrigals in honour of the king, Mme. de Montespan, and the author, one of which is attributed to Racine. The body of the work consists of the duke's letters, extracts from history, reflections drawn from his lessons, and a set of maxims of his own composition. To us, the most interesting thing is of course the dedication, which gives a very clear idea of the atmosphere in which a child of his rank grew up, and of the inculcation of the Sun-King cult in the nurseries of aristocratic France. When we see the sort of sentiments proper to a well-educated child of seven, we view with less surprise the France of twenty years later, in which La Feuillade[14] could successfully petition the king to allow him to erect a statue in honour of Louis, before which candles would be perpetually kept burning, and at whose plinth loyal subjects could prostrate themselves. The dedication is nominally to Mme. de Montespan, actually to the king himself, and begins with an appeal for the lady's protection of his works, from the youngest author in France. After touching on the happy circum-

[14] La Feuillade, Louis d'Aubusson, 4th Cte. and 1st Duc de, 1623–91, son of the 2nd Cte. and Isabelle Brachet; in 1666 made an absurd journey to Madrid, to challenge a Spaniard who had spoken slightingly of Louis XIV.

stances of his birth–no irony is apparently intended–he goes on to attribute his own merits to his parents, and then unpacks his wares:

"You will find in the work he offers you, some pretty enough things from ancient history; but he fears that in the throng of marvellous events which have happened in his own times, you will be little touched by anything he can tell you of past centuries. He fears it all the more because he has himself experienced the same thing in his reading. He sometimes finds it strange that men have considered it necessary to learn by heart authors who tell us of happenings so far below those which we can see for ourselves. How is he to be struck with the victories of the Greeks and Romans, and with all that Florus and Justinian tell him? His nurses from the cradle have told him of greater things. They tell him, as a prodigy, of a town which the Greeks took in ten years; he is not seven, and has heard *Te Deums* chanted in France for the taking of more than a hundred towns. All this disgusts him a little with antiquity . . ."

And us, not a little, with the writer of the passage.

We have unfortunately no details about the reception of the great work; Louis was not much of a reader, but this work we may be sure he read, as did anyone else who could come by a copy of it.

1679 is the last year of Maine's childhood, for at ten a man could not with decency remain any longer in leading strings, but passed from the hands of a governess to those of a governor. It seems to have been a singularly placid and uneventful year in his life. In fact only once do we catch sight of him, but this one appearance is satisfactory, as showing that increasing years had not diminished the reputation for wit which he had acquired in his younger days. His latest *mot*, addressed to the Great Condé, delighted the whole Court. The scene is a room at Versailles, Maine and a group of children romping; a door opens, and the terrible eagle face of the old soldier appears–"Less noise, you children," he shouts angrily; blank, dismayed, and guilty silence on the part of the children, until Maine retrieves the situation; he advances and makes his best bow: "Monseigneur, you who have already made so much noise in the world, might show a little indulgence to us children, who have not yet made any." Did he say it? Condé was as assiduous a courtier as the neediest Gascon cadet, and the reader must judge for himself.

At the turn of the year Mme. de Maintenon prepared herself with a heavy heart to hand over her beloved prince. In a letter to

M. de Montchevreuil,[15] his destined governor, dated 23rd January 1680, she gives some advice on the duke's treatment:

"I think I am leaving the prince in good health, and I am going to tell you what I think is needed to keep him so; you will sometimes be hindered, but you will often be the master (a hint I think, that the king spoilt him). He should never have less than nine hours in bed, it is little enough for a child of such a quick and lively temperament as his. Do not force him to eat in the morning if he is not hungry, though it sounds odd to keep a child fasting until two in the afternoon; but he has his supper so late that it is impossible for him to digest it, and it is better for him to reserve himself for his dinner. . . . You will find him accustomed to eat several kinds of soup, and I have always allowed it . . . it is a taste they all inherit from the king, and it is less hurtful than eating a lot of meat without bread. Most women who have charge of children make the mistake of crying out against sweets. They are not unhealthy after a meal, provided one eats them in moderation, and raw fruit is much more harmful. He dines so late that he should never have his *collation* before six; Mme. de Montespan wants them always to eat dry bread, but they all have such bad teeth that they would rather not eat at all than eat that, and when he has made a poor dinner, which happens often, I advise you to let him eat heartily at his *collation* rather than stuff himself with meat at eleven o'clock at night. If you are the master, give him raw fruit when his bowels are in order, but let it be fruits with plenty of water in them, such as pears; peaches and apples are not bad for him. . . . He does not catch cold easily in the open air; but an open door or a draught always gives him one. The sun, or a fire on the back of his head are very dangerous. . . . I forgot to mention that you must take particular care that people do not give him sweets, and that he does not slip sweets into his pocket to eat between meals. Watch the state of his fistula. . . .

"So much for the body, and now for his character. I cannot find any inclination to vice in him; his chief faults are laziness, and that he easily lets himself be discouraged. You must always pique him on the point of honour, and remember to talk to him everywhere and on every subject as if he was twenty years old. Do not be afraid to be familiar with him, and caress him as much as respect and decorum allow. . . . Discourage his chaff with his valets while he is dressing. . . . I expect you will be asked to see that he does not play cards; you yourself have little turn for jeux d' esprit, and while you are picking up that sort of thing, I would like you to turn his leisure thoughts to the subject of war, where you can teach him a thousand things that will be useful to him. Make him take the air as often as you possibly can. I have nothing to say about goodness,

[15] Montchevreuil, Henri de Mornay, 1st Marquis de, 1622–1706, son of the 3rd Seigneur de Montchevreuil; witness to Louis' secret marriage, 1684; Gentleman of the Chamber to Duc du Maine, 1692.

humanity, or liberality, for on those subjects you know more than I do; but be always diligent in setting the king before him as an example; not only do you pay your court in doing so, but you will inspire him with a respect, an esteem, a tenderness which he owes to his father, his king, and his master. Take care not to preach him long sermons; everything must be said in four words as and when the occasion calls for it, without strangers perceiving that you are prompting him, for it is the taste of those with whom you have to deal that everything should appear natural. . . . Lutin and Marcine can be of some use to you at the start; they saw their master born, and they know how I have ruled him, but when you ask them anything, let it always be in private. . . . Always be on your guard before the prince; he is full of discernment which he inherits from the king, and of the Mortemart wit. I should be more frightened of saying or doing a foolish thing in front of him than before anybody I can think of."

The letter inspires us with a good deal of sympathy for Montchevreuil, who is obviously expected to lean pretty heavily on Mme. de Maintenon in the execution of his duties, and who can hardly have been flattered by the blunt passing reference to his own deficiencies; but they were very old friends, and in fact no friction arose.

We have so far taken Maine's education rather for granted, but the time has now come to try to get some idea of what education meant for a boy of good family in the seventeenth century.

Education cannot be criticised in the abstract: we must know the result aimed at before we can consider its efficiency. Now the great object of the education of a French gentleman was to produce an *honnête homme*: not, let us be clear, to be translated "an honest man." The French phrase has a certain ambiguity which makes it easier to recognize an *honnête homme* than to define one. Perhaps Sir William Temple's is as good a definition as we are likely to find– "What we call an honest man, the Romans called a good man; and honesty, in their language, as well as in French, signifies a composition of those qualities which generally acquire honour and esteem to those who possess them." From which it follows that the emphasis in the character of an *honnête homme* rested rather on the social code of the day than on fundamental virtues, and it was lucky for the Duc du Maine and his contemporaries that religion and real piety were living forces in society at the time they were about to enter it. In the opinion of the worst of the worldly "a solid piety" was no bar to the character of *honnête homme*, and in the opinion of the best, it was the foundation of such a character.

But, with all his attractiveness, the *honnête homme* is an unsatisfactory person, for his character is built upon the shifting sand of fashionable manners and not on the rock of permanent values. Religion, or if you prefer it, a fixed code of morality, is not the foundation of the character, but one of its ingredients. "A devout courtier," says La Bruyère in his bitter way, "is a man who, under an impious king, would be an atheist." When we come to the Regency, we are shocked at the *honnête homme* of the Palais Royal, and are inclined to think that nothing remains of the type but the name; on the contrary, the change is perfectly logical. Scepticism had become the tone of good society, so the *honnête homme* was first a sceptic and then a debauchee. The change was of course neither clear-cut nor instantaneous, and there were bad old men, good young men, and coteries which clung to an older ideal. It is to the honour of the duke and his governess that he had been too well grounded in the practice of religion to change after the king's death; he remained a Christian during the Regency, unmoved by the sneers of those who could find nothing more disparaging to say of a man than that he "smelt of the old Court."

What were the qualities which the good tutor would look for, instil, and cultivate in his pupil in the year 1680?

Firstly, physical courage, without which all other inherited or acquired accomplishments would be not only useless, but worse than useless, serving merely to emphasize the lack of the one essential quality. Politeness: a knowledge of the world: piety, or at worst, a scrupulous observance of the externals of religion: an open-handed carelessness, real or simulated, in money matters: conformity to a standard of good taste high enough to enable one to offer intelligent criticism of a cook, a sermon, a jewel, a play, or the layout of a friend's garden. If nature has endowed you with any brains, so much the better, for you will have the much envied gift of being able to say a good thing, or of turning out an acceptable set of drawing room verses. But otherwise, the possession of brains is not a quality to be paraded, still less must you make a show of acquired knowledge; Chavigny, in 1705, published a conversation piece for the guidance of the would-be *honnête homme* which contains this significant bit of dialogue:

"Q. Is it necessary for persons of quality to understand painting, music, and architecture?

A. It is a good thing that they should be instructed in these matters . . . but they must not let it appear that they are skilled in them."

An affectation of amateurishness, in fact, is that which gives the final polish to the well-bred man's character.

This same Chavigny provides us with a formidable list of the subjects with which his imaginary pupil must have at least a bowing acquaintance–religion, astronomy, geography, history, chronology, fables, blazonry, war, and fortification. Of these, blazonry was by no means the least important; it was remarked of Buzenval[16] when he made his début in society, that he created an excellent impression because he knew the origin and alliances of every illustrious family, so that, "with a solid judgement and application, he also had everything that could serve for agreeable conversation, without descending to trivialities."

Let us now see how the educationalists set about producing their *honnête homme*.

[16] BUZENVAL, Nicholas Choart de, 1651–79; became Count-Bishop of Beauvais in 1651.

4. The Devil and Mme. de Montespan

SINCE the beginning of the century, the period during which a boy was kept in women's hands had lengthened. The Duc du Maine, as we have seen, did not leave his governess until his tenth year, whereas Dr. Jean Hérouard, physician to the child Louis XIII, recommends six as the age at which a boy's education should become the responsibility of a governor.

Between the ages of six and fourteen the child should lay the foundations of a good education; and eight very full years they must have been, if the doctor's syllabus was adhered to. The first lesson the child must learn, he says, is "to fear and obey. The second, to shun evil and love right." Reading and writing are to be taught him by a woman of correct speech and good hand, and if the elementary syllabus had included a little French grammar, no harm would have been done. Here is the opening sentence of a letter written by the Maréchal-Duc de Luxembourg in 1675–*Je sommes pauvres, monsieur, mais j'avons de l'honneur*: a sentence which incidentally contains in addition to three grammatical errors, two falsehoods. As regards the first books, the Proverbs of Solomon and the quatrains of Pibrac are recommended, followed by the historical books of the Bible and Aesop's fables. Pibrac, now completely forgotten, occupied the same educational position in sixteenth- and seventeenth-century France as did the Trimetrical Classic in old China; there were over a hundred quatrains in the book, each enforcing some point of morals or good manners, and a well-brought-up child was expected to have its Pibrac by heart before passing on to more serious things. Mme. de Maintenon, in the days when she watched her aunt's geese, was provided with a basket containing her lunch and her Pibrac, so that she could learn her quatrains before driving her flock home in the evening. She, it is true, had been unorthodox enough to begin her education with Plutarch, and she tells us that she and her brother, when alone, were strictly forbidden to talk about anything whatsoever except the things they had read in that book. Pibrac's sentiments are irreproachable, but his style lacks sparkle, and memorizing him must have been a heavy task. Here is a specimen of Pibrac at his best:

> "Ce que tu vois de l'homme n'est pas l'homme;
> C'est le prison ou il est enserré,
> C'est le tombeau ou il est enterré,
> Le lit branlant ou il dort un court somme."

At six, or at the latest seven, the boy began to learn Latin, his most important subject. Its literary importance was however secondary to its practical, for until well on into the century, Latin was the language of diplomacy, and the key to the world of the learned, many of whom were still writing in that tongue. The groundwork of arithmetic, music, and geometry were also now to be laid, to say nothing of poetry and philosophy. One regards with amazement the idea of a child of six studying philosophy, but not only does Hérouard mention it, he says that in this subject the child must be "a diligent disciple." Perhaps however, he did not tackle it until his course drew to an end in his fourteenth year, when, with history, "the real school of princes," it would provide the coping stone to his book-learning before he passed on to the study of riding, fencing, and courtly manners. One would have thought that there was little opportunity for anything but work in such a scheme of life, but in fact the timetable is by no means terrifying. "He should be up," says Hérouard, "and dressed by seven o'clock, and study until nine. Then to Church, and after Mass be free until eleven, at which hour he should dine. His lessons should begin again at one, and end at three. He should then be free until six o'clock supper, and he should go to bed at nine." This timetable cannot have been applicable to the Duc du Maine, for he, as we have seen, dined at two, had his *collation* at six, and supper at eleven, followed by nine hours in bed. But in the schoolroom, his early education was, one imagines, much the same, with perhaps a slightly less restricted choice of reading matter. As his education under his tutor advanced, it would doubtless follow closely on the lines laid down by the Jesuit controlled public schools, the more so since, some forty years earlier, these schools had gained a brilliant advertisement when the College of Bourges secured the great Condé as a pupil, prince of the blood though he was. This sound schooling Condé owed to the stinginess of his father,[1] who was as mean as he was greedy. He was sent to Bourges at the age of eight, though the decision "was in some quarters looked upon as hardly less than sacrilege." True, the prince's desk was surrounded by a gilt balustrade, and he appears to have had two private tutors, but still, the son of the First Prince of the Blood was receiving the education of a commoner; very luckily for him, if Mme. de Maintenon is correct in saying that of all educations available in seventeenth-century France, that offered to royal children was the worst. "No pupil has shone more brightly," says Condé's report for 1630. In 1633 he gained a prize: in April 1635 he is "preparing himself in the whole study of philosophy," and in the same year he passed brilliantly a nightmare leaving examination in which he sustained twenty-seven theses in Ethics, fifteen on Meteors, fifteen on the Transformation of Substances, and fifteen on Metaphysics. He was not yet sixteen, and we learn without surprise that it was found necessary to send him to the family place in the country for a complete rest. But Condé himself was evidently impressed with the value of a public school education, for when the time came, twenty years later, he sent his own eldest son, first to the College of Namur, and afterwards to Antwerp to read Philosophy.

Whether the timid, easily discouraged Duc du Maine would have profited by such an education is very doubtful, and in any case his health would probably not have supported its hardships; though a royal and tutorial education by no means exempted the victim from acute suffering. From that other dreadful schoolroom at

[1] Condé, Henri II de Bourbon, 3rd Prince de, 1588–1646, son of Henri I, 2nd Prince de Condé and Charlotte de La Trémouille; married 1609, Charlotte Marguerite de Montmorency, "the most beautiful girl in France"; by 1641, "a rapacious, intelligent little old man, so filthy that Richelieu used to send him word that he was to clean himself before visiting the king."

Versailles, where Maine's half-brother, the heir to the throne, was being educated by the brutal Duc de Montausier,[2] there issued at all hours of the day the sound of the cane and the screams of the Dauphin, the monotony of whose floggings was varied only by the tutor occasionally flinging away his cane and falling upon his pupil with his fists. The Duc du Maine must often have crossed himself when he compared his own lot with that of his august half-brother, for Montchevreuil was a very different man to Montausier. "Henri de Mornay, second Marquis de Montchevreuil," says St. Simon in his disagreeable way, "was of good family, without any sort of ability, and poor as a church mouse . . . a very honourable man, and, brave, but extremely stupid"–which, coming from the source it does, almost amounts to a glowing testimonial. Court circles, and particularly feminine circles, were not slow to explain the reasons for Montchevreuil's appointment; was he not first cousin to that rakehell Marquis de Villarceaux, whose goings on with the widow Scarron had been so notorious twenty years earlier? Nay more, did not old ladies know, on the authority of a dear friend who was a dear friend of someone else's, that Montchevreuil had had Villarceaux and the widow as guests at his house together, and that Villarceaux had paid the bill for all three? It was easy to see who had got the appointment for a Mornay. So they hissed and whispered behind their fans, whilst Mme. de Maintenon, as usual, said nothing at all; nor is there any evidence that she was even consulted about the appointment of Maine's tutor.

But, however he came to be appointed, Montchevreuil was by no means a bad Governor, and the Duc du Maine might have done much worse.

The duke's first appearance in 1680 is in circumstances which were to be of importance to him in after-life, however little he may have appreciated the situation at the time. Mlle. de Montpensier, the king's cousin, had, like so many others, been much taken with Maine and diverted by his childish wit; she was now fifty-three, a spinster, and the richest princess in Europe. By a complicated intrigue, which

[2] Montausier, Charles de St. Maure, 1st Duc de, 1610–90; Governor to the Dauphin, 1668.

this is not the place to unravel, she had been induced to make the Duc du Maine her heir in return for the release of her old lover, the Cte. de Lauzun, from the prison in which he had languished for several years–that same Lauzun, by the way, whom we have already met with the infant Duc du Maine in his arms, outside the gate of St. Germain. The bargain was honourably observed on both sides: Lauzun was released, and Maine was made Mademoiselle's heir. He shortly afterwards paid her a visit of thanks, at which he acquitted himself excellently, making his little speech with an adroitness and sincerity which he might well show, for if he made a good match, he now stood every chance of being richer than many sovereign princes.

April 1681 finds Maine once more on the weary road to Barèges, this time of course in charge of M. de Montchevreuil. Mme. de Maintenon, now lady-in-waiting to the newly arrived Dauphine,[3] remains at Versailles, from where she keeps up an anxious correspondence with the duke and his Governor; on 27th April she writes to the latter,

"You know my extreme tenderness for our duke, and that the least detail of his household touches me more than most of what happens here: you cannot tell me too much of his health, his studies, and his wit."

One change in the household we notice, and not I think for the better. M. Le Ragois has been replaced by the sixty-eight-year-old Urbain Chevreau, a learned bore in the opinion of his contemporaries, and the author of a number of works now happily forgotten, who had been palmed off on the Maine household by Madame Palatine, to whose father he had been a Councillor of State. Madame Palatine, we may remind ourselves, is the Duchesse d'Orléans, that eccentric German lady who goes for country walks, and sleeps with her windows open. We also notice that the duke has an addition to his suite this year; though he is only eleven, he now has his own private secretary, one Cato Le Cour or Le Court. On 23rd May Mme. de Maintenon writes to say that she is delighted to hear that the tutor has gone off on a holiday to Loudun: "this little rest will

[3] Dauphine, Marie Anne Christine de Bavière, 1660–90, daughter of the Elector of Bavaria, married *Monseigneur,* 1680; a sickly, retiring woman, who took no part in the life of the Court.

do my *mignon's* flux good. Kiss his hands on my behalf and talk to him of me as much as you can."

A week later she is highly indignant to hear of a proposal to bathe the duke at Bagnières, because the road to Barèges is not yet open:

"This is a strange reason, and one which I hope you will not admit. One must assuredly begin at Barèges and then go on to Bagnières . . . do not be in a hurry to move, let the servants grumble, some of them have no common sense, and others are impatient to return to a place to which they look for all their pleasure and prosperity. I am consoled for M. Chevreau's illness by the hope that it will give my *mignon* more of a rest, and that you and M. Le Court will thereby have more time to inspire him with those sentiments which are better than a knowledge of Latin . . . do not let the dear prince forget me."

But, full of love for Maine as the letters are, Mme. de Maintenon is by no means blind to his faults; in another letter, she says to Montchevreuil,

"I do not mind telling you that, whatever you do, he will be an ignoramus, and that if you teach him anything in spite of himself, he will either forget it, or pretend to have done so . . . I am not surprised at his laziness in writing, for he has got out of the way of it, and he is a creature of habit. When he was in my hands, writing stood him instead of study, and thus he took to letter writing with less repugnance . . . but he is certain to write well, speaking as he does. I am delighted at what you tell me about his Guards (toy soldiers?), and I will pay his court with this bit of news; there is his bent, and you must profit by it to get into his head something of the métier which he will have to practise."

Lutin we remember from earlier journeys, and there is a kindly message for him; "Tell old Lutin that I stood godmother to his son, with Bontemps[4] for godfather."

The letter closes with a reiteration of the advice to Montchevreuil not to be in a hurry to return to Versailles:

"I do not doubt that all your people prefer mountains at a distance to close at hand; stock yourself with patience and even obstinacy against the passion they will have to get away."

[4] Bontemps, Alexandre, 1626–1701, First *Valet de Chambre* to Louis XIV. He was privy to all Louis XIV's secrets, and "as silent as the tomb"; in charge of the secret police and intelligence service in all the royal residences; "he never injured anybody, and only used his favour to oblige people."

From the next letter we gather that a "machine" has been discovered, which is being tried on the unfortunate prince; this apparatus supplies the theme for several letters, all the more sinister because we never discover the nature of the appliance, or the method of its use. The treatment itself must have been tedious enough to the boy in the hot southern summer without the additional infliction of the "machine," for apparently after the bathe, taken every other morning, he was immediately hustled from the baths to his bed, muffled against the least breath of fresh air.

Not until the 4th of July does Mme. de Montespan seem to have been sufficiently interested in her son to write to Barèges, and when she does, it is a mere letter of compliment. On the 18th, there arrives from Mme. de Maintenon, a regular medical lecture on the treatment of the prince's case; she had no doubt received it from a Court doctor, and it is worth preserving as a specimen of the up-to-date medical theory of 1681. She begins by saying that the Barèges waters will recall the nourishment to his bad thigh, and goes on,

"we know from experience that at the same time, the waters cook the matter which exudes from his fistula, and we may hope that by putting his flesh in a condition to make the coction, the coction will cure him of itself by its natural heat, which will be increased by that of the waters, which are soft and kindly, do not heat except for the moment, do not prevent him from sleeping and in a word, cannot hurt. . . . One must fortify him by recalling the heat into an almost paralytic limb, and by dissolving the hindrances to this process. All this goes on inside him, and so far from strengthening the system, must of necessity enfeeble it a little. If, in spite of my reasons, you find him getting stronger, rely upon it, it is not Barèges, but the effect of the life he is leading, going to bed early, sleeping well, and eating sanely."

With her accustomed good sense, Mme. de Maintenon gets to the root of the matter; she may be wrong as to the cooking and coctions, but she at least understands that early hours in the country are better for a small boy than eleven o'clock suppers at Versailles.

Life at Court in the meantime was not proceeding so smoothly as the stately surface of the current would suggest. Mme. de Montespan, we hear on the 2nd of September, often has the vapours, and Mme. de Maintenon has only seen her once in the past month. From her, this hint is more valuable than a page of the garrulous

Mme. de Sévigné. The letter in which we find this information closes with an exhortation for the Duc du Maine:

"Tell him that he will kill me with grief if he disappoints the hopes which the king has formed of his merit; he has not much to console him in the rest of his family; please God, our prince may be his consolation for what is lacking in the others, and that in him he will find a true son. Spur him on to want to be superior by merit to everyone he sees, at the same time yielding to them because he is the youngest."

The passage is interesting as showing how completely even Mme. de Maintenon confounded Louis XIV's bastards with his legitimate children; there is in all this no sign of any distinction between the Dauphin and the Duc du Maine other than that conferred by seniority of birth.

The next letter throws an interesting light on the celebrated *Oeuvres d'un Auteur de sept ans* at which we have just been glancing; it does not, to be sure, absolutely convict Mme. de Maintenon of an imposture, but she does for once show a little less than her wonted discretion in this revelation of nursery secrets. Mlle. de Tours, the duke's sister, has just died at Bourbon, and Mme. de Maintenon writes to M. de Montchevreuil,

"I want the duke to write to the king and say that, knowing the extreme tenderness with which he honoured Mlle. de Tours, he feels that he ought to testify the share he feels in his sorrow in addition to that which he feels personally for the loss of a sister. . . . It should be easy for you to suggest this letter to him when you are alone with him, in such a way that he will imagine that he thought of it himself."

We spoke a moment ago of Mme. de Maintenon's inability to draw any distinction between the Queen's children and the royal bastards: in this she merely observed the climate of opinion which was now general, not only in society but all over France. By Mme. de Montespan it was naturally held more strongly than by anyone else, and, familiar though the point of view is in the abstract, we can still be astonished at the scene described by her in the following letter:

"I say nothing of my own sorrow: as for Mlle. de Nantes, she was afflicted as if she was twenty years old, and received the visits of the Queen, of Mme. La Dauphine, and of all the Court with a wonderful grace."

Imagine it. The Queen, in company with the wife of the heir to the Throne, goes to pay a formal visit of condolence to her husband's eight-year-old bastard daughter, and offers her her sympathy on the death of her bastard sister. We see at once how wrong we should be in imputing any sarcasm to the crowd of loyal peasants who had a few years earlier cheered the passing of a coach containing the Queen, Mme. de Montespan, and Mlle. de La Vallière with excited shouts of "Here comes the three Queens!" A lot has happened since the little establishment in the Rue Vaugirard was set up eleven years ago. In the late summer the Duc du Maine, whether prompted by some Court sycophant or acting on his own we do not know, wrote to his father begging permission to accompany him on his expedition to Strasbourg; and the petition was received by the king with such satisfaction that Mme. de Montespan writes to her son to pass on the good news: "He was so pleased that he told everybody about it, and I do not doubt that if you had been here, he would have taken you with him."

Had anyone mentioned the words "active service" in connection with the presence of a French army at Strasbourg in 1681, Louis would have been much annoyed, for he was busily engaged in attempting to persuade a frightened Europe that it was there merely to prevent disorder whilst France resumed possession of some Crown property which had reverted to its legal owner. He was in fact engaged upon another cold war even more stupefying in its impudence than that of 1667. By the Peace of Westphalia which had ended the Thirty Years War in 1648, France had gained several important towns on her Eastern frontier, "with their dependencies;" and now someone, perhaps Louis himself, had had the brilliant idea of doing a little historical research into what exactly these "dependencies" were. A Chamber of Reunions was set up for this purpose at Metz, and as a result of its scholarly investigations, it was found that five important towns on the western frontier of the Empire had in reality been French property since 1648: and by the time Vienna woke up to what was happening, Louis had already taken possession. He was now on the way to a sixth, and far more important place which had been "awarded" to him—Strasbourg, which, under the influence of bribes, threats, and a military blockade, admitted the validity of the French claims on 30th September. At the same time, whilst all eyes were on Strasbourg, Maréchal de Boufflers quietly possessed himself of the important fortress of Casale, dominating the entrance from France into Italy. It proved impossible to dislodge Louis from any of his conquests, but in September, Holland, the Empire, Sweden and Spain entered into a defensive alliance against France. Louis however not only remained unperturbed, but showed his opinion of the coalition by seizing Luxembourg, Dixmude, Courtrai and Oudenarde between April and June 1684: and by the Truce of Ratisbon in the following August, he was granted twenty years' possession of all the places "assigned" to him by his own Court of Reunions.

Mme. de Montespan in 1681 seems to have at last realized that the Duc du Maine was growing up, and that in a few years he would be a personage to be reckoned with: and she starts to impress him with his high destiny in the following remarkable homily:

"It is well that you should realize that you are happily saved from the mixed blood that is ordinarily the fate of persons of your class, and that, from whichever side one looks at you, one finds nobility, courage, and wit; this is a very advantageous circumstance for you, but it also imposes on you the obligation of making the very best of yourself."

This is a little obscure until we remember that the Mortemarts admitted only two houses in France to be noble, their own and that of La Rochefoucauld. So that, if there was any difference of station between the duke's parents, the advantage rested with the mother's family. It is true that the Mortemarts were too well bred to press these facts frequently on the royal notice, but Mme. de Thianges[5] more than once told the king to his face that the Bourbons were not one of the really old families of France. We shall not see much of Mme. de Thianges, but she is always worth meeting; she was as lovely and witty as her two sisters, and was possessed of a self-assurance which was rare, even in the House of Mortemart. "My

[5] THIANGES, Gabrielle de Rochechouart-Mortemart, Marquise de, sister of Mme. de Montespan, born about 1630; married, 1655, Claude Léonor de Damas, Marquis de Thianges; one of the king's inner circle; "in her anger, she would call the king names, and the more he laughed, the more furious she became"; died, 1693.

beauty," she was in the habit of saying, "and the perfection of my wit, are due to the difference which birth put between me and the commonalty of mankind." As for Mme. de Montespan, she was to linger on at Court for several years, but her day was now over; Louis had ceased to live with her since 1679, when he had taken a new mistress in secret, Mlle. de Fontanges;[6] and by April 1680 it was common knowledge that the official mistress was furious at her neglected state. Or perhaps only acted as if she were furious, for Mme. de Montespan was standing on the brink of a precipice, and knew it. She was a brave woman, still showing a smiling face to the Court, but for over a twelve-month she had been the prey of an unresting fear; the Affair of the Poisons, the most hideous scandal of the century, was approaching its denouement, and she was deeply implicated. Any day now might bring exposure, disgrace, perhaps even punishment: she knew it: she must have guessed that Louis knew it: and she was helpless.

The credit of revealing the horrors of the Paris underworld rests with one Gabriel Nicolas de La Reynie, a fifty-seven-year-old lawyer, whom Colbert had discovered in 1667, and had appointed Lieutenant of Police for the city of Paris. Colbert had a flair for picking men, and La Reynie was emphatically the right man in the right place. He was patient, incorruptible, able to sift conflicting evidence, remorseless on the track of a criminal, and with some real detective ability; in fact, the first modern police officer. He had the further advantage of enjoying the full confidence of Louis XIV.

La Reynie had been unhappy about the state of Paris ever since 1673, when the confessors of Nôtre Dâme had informed him that a startling number of women were accusing themselves of having poisoned one or more of their relatives; but it was not until 1677 that he got a lead. One Vanens was arrested in December of that year, proved to be a poisoner, and under interrogation, he "squeaked." His disclosures were followed by the arrest of the widow Bosse in 1678, who, under cover of keeping a cosmetic shop, proved to be another poisoner in a large way of business; and in 1679 La

[6] FONTANGES, Marie Angélique d'Escoraille de Rousille, Duchesse de, "beautiful as an angel and stupid as a basket"; died suddenly in 1681, not without suspicion of poison.

Reynie had enough evidence to pull in the bulk of the big operators in this and its allied trades.

He was, like most of his contemporaries, a hard-bitten man, but even he was sickened by the dossier of his own greatest case; for the evidence disclosed that not only was poisoning "big business" as we should say, but that its operators claimed some of the highest in the land for their clients. It was too, a highly specialized trade, the poison being manufactured by men posing as philosophers engaged in the transmutation of metals, and the retailers covering their activities by the sale of soaps, perfumes and toilet articles. An incidental disclosure was that when the demand for "succession powder" was slack, the manufacturers kept their establishments going by coining. The poisons most commonly used were arsenic, opium, antimony, and hemlock, but chiefly arsenic, which its makers advertised as "the king of poisons;" and so indeed it was, for it was potent, easily administered in a variety of ways, could produce slow or quick death, and in the then state of medical science could not be detected by post-mortem examination of the organs. It was a further shock to La Reynie to discover just how easy it was to buy poison; all these bogus beauty parlour criminals confessed to doing a little harmless fortune telling in their back rooms to amuse their customers, and, once in the back room, any woman with money had no great difficulty in getting what she wanted; though, as there was a heavy fee for each consultation, she would not get it in a hurry. A woman for example who had an inconvenient husband would be recommended at the first visit to pray for a week to St. Anthony of Padua. The poison-seller would during this week make enquiries among her colleagues, and if the woman's story was genuine and she seemed "safe," she would on her next visit be asked to bring the poisoner one of the husband's shirts. This would then be washed in arsenic soap, and the poisoned garment would sooner or later kill the victim. If for any reason the use of arsenic soap was impracticable, liquid arsenic in graduated doses could be bought, with instructions in mixing it with your husband's food.

All this was bad enough, but there was worse to follow; in the spring of 1679 the Abbé Guibourg fell into La Reynie's hands, and under steady pressure and confrontations disclosed the fact that devil-worship and the horrors of the Black Mass were common in Paris, yielding a handsome profit to the officiating priest and the illegal midwives who provided the sacrificial victims; and Guibourg too insisted that his clientèle was drawn from the nobility rather than from the bourgeoisie. At first sight it would appear that there was nothing in common between the activities of the poisoners and the wretches who celebrated the Black Mass, but in fact they played into each other's hands. Women endeavouring to retain a faithless lover by means of the Black Mass, and failing to do so, would be sent to buy revenge at the poisoners: and a poisoner who saw that a client was not yet worked up to the pitch of compassing the death of a lover, would quietly recommend the good offices of Father X, giving the woman a "sympathetic powder," usually an aphrodisiac. This the Black priest would bless, making the sign of the Cross over it, and it was then mixed with the desired one's food. If this failed to work, the next step down into the Pit was to write your own name and that of the person to be bewitched on a wafer, which the priest consecrated at a real Mass, and which was also given to the victim in his food. The last resort was the Black Mass, celebrated by night, preferably in a chapel, but if that was impossible, in cellars in obscure corners of Paris. An altar with black hangings, embroidered with acorns: an inverted black crucifix: and six candles, also black, made from the grease of a man who had been hanged, were the essential properties. The priest, naked except for his vestments, with a witch as server, then received the woman on whose behalf the mass was being offered, she being entirely naked except for her head, which was wrapped in black muslin. The woman was laid on her back on the altar and the chalice placed on her belly. The priest then said the true Mass backwards, a wafer was desecrated, the throat of an infant cut, and its blood poured into the chalice; after which the priest kissed the woman's body instead of the altar, and both partook of the wafer and the blood[7]. And, to me, not the least horrible part of the whole business is that here is

[7] This is an expurgated version of the ceremony; the full details are unprintable.

4. LOUISE FRANÇOISE, DUCHESSE DE BOURBON
MAINE'S FAVOURITE SISTER

From a painting attributed to Largillière

5. MARIE THÉRÈSE, QUEEN OF LOUIS XIV

no case of utterly corrupted scoundrels trading on the credulity of foolish and wicked women. The whole disgusting crew, Black priests, witches, wizards and the rest, believed as firmly as did their clients that the Devil, in return for their souls, had really conferred upon them a portion of his power.

It was with a sad heart that La Reynie laid his evidence before a horrified Louis XIV, who on 10th April 1679 established a special court, the *Chambre Ardente*, to deal with the matter, laying it down "in clear, emphatic tones" that strict justice was to be done "without distinctions of rank, persons, or sex." La Reynie was to prosecute.

But poor La Reynie was only at the beginning of his troubles; as he sifted and considered the steadily growing mass of evidence, leads began to appear in several of the accused's statements pointing to Mme. de Montespan as one of the great ladies who was implicated, and by the summer of 1680 it was impossible for him to disguise from himself that the weight of presumptive evidence against her was impressive. But what was he to do? To cite the mother of the king's children to appear before the *Chambre Ardente* was an obvious impossibility; and in any case, if he preferred a charge against her and she was acquitted, what then would be La Reynie's position? He would undoubtedly be made a scapegoat for the king's fury at the horrible scandal which he had provoked. He solved his problem by a series of written reports to Louvois, which he knew would be shown to the king: reports of an exquisite verbal dexterity in which Mme. de Montespan is never named, but from which no one reading between the lines can have any doubt that La Reynie was convinced that there was sufficient evidence to put the Marquise on her trial. And, as we shall see in a moment, Louis agreed with him.

The gist of the evidence against Mme. de Montespan, reduced to its bare essentials, was as follows: From 1667, Mme. de Montespan was a client of the poisoner Lavoisin senior, who had employed Mariette, a renegade priest, on her behalf to "make conjurations" whereby she should win the love of the king. Lesage, another renegade priest, deposed that he had blessed love philtres for her and placed them under the chalice at a real Mass. Mariette confessed that in 1668 he had received two pigeon's hearts from Mme. de Montespan, in order "to say Mass over them and put them under the chalice." This "conjuration" was intended to bring about the death or banishment of La Vallière. The Abbé Guibourg, corroborated by Lavoisin junior, confessed that in 1673 he had said three Black Masses for Mme. de Montespan, and further, that he was told that the naked woman on the altar was Mme. de Montespan herself. After the ceremony, the naked woman took away the desecrated Host and some of an infant's blood, in a glass phial. He further stated that Mme. de Montespan had expressed her conviction that she owed her recognition as the king's mistress in 1674 to the aid of the Devil.

In 1675 Mme. de Montespan ordered a further Black Mass, this time to rid herself of the rivalry of Mme. de Soubise.[8]

Guibourg deposed that in 1677 and 1678 he celebrated further Black Masses at Mme. de Montespan's request, that of 1677 being with the object of procuring the death of the king if he was unfaithful to her. Lavoisin junior, corroborating, stated that at this Mass Mme. de Montespan was on the altar, "quite naked on a mattress, her head hanging back on a pillow on an upturned chair, her legs hanging down, a napkin on her belly, and the chalice on the napkin." (A deposition whose vividness gives it a convincing ring of truth.)

In 1679–80 there were, according to Lavoisin junior, further Black Masses, and Mme. de Montespan "wished to carry things to extremes and engage Lavoisin senior in things which she felt great reluctance to do." (To poison the king who had now openly and entirely deserted her?) Lavoisin junior further deposed that Mlle. des Oeillets, Montespan's waiting-woman, frequently visited Lavoisin senior and took away with her packages which neither woman ever touched ungloved: and it is rather damaging to Mme. de Montespan to note that at a subsequent identification parade, all

[8] SOUBISE, Anne de Rohan, Princesse de, eldest daughter of the 2nd Duc de Rohan, by his wife Marguerite de Rohan, born 1648; married, 1663, her cousin, François de Rohan, Prince de Soubise; her liaison with Louis XIV, which perhaps began as early as 1671, was kept a close secret; Louis XIV was probably the father of her son, the Cardinal de Rohan; she died in 1709.

the poisoners unhesitatingly picked out Mlle. des Oeillets as one with whom they had had dealings.

We shall never know now if Athenäis did really commit all the vilenesses of which she was suspected, but this much at least is clear; La Reynie at the time, and Ravaisson in the nineteenth century, were both convinced that she was guilty of administering love philtres to the king. As regards the deeper infamies, La Reynie refuses to give a judgement; but though he did not say in so many words that she was guilty, he certainly does not acquit her: had he been a Scot, I think he would have brought in a verdict of "not proven," Ravaisson on the other hand, the leading authority on the subject in modern times, seems to me to think the evidence of her guilt on all counts conclusive. That Louis was convinced of her guilt seems obvious from the action which he took; after discussing the matter with Louvois and Colbert, he gave orders that when preliminary evidence, taken in chambers, disclosed anything to the prejudice of Mme. de Montespan, that evidence was not to be laid before the Court: orders which reduced the proceedings of the *Chambre Ardente* to a farce, though it was not dissolved until 1682. Many people who would have been much the better for burning thus escaped with their lives; it was too dangerous to let them speak in their own defence in open Court, proceedings against them were dropped, and they were dispersed amongst various provincial prisons on *lettres de cachet*.

As for Mme. de Montespan, she remained at Court, in order that the scandal might have no fresh material to feed upon: nominally the king's mistress still, actually deprived of all position and influence. She received a daily formal visit from the king, who, if he believed the charges against her, must have viewed the still beautiful, smiling woman with a shuddering disgust. So far as I know he never saw her again after 1680 except in the presence of one or more witnesses.

Sick of Mme. de Montespan, bored by Mlle. de Fontanges, Louis was turning more and more to Mme. de Maintenon for amusement:

"He (the King) very often passes two hours after dinner in Mme. de Maintenon's room, chatting with a friendship and a natural air which makes the room one of the most desirable places in the world."

By June the visits have lengthened to four hours, and inopportune blunderers calling on Mme. de Maintenon find her and the king, "each in an arm chair, and as soon as the visit ends, they take up the thread of the conversation where they dropped it:" hardly possible to make one's visit too short in these circumstances, one imagines. We, brought up in a different world, take the two arm-chairs for granted, but it was the chairs, and not the visit, which so startled contemporaries, for the queen was the only woman in France allowed to sit in a chair with arms in the presence of the king.

We lose sight of the Duc du Maine until 1683, in which year his mother suffered the further humiliation of being civilly deprived of her rooms at Versailles. In this year we find Maine writing to Mme. de Maintenon,

> "I will try to correct the mistakes which you point out in my first letter, and I ask you to forgive me if this one is no more to your taste. I am afraid it is difficult for me to avoid using big phrases, but I will do what I can. I snatch an opportunity to write to you between mathematics, Bible reading, and a trip to Glatigny, where I saw (and here follows a list of his dogs). So you are now better informed of my kennel than of my progress, for which I fear you will not be best pleased with me today."

In this year occurred an event whose importance cannot have been immediately apparent to the duke, but which was to make a considerable difference to his future. On the 30th of July, Marie Thérèse of Austria, Queen of France, died in the arms of Mme. de Maintenon. Poor little woman, it would be a hard heart which did not pity her, and yet it is impossible to help laughing at her; she had been a stupid girl, and she grew into a stupid woman. And stupidity was at Versailles the one sin for which there was no forgiveness. To crown her misfortunes, she fell passionately in love with her husband on her wedding night, and remained passionately in love with him to the end of her days; she was by no means unattractive, this "little, fair, plump woman with the lovely eyes, and a beautifully modelled face, who however somehow failed to please or touch the heart," as a contemporary connoisseur puts it; and she bored the king more than any woman in France, though he treated her with an unvarying courtesy and even kindliness. Well, it was all over now, and Louis, weeping, turned from the poor clay to his assembled courtiers—"This is the first annoyance she has ever given me," said the tearful and naïf royal egoist as he left the room with Mme. de Maintenon.

For the next two or three years the Duc du Maine cuts an obscure figure at Court, for a reason which is not hard to seek. He is no longer the infant prodigy whose latest *mot* circulates through the salons, nor is he a man, he is in the doldrums of boyhood. His letters have ceased to have any childish charm, and, as he has nothing to say, have become tedious reading to all save his old governess. We will leave him to get himself fledged, and return to the king.

From the time of the queen's death, a change, dramatic in its suddenness, comes over Louis, and almost within a matter of weeks, the whole tone of the Court begins to alter. Mme. de Maintenon is at last triumphant, and the whole of her rapidly growing influence begins to exert itself to produce a cleaner and better Court. By 1685 the king, who ten years earlier was living in mortal sin, who twenty years earlier was spending his nights climbing about the roof of the Louvre to get into the maids' bedrooms, is exhorting women to live devoutly, and "speaks so well against patches that even the greatest coquette dare not wear them." Nay more, a sober suit now ensures a man a welcome at Court, whereas to be gaily dressed will earn you a slightly, but perceptibly, chilly reception. Absence from Mass, or any irregularities in Lent, you now commit at your peril, be you man of the sword or man of the gown. The Edict of Nantes has just been revoked, converts are pouring back into the Church all over France, and Louis, married to Mme. de Maintenon, has settled down at last.

We have got somewhat ahead of the actual marriage, but in doing so we preserve the unities, for it was only gradually that the truth dawned upon France. To this day no positive proof of the marriage has come to light, but there is an impressive weight of evidence for its having taken place; for example, the Bishop of Chârtres, Mme. de Maintenon's confessor, writing in 1697, says that God has chosen her to be elevated for the sanctification of him who has raised her to occupy the place of a queen—"Offer yourself entirely to God," he says, "and to the king for the love of God, who has chosen you for his consolation and in order that you may obey him." The Bishop was a man quite incapable of writing such words to any woman who was not a wife. Languet de Gergy, another impeccable witness, states positively that the marriage took place, and amongst the moderns, Lavallée pronounces that the wedding was celebrated at a midnight Mass at Versailles on 12th June 1684. But perhaps no evidence is more important than that of St. Simon, who, like everyone else at the time, accepted the fact of the marriage; only think how he would have dealt with the matter if he could have got the faintest hint that the hated old sorceress was a mistress, and not a wife.

For the Duc du Maine the marriage was a strengthening of his position; the woman who was his mother in every sense save the physical was now his father's wife: he loved them both: they both loved him. He was no longer a lodger in Mme. de Montespan's rooms, but a son with a home of his own. The duke is now sixteen, and by the standards of his time a man, leading the ordinary life of a courtier, though still under the eye of Mme. de Maintenon, who is apparently anything but satisfied with his début in society. The duke is beginning to find apparently that there is all the difference in the world between handsome expectations and an adequate income, and we can easily guess from the letter which follows that his old governess has had to settle a card debt for him:

"I am in despair to see you blush for me; from this moment I will give up trictrac; if you like, I will also give up hunting, which is my only pleasure and billiards too, if I must; you have only to say what you want me to do. I told the king that I would hunt tomorrow, but I will not go. There is in fact nothing that I won't do to prevent your using the phrase 'breaking with me.' Without thinking of the harm which it would do me in the world, I could not live without your love."

Later in the same year he has once more to appeal to Mme. de Maintenon, and this time he adopts what may be called the despairingly jaunty style:

"As one should always finish by taking one's sins to one's confessor, I write to tell you of my debts. The fear of your just reprimands, which frightens me more than those of Mme. de Montespan because they are always founded on reason, forces me to tell you about this by letter. The same fear which hinders me from telling you things face to face has always prevented me from asking you for money when I am with you. It is impossible to go to Marly without playing, and yesterday, not finding anyone who would play for small stakes, I lost fifty pistoles to Richelieu[9] and the same amount to Gramont."[10]

Then follow fervent protestations and regrets. Needless to say the young man has not acknowledged the total of his debts: what young man ever did? And his method of dealing with the difficulty has a certain ingenuity; he has absent-mindedly pencilled a little sum on the paper, in such a position that the first thing which Mme. de Maintenon will see on opening the letter is a total of 1,200 livres, which is rather more than a hundred pistoles.

We catch another glimpse of him this year, at one of the king's parties at Marly, where Shops of the Four Seasons have been set up, and the Court is drawing a lottery for their contents; Maine, jointly with Mme. de Maintenon, kept the Shop of Winter, where was everything that a courtier could need for that season, and when the tickets had drawn their prizes, the king and *Monseigneur* gave away what was left over.

Already something of the promise of Maine's early youth is fading, he does not stand out from the rank and file of the Court except in so far as he is brought forward by the king and flattered by far-seeing nobles who regard him in the light of a speculative investment carrying a chance of handsome future dividends. He is present, and that is all; his name appears in small type as it were, high up on the list of guests at each fête, comedy or masquerade, and he conscientiously follows the prescribed routine for a courtier and a son. He is at the king's *lever* each morning at eight o'clock, he has the priceless privilege of following him into his private room and of joining the tail which he leads to Mass: where the king behaved "very respectfully . . . he remained on his knees the whole time,

[9] RICHELIEU, Armand Jean de Vignerot, 2nd Duc de, 1629–1715, great-nephew of Cardinal de Richelieu, whose duchy he inherited by marriage, on the death of the Cardinal in 1642.

[10] Most probably Philibert, Cte. de Gramont, 1621–1707, the notorious hero of Hamilton's Gramont Memoirs.

except during the reading of the Gospel:" as no doubt did everyone else. Mass over, Maine has a spell of freedom, much of which he no doubt spends in Mme. de Maintenon's room, where he finds himself more at home than in gossiping with the men, and then comes the king's dinner at one o'clock. The Duke, the Dauphin, all in fact who are present, stand bareheaded during the meal, answering the king's occasional remarks with a profound bow. In the afternoon there will be a hunt, perhaps shooting, possibly a walk in the gardens, but always in as close attendance on the king as can be managed; then another spell of leisure until duty–"pleasure" they call it– summons him to the evening's entertainment, comedy, cards, billiards, or dancing until ten o'clock, when comes what is the crown of the day for Louis XIV, the gargantuan royal supper, a family meal, with the king in the centre of the long table. Then follows the *coucher*, and between twelve and one the limping, footsore Duc du Maine, having bidden his father goodnight, may drag his weary limbs to his bedroom. A bleak, splendid, comfortless existence, whose tediousness was well-nigh unendurable, even to a tough generation, and whose only sweetness lay in savouring the unconcealed envy of those who were not permitted to share it. It is into the pattern of this day that we must picture the duke fitting his own slightly more complicated one: more complicated owing to the fact that every prince of the blood, every duke, every courtier, was himself a little Louis XIV with his own *lever* and *coucher*. Maine, in order to be at the king's *lever* at eight, probably held his at seven; Montchevreuil's *lever* would be at six, to enable him to attend Maine's before they went on together to the king's, and so on down through the hierarchy to the Gascon squireen who, after a couple of hours in bed, would be up in the black night to form, with their joint peasant valet, a court at his elder brother's bedside long before dawn. And it was to this tedious and despicable life that the French nobility had sunk; the creation of the courtier was the Bourbon revenge for the Fronde.

Louis was an adept at the application of the maxim *ce n'est que le premier pas qui côute*. He had at first done his best to conceal the existence of his bastard family; he had then used the Longueville precedent[11] for their legitimization; the reaction of public opinion had been tested by the Duc du Maine's travels through the kingdom, and, satisfied that he had nothing to fear from his people, the king had begun to build up a position for his favourite son which was not to be distinguished from that of a prince of the blood. In 1682 the duke had been appointed Governor of Languedoc; in 1684 he stood proxy for the Duke of Savoy at his marriage with Mlle. d'Orléans; and in this year he was given the Order of the Holy Ghost. Trifles all of them, but skilfully chosen trifles, each marking a slight step forward in Maine's pretentions. Languedoc was in every sense a royal government, one of the best in the king's gift, but it had been held by commoners, and the proxy for the groom at a royal wedding was usually, but not invariably, a prince of the blood. But admission to *The Order*, as it was usually called, was on a different footing, for only princes of the blood were admitted as knights before the age of twenty-three. Something more had happened than the gift of a jewelled star to a boy of sixteen; it was a tacit declaration by the king to all France, indeed all Europe, that Louis Auguste de Bourbon was a recognized Son of France. As the youth murmured the rubrical *Domine, non dignus sum*, did any suspicion cross the minds of the Chapter that this was no mere formula, but a statement of fact? Probably not. Choisy's account of the ceremony makes it clear that Maine's admission to The Order was accepted as being as much a thing of course as that of his three fellow recipients, Chârtres, Bourbon, and Conti, the first a Grandson of France, and the other two princes of the blood.[12,13,14]

During the winter of 1686, Court routine was disturbed by the

[11] About 1670 the Maréchale de La Ferté bore a bastard son to the 4th Duc de Longueville; the lady's husband was alive at the time, and Louis granted the Longueville family's request that the son should be legitimized without mention of the mother's name.

[12] CHÂRTRES, Philippe de France, Duc de, 1674–1723, son of *Monsieur*, brother of Louis XIV, and of Madame Palatine, his wife; Regent of France, 1715.

[13] BOURBON, Louis III, Duc de, 1668–1710, son of Henri Jules, 5th Prince de Conde, married Louise Françoise, *legitimée de France*, 1685; a brutal drunkard; died of a tumour on the brain.

[14] CONTI, François Louis de Bourbon, 4th Prince de, 1664–1709, second son of Armand, 2nd Prince de Conti and Anne Martinozzi, his wife; elected King of Poland, 1697, but was driven out before the end of the year; "his circle was the mark of the highest fashion."

serious illness of the king, who on 18th November was operated on for a fistula; he showed his accustomed courage during the operation, and stoicism afterwards, refusing to omit such of his daily tasks as could be performed in bed, even on the day after the operation. But he was in pain and he was bored, for he had given strict orders that the usual life of the Court was to continue in his enforced absence exactly as if he were present. Maine and his sister came to his rescue with masquerades and comedies, acted at the foot of his bed, and the days of convalescence bound father and son more closely together. We have not seen much so far of *Mme. La Duchesse*, Maine's favourite sister; she is that Mlle. de Nantes who so decorously received the queen's visit of condolence at the time of the death of her sister, Mlle. de Tours. Now fourteen, and for the last eighteen months the wife of the heir of the house of Condé, *M. Le Duc*, she nearly died of smallpox at Fontainebleau this year, but has emerged from the ordeal with her beauty unspoilt. Not only was she beautiful, even by non-royal standards, but she more than held her own with the wits of her day, for she was the prettiest, wittiest, and naughtiest of the fast set in the latter half of the reign, and was in constant hot water. Her comic verse, too often indecent, was genuinely amusing, except to the victims, and the king was not at all amused at a set which she had written on his august self; and when, soon afterwards, she was found filling the royal sanctum with tobacco smoke after borrowing a pipe from the guard room, she got a scolding which concluded with some ominous remarks on the benefits of change of air, and the uselessness of maintaining country houses for princesses who never used them. St. Simon, no admirer of the royal family, says that it was impossible to refrain from trying to please *Mme. La Duchesse*, and that her whole appearance showed her to be "the offspring of the tenderest love." For the rest, she was always in a good temper, was reproached with having a gizzard instead of a heart, and could drink any woman, and most men, under the table. With the connivance of a Court which adored her, and by her own dexterity, she managed to satisfy her husband of her devotion to him, while she was in fact the mistress of her brother-in-law; so we may surmise that whatever may have been her qualities as an actress in the king's bedroom, in her own they must have been of a high order.

The Duc du Maine is now of an age at which his contemporaries were launched in life, but he we find is still clinging to Mme. de Maintenon's skirts, still *le mignon*, reluctant to leave that cosy nest where alone he is appreciated and cossetted as he loves to be. In 1687, now seventeen, he is asking her advice about offering himself as a guest at Trianon:

"Since you told me the first time the king dined there I ought not to go, I took it that I should do likewise whenever he went there for a meal, and that is why I have not shown myself there; but I see it is becoming the fashion to go, and that one pays one's court ill by absenting oneself. I give you the facts, it is for you to judge and advise me."

It is a dispiriting picture of a youth who seems to be developing no self-reliance, and the extent to which he is still Mme. de Maintenon's docile pupil is even more evident in a later letter, obviously written in answer to a scolding:

"I am grateful for the means you have adopted to let me know that my conduct is not good; but I am astonished and annoyed that, having found it so, you did not let me know of it sooner. . . . You will remember that when Mme. de Montespan came back, I asked you to find out what line of study I should keep up. I promised you that until Mme. de Montespan decided, I would go on with mathematics. I have not missed, at the outside, more than four lessons. You told me to call once a week on the Dauphine, I have been more often. . . . It is only five days since I last saw *Monsieur*: three since I saw *Mademoiselle*. . . . I admit I am to blame about M. Le Prince de Conti. Four days ago I lost some money to him. I expected to get my allowance yesterday, and would then have paid him at once. I did not tell you about it, because I know you do not like me to gamble, and I had hoped you would not hear anything about it."

Then there follows an involved defence of his action in bothering the king's confessor for preferment for one Malézieux, a gentleman we shall be seeing more of in years to come; and by this time he has warmed his courage up sufficiently to venture on what is obviously a sarcastic quotation from Mme. de Maintenon's last letter:

"I know very well that I am only a country gentleman who passes his life far from the world and its pleasures, always in the woods with M. La Rochette. . . . But let that pass; I only hunt three days a week. . . . It is true that I do not take people with me, but that is easily remedied.

Hunting apart, Rochette hardly ever visits me, has done so perhaps a couple of times, and then I was with my gentlemen. As he does not understand anything except hunting, I naturally talk to him about it."

Mme. de Maintenon knew her world better than we can know it, and no doubt was doing the best she could for her favourite; yet our sympathies in the argument are with the duke. In his place we feel that we too would prefer the forest and the society of Squire Western-Rochette to a day spent in painfully dragging a lame leg over the endless parquetry of Versailles.

But in any case, the days of the forest and the salon were drawing to a close.

5. *Cavalry Commander*

THE high tide year for Louis XIV was 1684. He had robbed the Empire with impunity, Spain had, except by courtesy, ceased to be a first-class power, Holland was too weak to cause any anxiety; Charles II of England was his pensioner, thus securing the French left flank for any future operations; France held the east bank of the upper Rhine; French influence was predominant throughout Europe; and Louis commanded the finest army in the world.

But on the 6th of February 1685 Charles II died, and from that moment Louis' fortunes begin to ebb. Charles had not been, from Louis' point of view, by any means the ideal king of England, but he was perfection itself compared with his brother James II, whose mulish obstinacy and incredible ineptitude maddened every statesman in Europe. Charles had at least understood his own interests and acted accordingly, whereas it was speedily evident that the only certainty about James was that he could always be relied upon to do the wrong thing, in the wrong way, and at the wrong time.

Louis had always been feared by his neighbours, and to that emotion hatred was added over a large part of Europe when in 1685 he set to work to extirpate French Protestantism. 1686 was a crisis year, such as is only too familiar to our own generation; on July 17th Holland, the Empire, Spain, Sweden, and Bavaria signed the League of Augsburg, nominally to maintain the status established by the Treaty of Westphalia, actually, as indeed Louis and everyone else knew perfectly well, to humble France by force of arms on the first opportunity.

1688 came in with a welter of manifestoes, justifications, and high-sounding sentiments about world peace and the rights of peoples. Whilst Louis perfected the details of the offensive-defensive war which, in his view, was being forced upon him by little men, jealous of his glory, Louvois[1] was working night and day to put the finishing touches to his great military machine. This Louvois whose work adds such a lustre to the Grand Siècle was anything but an agreeable person; those who are successful in cleansing Augean stables are rarely pleasant company, especially if you yourself happen to be one of the abuses which need cleansing. And as nearly all France, all talking and writing France at any rate, was in Louvois' eyes an abuse, an anachronism, or a downright fraud, he has left behind him an impressive legacy of hatred. For he was remorseless in his disregard of vested interests, in stamping out nepotism, insubordination, corruption, and inefficiency, and he cared nothing for the screams of those whose corns he trod on. Brute though he was, he was also a genius; when he became Secretary for War in 1662, he found France with a feudal army; when he died in 1691, he left it with the first of the modern ones.

Events now began to move swiftly. England decided that it had had more of James II than it could stand, and on the last day of June 1688, a group of Whigs invited William of Orange to invade their country; in September, Louis issued a manifesto exposing what he would have called his "just griefs," and in which he shed a few crocodile tears at the necessity which provoked him to take up arms in defence of his patrimony: on the 5th of November, William of Orange landed at Torbay, and on Christmas Day, James II, having lost three crowns in as many years, landed in France to begin his life-exile. On the 22nd of September *Monseigneur* was appointed to command the Army of the Rhine, and two days later Louis declared war on the Emperor. On the 25th *Monseigneur* left Paris for the front, taking in his suite the Duc de Bourbon, the Prince de Conti, and the Duc du Maine.

The first campaign was the finishing course of a French gentleman's education–"he goes to make his proofs," was the expression usually applied to the process. For good or ill, the Duc du Maine

[1] Louvois, François Michel Le Tellier, Marquis de, second son of Michel Le Tellier and Elizabeth Turpin, his wife, born 1641; remodelled French army, 1668–72; Minister of State, 1672; "the greatest clerk and the greatest brute that ever lived," he encouraged Louis in his policy of calculated aggression, and was responsible for some of the worst crimes of the reign; died, perhaps poisoned, 1691.

who returned to Court in the autumn would not be the same man who had left it in September. It is a suitable moment to take further stock of him.

There is already a difference of opinion about the king's favourite son; there is no longer that universal chorus of praise which was to be heard a few years earlier. Dubois,[2] who met him for the first time this year, is supposed to have said that he was vulgar looking and deceitful, with "a smile that was an epigram;" the report is however of doubtful authenticity, and it seems unlikely that a son of Louis XIV and Mme. de Montespan could have looked vulgar: plain perhaps, but not vulgar. Madame Palatine indeed describes him as "frightfully ugly," but then she is writing in a passion of unfounded fear that the king was about to marry the duke to her daughter, and the most interesting fact in her letter is the involuntary testimonial which she writes for Mme. de Maintenon–"She loves this wicked cripple as if he were her own child." Lavallée's verdict on the duke in his eighteenth year is that he has turned into an affected chatterer, from whom no great things are to be hoped. Mme. de Caylus, who knew him well, deals more sympathetically with him; it would have been a happy chance, she says, if Mme. de Maintenon had completed his education as well as beginning it, for she would have no doubt imparted to him some of her own drive and moral courage, and would have impressed upon him the necessity of holding his own amongst the men of his generation; whereas all his life, he was thrown back on a little clique, predominantly feminine, and in which alone he was at his ease, by "his looks, his natural timidity and the king's liking for him;" for Louis frowned upon those whom he admitted into his intimate friendship mixing freely in general society. "Shyness makes men farouche, and specially when they make it a point of duty not to overcome it." Spanheim is a witness of considerable importance, for he has no axe to grind, but as a professional diplomat stationed at Versailles, limits himself to reporting what he thinks to be the facts–"He has a handsome

[2] Dubois, Guillaume, son of a chemist, servant in a Paris college, born 1656; emerged from obscurity about 1684 as preceptor to the Duc de Châtres, and was later his Governor; Prime Minister under the Regency; Archbishop of Cambrai, 1717; Cardinal, 1721; died of syphilis, 1723.

face and a happy expression, an agreeable approach, and a wit of uncommon charm and knowledge. . . . He made great progress rare for a man of his rank, in belles lettres, history, antiquity, and mathematics. . . . Good, pious, and generous." The negative begins to develop. We see the picture of a strong-minded woman's ideal boy, habitually good and submissive, the perfect child, who was to remain a perfect child long after he should have the virility, even the touch of brutality, needed for the part he was to play; a man of colourless virtue, without positive vices, in whom the physical lassitude of prolonged illness had induced a corresponding lethargy of character, aggravated by the inferiority complex resulting from his physical deformity, and manifesting itself in an ivy-like clinging to the nearest strong character. In short, a misfit. With his shy disposition, he had in himself no qualities necessary to sustain his usurped rôle of prince of the blood, nor even that of a bastard of France. For this too was a traditional part under the ancien régime; but the tradition unfortunately called for a certain swaggering bravery, which was utterly alien to his temperament; and, that the scale might be fully weighted against him, there was the ever present contrast between himself and the head of Henri IV's bastard family, the popular and successful Duc de Vendôme;[3] or, if he turned to the house of Stuart and to his own generation, what a poor figure he cuts beside the Duke of Berwick,[4] his own age, and destined to die a Marshal of France, with a well-earned bâton. In how much pleasanter places would his lines have fallen if his father, recognizing the weakness of his body and character, had found him a more appropriate niche in life, in the Church for instance. With his sincere but easy piety and his innate purity, he would have grown to manhood peaceably under the shadow of the cloister. Some rich abbey would have been found for him, far from Court, where his life would have worked itself out in the service of his order. Even happier perhaps

[3] Vendôme, Louis Joseph de Bourbon, 3rd Duc de, 1654–1712, son of Louis, 2nd Duc, and Laure Mancini; one of the best generals of his day; his victory at Villaviciosa, 1710, saved the Spanish Bourbons; died whilst commanding in Spain, 1712.

[4] Berwick, James FitzJames, Duke of, 1670–1734, son of James II and Arabella Churchill, sister of the Duke of Marlborough; naturalized French subject, 1703; killed in action at Philipsburg.

6. MADAME DE MAINTENON

7. LOUIS ALEXANDRE DE BOURBON, COMTE DE TOULOUSE

had he been the Bishop of some not very important See, for he shares with Cowper and Richardson something of their chaste craving for constant and intimate female companionship. His piety, his conversational charm, the very shyness which so handicapped him in the world, would in more fortunate circumstances have made him the focal point and oracle of a circle of elderly ladies—"the dear Bishop's Tuesdays"—we can almost hear the conversation.

But no such ideas had ever crossed Louis XIV's mind. On the contrary, Maine was to be a prince of the blood: he was to be a general: he was to play a great part. How he played it remains to be seen.

While the duke was en route for the front, another windfall came his way; his uncle, the Duc de Vivonne,[5] had just died, and the king gave his son the vacant office of General of the Galleys. What did Maine know about the administration of that sinister fleet? Nothing, nor was it expected that he should make himself conversant with the subject, for the appointment was a sinecure: and let us note, a sinecure in that golden age was not an honorary post to which no salary was attached, but meant a handsome salary for which no service was rendered. A very comfortable thing for a young man who did not always find it convenient to settle his card debts on the nail.

By 1st October the headquarter staff had reached Toul, from where the duke writes to Mme. de Maintenon:

"We arrived here yesterday, very tired after our long journey. I can assure you, Madame, that I am on the best of terms with *Monseigneur*, and hardly ever leave his side. We are all very anxious to get to Philipsburg, and I think that the discomfort of the road contributes somewhat to the impatience we have."

By the next post, he hears from Mme. de Maintenon, whose letter, judging by the reply, has not been a comfortable one:

"I assure you, Madame, that I do not deserve your reproaches; I was deeply touched when I said goodbye to the king and you. . . . It is not possible for me to write as frequently as you seem to imagine I can: and from Meaux, having only bagatelles to send, I wrote to *Mme. La Duchesse*, and begged her to make you my compliments."

[5] VIVONNE, Louis Victor de Rochechouart-Mortemart, Duc de, 1636–88, son of 1st Duc de Mortemart; "he had, in an eminent degree, the wit of the Mortemarts."

On 7th October he arrives at Philipsburg, the capture of which town is the first objective of the army of the Rhine:

"We arrived here yesterday evening very tired; *Monseigneur* admitted that he was at the end of his tether, he was in fact so tired that he could not eat; for myself, my fatigue did not take away my appetite, and having supped, I slept perfectly for ten hours on some straw. . . . I cannot tell you how joyful I am to be here, nor of my impatience to see the place from a closer viewpoint, for yesterday M. de Duras[6] made us pass it pretty far off, except for two or three points. . . ."

The rest of the day was spent in looking into matters of supply, bridges, artillery and so forth, and the duke goes on to tell with great pride that he has already been under fire;

"I advanced alone with *Monseigneur*; we were in full view of the place, and the enemy fired on us with two cannon; the bullet from the first fell in the Rhine, and that from the second went straight over our heads; four peasants who were behind us threw themselves on their faces, and the ball was found about three hundred paces away."

By 20th October he is able to report that the *Maréchal* treats him with the utmost distinction, and that he has hopes of succeeding in the profession of an officer. Duras had presumably sent a favourable report on him to the king, for on the 23rd Louis writes, not to Maine but to his Governor, to say that "the countenance of the Duc du Maine gives me great pleasure." On the 19th, the duke writes to enlist Mme. de Maintenon's sympathy for the numerous family of a Brigadier who has that morning been killed in the trenches; and we learn from Dangeau that, owing to Maine's intervention, the dead man's son was immediately given command of a regiment. On the 25th the duke writes in a strain only too familiar to those whose lot it has been to write home from the front:

"Every day, Madame, we get reprimands for not writing, and we in fact write regularly every day. It is very hard to kill oneself to find news, and then to find that no one is contented with our efforts. Since you directed me to send my letters through St. Pouanges, I have always done so, and apparently they are still going astray. It is none the less true that what with writing letters, I have not the time to eat or drink. As soon as I get up, I

[6] DURAS, Jacques Henri de Durfort, 1620–1704, 1st duc de, son of Guy, 2nd Marquis de Duras and Elizabeth de La Tour d'Auvergne; "he was on such a footing with the king that he could say anything he liked".

write; as soon as I get off my horse I write; in fact I seem to do nothing else, and I am furious to find that the trouble I take, and trouble which you cannot imagine, is so much time lost. . . . Since I have been here I have written to the king six times. *Monseigneur* is my witness. . . . I would not have believed that the negligence of a miserable courier could have effected such a change in your sentiments towards me, but I very well see that as soon as you do not hear from me, you forget the good you have heard of me. . . . Instead of encouraging me when I am in danger, you go out of your way to depress me."

The siege of Philipsburg proved an unexpectedly easy one; Starhemberg,[7] the Governor, was in ill-health and capitulated on 1st November. On the 3rd the duke sends news to Mme. de Maintenon, and we gather casually that he is already colonel of a cavalry regiment stationed at Metz–"I have asked *Monseigneur* to inspect my cavalry regiment on the way back, and he is going to do so." By the 9th Maine is preparing to take duty in the trenches below the citadel of Philipsburg, a duty in which, on his own showing, he had not distinguished himself on a previous occasion–"I shall mount guard on Wednesday in the trenches," he writes, "and I assure you that I shall not do as I did the other time and leave the trench before the battalion does." Philipsburg having fallen on the 1st, this reference to continuing siege operations may be obscure to those unacquainted with the etiquette of a seventeenth-century siege. It was in two distinct stages, first the siege of the town, which was held until the defender decided that it could be taken by assault; he would then surrender the town and withdraw into the fortress itself, which the assailants were obliged to reduce, and which was usually defended under a clause inserted in the articles of capitulation for the town, to the effect that if the fortress were not succoured within a given period, it also would be surrendered.

The taking of Philipsburg was the only important feat accomplished by the Rhine Army in 1688, and with the capture of Mannheim, a few days later, the campaign closed. On Sunday 27th November, *Monseigneur* and his retinue of princes arrived at Versailles.

We know nothing of how the Duc du Maine spent the winter,

[7] STARHEMBERG, Guidobaldo, Count von, 1657–1737.

but we may assume that his new prestige as an officer on leave from the front facilitated his spending a few days in the woods with his hounds and his La Rochette, of whom Mme. de Maintenon so disapproves; all was going well at the front, and the king would be in an expansive mood, renewing his own youth in his son, and full of stories of his own first campaign, and "how things were done in my time." Let us hope that the duke quieted the loving jealousy of Mme. de Maintenon on the vexed question of those missing letters, and that his pay and allowances were sufficient for a flutter at the card table.

On 21st May 1689 he left again for Flanders, where this year he was to take command of his own regiment, and on the following day wrote to Mme. de Maintenon from Laon:

"I was so touched and moved by the king's farewell that I was not able to say a word to him. . . . I picked up all my people here, and all were pleased to see me. I am lodged in the Archbishop's palace, where I found, without including five harangues, the Duc and Duchesse d'Estrées[8] with their daughters, and Mme. de Vaubrun. The crowd of people who came out from Laon to meet me would have delighted *Monsieur*, but for my part I was quite ashamed."

He writes again from Rocroi on the 24th:

"I am writing to the king without ceremony, just as I did last year, and I tell him that I hope to join M. le Marèchal d'Humiéres[9] the day after tomorrow at Bussière."

Once at the front, he is eager to impress those at home with the hardships which he is enduring:

"I am beginning to feel the fatigues of war, for I have been three days without changing my shirt, and two nights; but, as you so well foresaw, it is doing me no harm. There are so many overcoats here that I do not doubt that this will be known as the overcoat campaign."

By 31st May he is in camp at Pictou, and in good spirits:

"I am as well as I can possibly be, and my valets tell me that I am visibly fatter. The air of the front seems to be doing me good; I am eating and sleeping well, and drinking nothing. The officers appear to be satisfied

[8] Estrées, François Annibal, 3rd Duc d', 1649–98, son of François Annibal, 2nd duke, and Catherine de Lauzières.

[9] Humières, Louis de Crévent, 4th Marquis and 1st Duc d', 1628–94, son of Louis, 3rd Marquis, and Isabeau Phélypéaux; "a good courtier and a bad general."

with me. When I left I forgot to ask the king if the Swiss Guards should beat the general salute for me. Will you please speak to him about it, and let me know what his intention is. It is important to start right. . . . It is a bad joke of yours to tell me that you have seen the object of my passion. I am none the wiser, and I do not know whom you are talking about."

The reference to the Swiss Guards is explained by the fact that Maine had been their Colonel-General since childhood, and he wants to know if he is to be officially recognized as such. On 8th July he is trying to get Mme. de Maintenon to hint that the time has come when he ought to be promoted, a rather cool request when we remember that he has not been a Colonel for a complete year, and has not, so far as we know, been in action in that capacity; for the army of Flanders has orders to act on the defensive, and has not yet been in contact with the enemy:

"I still have the same anxiety to be a Brigadier; and, if I may say so, my attention to duty might win me this favour. . . . But, to speak frankly, I have no hopes, for I do not seem to be too well in favour at Court. I am consoled however by the thought that I have nothing with which to reproach myself. I begin to appreciate the truth of the old proverb, *les absents ont toujours tort.*"

The next letter shows vividly how curiously disappointing is the development of this formerly clever, or supposedly clever, child; he is now nineteen, yet he can write to his old governess,

"You would do me a great service if you would furnish me with a few compliments, for that sort of thing is not in my line, and I beg of you not to betray me when in due course you recognize them for your own, word for word."

I suspect him of having got into some sort of trouble in August, for he then writes again to Mme. de Maintenon,

"I am afraid you were in a bad temper when you wrote to me; I cannot see what cause I can have given you, unless it is that I spoke too strongly in rebutting the falsehoods which you were told of me; I shall be in despair if you have taken it in bad part. I do not know if the king is content with my recent letters, but I do know that I had a great deal of trouble in writing them."

And he concludes, rather ineptly one would imagine at such a moment, in pressing for promotion for the army commander under whom he is serving, finishing off with a hardly convincing assurance that he writes entirely without the army commander's knowledge.

Front line rumour was apparently as unreliable then as now, even when emanating from those in a position to pick up the latest gossip at headquarters. On 9th August the duke writes, "Today we have pretty good news from Ireland, for we hear that Rosen[10] has refused to receive the surrender of Londonderry." Rosen had never been offered the surrender of Londonderry, and eight days before the duke's letter was written, he had lost Ulster for King James by raising the siege. The letter concludes with another depressing illustration of the blight which seems to have fallen on the writer's mental development: "Please be so good as to supply me with some more endings for letters, I have only two." A fortnight later he writes in great excitement,

"I am as pleased as Punch. The king having sanctioned our undertaking the offensive, I asked the Marshal what duty he intended for me. He replied that, with a command of eight squadrons, I ought to be an acting Brigadier; but not being one, I dare not undertake the duties without the king's permission. I beg of you to ask what his intentions are, and to let me know. I await your reply with impatience."

There is a welcome touch of manliness, and some pathos, in his next letter:

"I was much alarmed when I saw in your letter to M. Le Court that you hope to see me as soon as you get back from Fontainebleau. Although I am not doing much here that is worth while, I am doing more than I would be at Court, where I do nothing except hobble about in front of those to whom I am a disagreeable spectacle; here, I am learning my métier, and I do not see *Mme. La Duchesse*, who you are always afraid spoils me. So I do not lack reasons for asking to stay at the front, without speaking of the great desire I have to do so."

A skirmish or two at the head of his regiment had given the young man a naïf self-confidence, which must have brought a sour smile to the face of War-Secretary Louvois if the following letter came under his eyes:

"My thoughts, Madame, are entirely centered on the prospect of getting some more responsible post next year. I have learnt cavalry soldiering in

[10] Rosen, Livonian soldier of fortune, 1627–1714. "One would not have cared to meet him at the corner of a wood on a dark night."

this campaign, and, without being assuming, I feel able to ask for the command of the cavalry next year in the army of one of my friends, that is to say M. d'Humières or M. de Luxembourg,[11] if the king wishes to make use of my services."

Even more naïf perhaps is the concluding paragraph of his letter, in which he takes upon himself to recommend these two generals as being the best choice open to the king for high command in the ensuing spring. He shows as little grasp of the implications of domestic politics as he does of his own military abilities; Pelletier,[12] Controller-General of Finances, one of the most important officials in the kingdom, was in this year replaced by Pontchartrain;[13] Mme. de Maintenon tries to draw out the Duc du Maine on this momentous piece of news, but she strikes no spark from him: "... Provided that I draw my pension, I do not take the least interest in whether it is paid me by M. de Pontchartrain or M. Le Pelletier ..." But we must give him some credit for a genuine desire to make himself an efficient officer. On 3rd October he learns

"with great pleasure that when Mme. de Montespan asked the king when she would see me again, the king answered that the campaign was not over yet. I am very keen to make myself something worth while."

And if the duke was no great soldier, he was at any rate a loyal comrade; his help is by no means indiscriminately given, but his letters are full of requests for help for brother officers, often quite obscure people. On 6th October he notices Captain de Jussac "looking sadder and more melancholy than usual;" the Captain has had to tell his wife to keep away from Fontainebleau "because her affair has not yet been decided." Cannot Mme. de Maintenon

[11] LUXEMBOURG, François Henri de Montmorency-Boutteville, Maréchal and 1st Duc de, of the new creation, son of François, Cte. de Boutteville, and Elizabeth Angèlique de Vienne; Marshal of France, 1675; in 1679, implicated in the poisoning scandals, and in the Bastille until 1681. Without morals or principles, pitiless, perhaps a poisoner; certainly a practiser of the Black Mass; homosexual; and a brilliant general, the last of the great seventeenth-century soldiers.

[12] PELLETIER, Claude, 1631–1711, grandson of a tanner, son of a barrister; Controller-General of Finances, 1683; Minister of State, 1689; "the king liked and esteemed him, and when he retired, insisted that he should come and see him privately, two or three times a year."

[13] PONTCHARTRAIN, Louis Phélypéaux, 1st Cte. de, 1643–1727, member of an hereditary ministerial family, which held important posts for a hundred and fifty years without a break.

do something for her? The duke, though still in considerable awe of Mme. de Maintenon, is not going to be bullied by her into giving up his charming sister, *Mme. La Duchesse.* We must not however blame Mme. de Maintenon for trying to withdraw Maine from his sister's influence; she had brought up both children, knew the weakness of the duke's fibre, and was under no illusions about *Mme. La Duchesse*; she had had enough of the famous Mortemart wit to last her a lifetime, and in addition suspected the duchess of levity, or worse.

"My absence has done nothing to lessen my fondness for *Mme. La Duchesse.* It is so natural for me to love my sister that I am sure it would give me great pain not to see her frequently. I begin to be persuaded that all the good offices which have been rendered me will only damage me; for the manners of this world, where one sees only men, are very different to those of the Court, where one is surrounded by women."

To which he adds a hasty parenthesis, "of whom all have not your solidity of character."

A fit of economy has overtaken the duke as the time draws near for him to come home on leave. He has decided to comb out his hunting establishment, and sends orders to that effect to his equerry. Commencing with a prelude on the gravity of the times which would do credit to a State paper, he then proceeds,

"In future, there will be a paid huntsman, two whippers-in, three kennel-men for the bloodhounds, five grooms, including Alexandre, and seven men to look after the hounds. It is not becoming that a man of my quality, with an infinite number of servants, should be waited upon whilst travelling by persons whom everyone knows to be kennelmen. My hunting establishment does not need a paymaster . . . and besides, he is a very proper person to have the conduct of my equipage on active service. . . ."

And so on. It is easy to smile at this, but it is all very natural; up to this time the youth has been on an allowance, but he has just become his own master, stands on his own feet as a man of property; Dangeau gives us the details:

"M. le Duc du Maine, whose household the king has just regulated, now manages his own affairs; he has about 350,000 livres of rent, namely 100,000 from the Government of Languedoc, 25,000 crowns of pension from the king, 48,000 as General of the Galleys, and 100,000 as Colonel-General of the Swiss Guards. . . ."

He had in fact, in the money of 1914, an income of between £16,000 and £17,000 a year. Even so, he was no doubt prudent to retrench on his hunting establishment, for in the seventeenth century the expense of hunting on a royal scale was enormous. In 1665 Louis XIV was far from having everything handsome about him, as he had in the latter half of the reign; and yet we find that he was then maintaining three hunting establishments, under the Grand Huntsman, the Grand Falconer, and the Master of the Wolf Hounds respectively. The first had, in addition to the Grand Huntsman, four Lieutenants of the Hunt, all salaried posts of course, and a small army of hunt servants proper; nor does this include the captains and keepers of the many royal forests. The Grand Falconer, "exclusive of the necessary officers," had under him fifteen salaried gentlemen. The Master of the Wolf Hounds contents himself with a salaried staff of thirty-five, amongst whom we notice "a baker to bake bread for the hounds" at £7 a year. One's hunting must necessarily have been on a modest scale if one were a mere minor royalty on £16,000 a year.

The campaign of 1689 ended late, and it was not until 31st October that the duke writes from the camp of Quiévran to say that the troops go into winter quarters on the following day;

"If the king intends to spend St. Hubert's Day at Marly, as I think he does, please keep a room for me. I hope you will do this much to give pleasure to a poor Colonel of Cavalry, whom you will find very rusty on everything appertaining to the Court."

In 1690, the campaign opened in May, and Louis, though nearly at full stretch was able to put five armies in the field: the Army of the Rhine, *Monseigneur* commanding, the Army of the Moselle, Boufflers,[14] the Army of Flanders, Luxembourg, the Army of Catalonia, Noailles,[15] and the Army of Dauphiné, Catinat:[16] a total

[14] Boufflers, Louis François, Maréchal and 1st Duc de, 1644–1711; Marshal of France, 1693; his defence of Namur, 1695, much admired; his defence of Lille, 1708, his most brilliant feat.

[15] Noailles, Louis Anne Jules, Maréchal and 2nd Duc de, 1650–1708, son of Anne, 1st duke, and Louise Boyer; Marshal of France, 1693.

[16] Catinat, Nicolas, 1638–1712, fifth of the seven sons of Pierre Catinat and Françoise Poisle; called to the Bar, gave up the law, and entered the Foot Guards, 1661; Marshal of France, 1693; "a good general, not popular with his officers . . . had made his way by sheer merit . . . looked upon contemptuously at Court, because he was . . . of obscure birth, modest, and unskilled in intrigue."

of 350,000 of the best troops in Europe, an immense effort for those days.

Maine, contrary to expectation, got his heart's desire, and went to the front to command the ninety-one squadrons of cavalry in Luxembourg's army of Flanders. He is no longer a subaltern officer, but is about to make his début before a highly critical audience, the star players in Europe's favourite game, who will not, whether friend or foe, be in the least disposed to make any concessions to his rank if he fails; a good deal of his self-satisfaction must have evaporated as he drew nearer to the front, and felt for the first time something of the loneliness of command. True, he called Luxembourg his friend; but in the solitude of his travelling carriage, he may well have wondered just what the friendship of that utterly corrupt, polished cynical hunchback with the snake's eyes and the dead white face would prove to be worth in a crisis.

By 14th June, Maine had arrived at the front, and from the camp of Deinsse writes gratefully, even fulsomely to Mme. de Maintenon; his mind is still entirely preoccupied with his recent promotion, and underneath his rather commonplace flow of compliment we can detect a real gratitude to his father for having given him his chance. He had not long to wait. The morning of 1st July found him at the head of his squadrons, contemplating with a quickening heartbeat what he had never yet seen, a hostile army drawn up in line of battle–the polyglot allied force of Dutch, Spanish, English, Swedish, and German troops, commanded by the Prince of Waldeck,[17] a moderate general, of the straitest sect of military orthodoxy, unlikely to be a match for the Maréchal de Luxembourg. Maine was not given to introspection, and we can only imagine what were his thoughts and feelings as he waited for orders at the head of his force; there would be, one guesses, an uncomfortable dryness of the mouth, and a tendency to fidget with his stirrup leathers; and a prayer or two, for he was never a man to be ashamed that he should be seen praying; above all, there would have been the fear of those outwardly deferential critics at the head of their squadrons, whose

[17] Waldeck, George Frederick, Prince von, 1620–92, German free-lance soldier and diplomatist.

low-voiced laughter would reach him in his isolation, with the clink of horse's bits, the squeal of a kicked charger, and the muttered oath of its rider.

But he need have had no fears, for he too was to have his day of glory as well as Luxembourg. It was all over by sunset, though the enemy fought well and bravely. But when night came, the French were the victors of Fleurus and the allies were in full retreat, leaving behind them eight thousand dead, nearly the same number of prisoners, six hundred colours, and forty-nine guns. Leaving behind them, too, a Duc du Maine very considerably surprised to find himself alive, and whose joy at having "made his proofs" knew no bounds. "The Duc du Maine," says the Gazette, "as General of the Cavalry, charged at the head of his squadrons several times, was confounded in the enemy ranks, had a horse killed under him, and behaved with great bravery; but he was during a part of the action exposed to a heavy infantry fire, during which the Cte. de Jussac, the Marquis de Villarceaux, and the Chevalier de Soyecourt were killed." Poor Jussac and his wife's affair, what does it all concern him tonight?

Maine's own account, written forty-eight hours after the battle, has in it a pleasant note of modesty:

"I am delighted, Madame, I have seen a battle; a great piece of good luck. I am quite well, God be thanked. I should never finish if I once began to praise all those who deserve it. I will content myself with saying that Vandreuil well deserves to be promoted Major-General, and that personally I shall consider myself lucky if the king proves to be satisfied with the services of a cripple, and if he finds that I am beginning to make him some return for his kindnesses to me."

The letters of 1690 make altogether pleasanter reading than those of 1689; there is a savoir faire, a maturity, a modesty, which were lacking in the previous campaign. He is in fact at last a man, and feels himself to be one; he has been tried, and not found wanting. On 9th July he writes again,

"I am really ashamed at all the praise, and compliments which are given to me. It will give a bad impression of us French to hear people *crier au miracle* about a man who has simply done his duty. . . . But what a pleasure it will be to take you in my arms, and to see joy painted on the king's majestic face."

But General Officer, victorious General Officer though he was, he had by no means escaped from Mme. de Maintenon's tutelage, and he shows himself as anxious to keep in her good books as he would have been ten years earlier;

"I am surprised that you think me plunged in debauchery the moment you hear that I have let a feast day pass without communicating. If I had ceased to be a decent-living man by nature, I should not be such a fool as to let the fact be self-evident. I hear Mass every day, with the exception of those on which I am on horseback by three in the morning and do not dismount until noon. So far as possible I insist on an attention to their religious duties from those under my command. I assist the suffering, I compose quarrels, and I have not done a bad turn to anyone, even to those who deserve it. In addition, I may tell you that I never get up or go to bed but I reflect that I may die at any moment. . . . I flatter myself, Madame, that I really am an *honnête homme*, and I shall be much grieved if you think me a libertine at an age at which, if I may venture to say so, I deserve some praise for conducting myself as I do."

The young man may fairly be allowed this bit of boasting, for at an age when all was forgiven to a prince, not even his bitterest enemy brings against him any accusation of sexual immorality; so far as we can find out, he never kept a mistress, or even indulged himself in those amourettes which were a thing of course amongst his contemporaries.

On the following morning he finds himself a little uneasy about the tone of his previous day's letter, and thinks it well to soften it a trifle;

"I am afraid, Madame, you may have found my recent letters a little strongly worded. Please forgive me the vivacity of my temperament, and my sensitiveness on certain subjects. . . . My conduct is, thank God, without reproach, and I am sure it would be only a bad man who would assert the contrary. As long as you give me your love, all will be well. . . . We expect the Household Cavalry back here today, and their return will be a great satisfaction to everyone. Please bring my general's name to the king's notice; he is more attentive to me than you can imagine, and so are all our other generals."

At the beginning of August, Luxembourg is back in his old camp at Quiévran, from where the duke writes about replacing his Equerry, de Jussac, killed at Fleurus.

I hear all sorts of people are putting themselves forward to fill Jussac's lace on my staff. Try to see that no one is sent who would not be pleasing o me, and to all other decent people. You would do me a great pleasure f you could let me have a list of those in the running."

For a young man on active service, Mme. de Maintenon was an xacting correspondent; on the 20th the duke writes her a letter in vhich there is an undercurrent of weariness;

My style, Madame, must have become very confused when you find it ecessary to make use of the king to get me to explain to you matters n which I thought I had already replied . . . nor must you think that a attle, of which no one talks any longer, has turned my head. But you nust think me greatly changed if you assume that I am sulking because, ot being able to find the time, I obey your orders not to write to you. . . Good gracious, Madame, be your own natural self again, and follow our own advice, that one should always employ one ear in listening to vhat good is said of people."

Though Luxembourg had made himself master of Flanders, it vas not until October that he had put his army into winter quarters, eaving the Duc du Maine free to enjoy his triumph at Versailles. His reception there was such as he had a right to expect, and he vould have been more than human if he had not thoroughly ppreciated the odour of Court incense. He probably never heard he one jarring note, which was contributed by his father. Louis XIV was an unrivalled judge of men, though it was rarely that he ould be brought to express an opinion, for he had a remarkable apacity for keeping his own counsel. This winter however, he let lip, before his surgeon Maréschal,[18] his verdict on his favourite son: "The Duc du Maine certainly has plenty of brains and ability, but e will never be able to make any use of them."

The most remarkable event of the winter season at Versailles was he final retirement of Maine's mother, Mme. de Montespan. The urprising thing is that she had not withdrawn earlier, and that the Mortemart pride had not driven her from a position whose humilia-ions would, one imagines, have proved intolerable. It was now welve years since she had lived with the king, seven since she had

[18] Maréschal, Georges, 1658–1736, son of an Irish refugee; First Surgeon of rance, 1703; ennobled, 1707; "honourable, straightforward, and outspoken . . . he ecame a sort of personage."

seen him happily married; and still she lingered on, treated with
perfunctory politeness and consideration more mortifying tha
any neglect. Why did she do so? Presumably from a feminin
desire to turn the kinfe in her own wound, and from a maliciou
pleasure in observing the ennui which her daily presence caused th
king. A trifle brought about the final scene. Her youngest daughte
Mlle. de Blois, now fourteen, was removed from her keeping an
put into the hands of a governess, without Mme. de Montespa
being consulted. The governess was M. de Montchevreuil's wif
and in the arrangement we may well suspect the hand of Mme. d
Maintenon; indeed we may go further and suspect that she foresaw
what would be the result of the appointment. But who can blam
her if she did in fact engineer the transaction? She had suffered muc
from Mme. de Montespan for many years past, and her continue
presence at Court must have been a perpetual thorn in her flesh
But however that may be, the removal of her daughter's educatio
from her hands proved to be the final straw to Mme. de Montespan
she commissioned Bossuet to see the king, charged with a bitte
message requesting permission to retire to the convent of St. Joseph
at Paris. It was immediately given her, and, that there might be n
afterthoughts, the king announced at the same time that he ha
allotted Mme. de Montespan's rooms to the Duc du Maine, an
those of the Duc du Maine to Mlle. de Blois. "Mme. de Monte
span," writes Dangeau on 15th March 1691, "has caused the kin
to be informed . . . that her retirement is permanent; she will spen
half the year at Fontevrault (where it will be remembered her siste
Gabrielle was the Abbess), and the other half at St. Joseph." But th
king had shown his usual wisdom in the prompt reallocation of he
rooms at Versailles, for a month later we hear a remark which throw
some doubt on the sincerity of Mme. de Montespan's resolve t
leave the Court for ever; she is still at Paris, and she is complainin
of "the unseemly haste with which her Versailles rooms have bee
dismantled." Our old friend St. Simon seizes upon this complain
and skilfully works it up into a telling picture against the Duc d
Maine; as usual, his mud sticks, and his account of the incident i
still being used as evidence against the duke;

"The Duc du Maine employed himself in the matter of her banishment with great harshness, and, at the finish, told her, without any beating about the bush, that he had orders from the king that she was to be gone. He was in such haste to occupy her rooms that he had her furniture flung out of the windows."

St. Simon is our only authority for both statements; why does not the tiresomely minute Dangeau tell us anything about it? We have seen that there never was any question of "orders to Mme. de Montespan to be gone," and as for the second accusation, Versailles was a crowded spot, and cascades of furniture erupting from its windows an unusual spectacle; what a scoop for St. Simon that he was the only one of all those thousands to see it. We would wager a good sum that we know what really happened. St. Simon, prowling morosely about the grounds, sees the tall French windows of Mme. de Montespan's suite open on to the terrace, and porters emerge staggering under the heavy furniture of the period. What's all this? By orders of the Duc du Maine?

So impatient to get in that he must throw his mother's furniture out of the windows, must he? And off goes St. Simon to his windowless room in the entresol to record his version of the matter, all piping hot and peppered, for the benefit of posterity.

We shall not be meeting Mme. de Montespan again, so we shall take this opportunity to see how she fared in retirement, where her conduct became as edifying as it had formerly been the reverse, her conversion as spectacular as that of any of the other notorious sinners of the age. The new Mme. de Montespan was liberal in the giving of alms, and never said one word which savoured of scepticism or impiety; several hours a day she devoted to making shirts for the poor, and she, who had been famous as a gourmet, now lived on the plainest and coarsest food; her underclothes and bed linen were made of the roughest materials procurable, and, severest self-conquest of all to a Mortemart, her tongue was kept under a rigorous control. Death came for her at Bourbon, where she was taking the waters, but she had some hours' warning of his coming; before taking the Sacrament for the last time, she sent for all her servants, even the humblest of them, and in their presence confessed her sins, afterwards asking their forgiveness for the scandal of her life. The end came very suddenly, on the morning of 27th May 1707, and found her "with her thoughts turned only to eternity and to her condition as a sinner, whose fears were relieved by a pious trust in God's mercy." She was in the sixty-sixth year of her age.

6. *Ludovise*

LOUIS XIV, taking stock at the end of 1690, had on the whole every reason to feel satisfied with himself. The fall of James II in 1688 had certainly been a severe blow, and the French declaration of war on the Empire had, as Louis foresaw, involved him with most of the States which resented his dominant position in Europe. He had indeed forestalled his potential enemies by declaring war upon them at what seemed to him the psychological moment: against Holland in November 1688: against Spain in April 1689, and against England in July. Further, the Duke of Savoy[1] had taken the opportunity of a European war to shake off the French yoke and was now fighting for the allies. He had however been given a sharp lesson, and Louis hoped that he would shortly see the error of his ways.

But what had this formidable coalition accomplished? Luxembourg had beaten the allies in the vital theatre, Flanders; Tourville[2] had beaten the English fleet off Beachy Head; the expeditionary force shipped to Ireland to set James II on one of his thrones again had effected a considerable diversion of England's war effort; and in Italy, Catinat had routed the treacherous Duke of Savoy. Prospects for 1691, thought Louis, were decidedly bright, and he resolved to use the initiative gained in 1690 by an early surprise attack in great strength on Mons, the fortress covering the gap of the Oise, and a potential enemy bridgehead for the shortest route to Paris. Plans were prepared in great secrecy, and on 17th March the

[1] SAVOY, Victor Amadeus II, 14th Duke of, son of Charles Emmanuel II, 13th Duke, and Françoise de Bourbon, Mlle. de Valois, born 1666; "geography prevented him from being an honest man"; in this and the succeeding war, by a policy of well-timed treachery, frequently repeated, he added greatly to the political strength of his country; married, 1684, a niece of Louis XIV's; died 1732; "he would have won the approval of Macchiavelli."

[2] TOURVILLE, Anne Hilarion de Cotentin, Maréchal and 2nd Cte. de, son of César, 1st Cte. by his wife Lucie de La Rochefoucauld, born 1642; won battle of Beachy Head, 1690; beaten at La Hogue, 1692; "the most modest of men."

king left for the front to assume the supreme command. With him went the Duc du Maine, serving as a Major-General on the Headquarters Staff. By 20th March he had reached Quesnoy, from where the duke hastens to write to Mme. de Maintenon:

"There will be work for us tomorrow, Madame, when we shall see the enemy. I do not know if he will enjoy it as much as we shall. The King is in great spirits and in the best of health, as are all who follow him. . . . I fear you will be uneasy so long as you know that the cannon of the fortress are still in action. But once we get our batteries built we shall soon silence them, and after that there will be only musketry fire, which no one bothers about."

On the 21st the army arrived before Mons, where Maine's younger brother, now aged thirteen, received his baptism of fire. We shall be seeing a good deal of the Cte. de Toulouse in years to come, so here we will only remark that he was to develop into a very different man from his brother. He had, we may recollect, been brought up by Mme. de Louvois, not by Mme. de Maintenon, and was thereby both a loser and a gainer; if he lacked the Duc du Maine's early charm, he had in compensation a far greater share of the Bourbon insensibility to danger, hardship, and the world's opinion. He was much the more popular of the brothers in France, and developed in time into a really competent admiral. His first recorded remark foreshadows the man who was to earn the respect of English sea captains in the next big war. On the outskirts of Mons a cannon ball kills the horse of La Chesnaye, by whose side he is riding in the king's entourage. The thirteen-year-old Count turns in his saddle and says, "Another horse for M. La Chesnaye," and remarks to his companions, "So that is what they call a cannon shot, is it? Is that all?"

The Duc du Maine was perhaps not without a twinge of jealousy at the success of his young brother's début, for he writes to Mme. de Maintenon a few days later,

"It seems to me, Madame, that the king is content with me, but it would set me at ease to hear from you that such is the case. . . . He is not keeping his word to you, for, apart from the way he fatigues himself, he also thrusts into danger like, if I may dare to say so, a young fool who has his reputation to make, and who has to show that he is not afraid. I beg you to speak to him about it, for he gets angry if any of us do so. My own health is good, though I am very fatigued. I shall be in the trenches tomorrow."

We may surmise that Maine's rather clumsy piece of flattery reached his father by return of post, for on 2nd April he writes to tell Mme. de Maintenon that "the king continues to show his kindness to me, and I continue to be grateful for it." And he goes on, doubtless warned by his experience in previous years, to forestall any complaints about his own letters;

"I have so little time for writing that it is hardly possible that my style should not suffer. . . . It would be absurd for me to attempt to send you any news, for I daresay you know a great many things that we do not know here."

And the letter ends with his thanks for the kindness which Mme. de Maintenon is showing to his young sister, Mlle. de Blois, who is apparently a boarder at St. Cyr. On 9th April, at half past one in the morning, Louis sits down to scribble a note to Mme. de Maintenon, one of the few which have survived;

"The capitulation is signed, so here is an important affair concluded. I shall take over one of the gates at midday today, and tomorrow, Tuesday, the garrison marches out. Thank God for His goodness to me. I feel sure that you will do so with pleasure.

LOUIS."

The siege over, the Duc du Maine and most of the other senior officers followed the king back to Versailles for summer leave, an unusual break in the accustomed routine of the campaigning season. We know nothing of the duke's movements except that on 9th April he writes from Mons to say that he is on the point of leaving for Paris, and then on 1st June we find him at the front again, at Halle, where he is serving on Luxembourg's staff in the Army of Flanders. His first letter from Halle is not uninteresting, for it gives us his impressions of one who was to play a big part in his later life, Philippe, Duc de Chârtres, afterwards Regent of France.

"M. le Duc de Chârtres has joined us, and has repeated to me all the advice you gave him when he was leaving, and the promise he made to correct his conduct in certain little matters. You should be contented with him, and believe that he is a man of his word. He is very friendly with me, and I respond, as is seemly, with respect, but without affectation. I think I ought to tell you that since he has been here, he has not mentioned the name of Mlle. . . . I have had him to dinner, and he has been to supper with M. de Luxembourg; he too has given us a meal. He was full of excitement when he saw the enemy; in short, he is doing marvels."

Châtres is only seventeen, but there is already ample scope for him to "correct his conduct in certain little matters." As the most famous debauchee of the period, he had already made a promising start by becoming the father of an illegitimate child before he was fourteen, and Mme. de Maintenon may well have wondered what he would do when he put away childish things and came to man's estate. It is as well to succumb to Philippe without a struggle, let conscience say what it will. He was a far more likeable version of our own second Duke of Buckingham, and the most good-natured man in France since Louis le Debonnaire, as St. Simon once told him in a fit of exasperation. The fairies, his mother used to say, had given him every gift at his birth, and the one fairy she had forgotten to invite had in revenge decreed that her sisters' gifts should all be useless to him. He might, if he had not been born a Grandson of France, have attained a modest degree of distinction as a musician, a librettist, a portrait painter, or a chemist. He had it in him to have been a successful ruler of France. He came near to being in the front rank of contemporary generals. "His generosity," says St. Simon, who knew him intimately, "amounted to a diarrhoea." And as Regent most of his wit and energy was devoted to finding plausible reasons for the bestowal of rewards and the pardoning of criminals. He was shortly to marry the Duc du Maine's sister, Mlle. de Blois, who was to bear him a family of daughters whose exploits make the *chronique scandaleuse* of Louis XIV's reign very small beer. In spite of the tone in which Maine writes of him, it is hard to believe that even at that early age the two young men can have liked each other, for their characters were antipathetic, and, even then, each must have sensed in the other, if not a rival, at least an inconvenience. The Duc du Maine goes on to say that he is on the best of terms with M. d'Arcy,[3] Châtres' Governor, and with the Abbé Dubois, his

[3] Arcy, Réné Martel, Marquis d', ob. 1694; Governor to Duc de Châtres, 1690; his death "was a great misfortune for the Duc de Châtres, for he had acquired the respect and esteem of his pupil, and gave him nothing but good advice."

tutor. He was to have reason to alter his favourable opinion of the latter in years to come.

Maine's next letter is, I suspect, inspired by Luxembourg, who adopts this method of hinting that he hopes to be given a free hand by the king; the moment was an appropriate one for making the attempt, for Louvois was just dead, and his son, Barbézieux,[4] who had succeeded him, was still young and inexperienced.

"It is true that since the enemy crossed the Sambre, we have not had much leisure. The Prince of Orange keeps close to us, but I think he only wants to annoy us, and fears to take decisive action. One way and another, everything is working out just the way the king would wish. God preserve him to us. Prevent him, Madame, from working too hard; for if he injures his health, he will do our affairs more harm than will be caused by his applying himself a little less closely to business."

Luxembourg, whose one preoccupation was the retention of Mons, spent the rest of 1691 in barring William's approach to that fortress, and in declining his somewhat clumsy efforts to entice him to battle. It was a pretty campaign, but doubtless very boring to Maine and his fellow generals, who thirsted for another Fleurus. Maine writes at the beginning of August:

"I am ashamed of having been so long without writing, but so very little happens here that this letter is merely to let you know that I am still in the world. . . . I am delighted that the king should still be pleased with me, for my one ambition is to be worthy of his kindness. I have sent him, by M. de Luxembourg's orders, a report of a little tour which I have just made to Dinant." (Where presumably he had been acting as the Commander-in-Chief's deputy on inspection duty.)

This is the duke's last letter from the front during this campaign. The rest of the field operations present no feature of interest to the junior officers or to the public, and Luxembourg had to put his army into winter quarters with no other consolation than that of having given an exhibition of professional skill which won the reluctant admiration of the allied generals.

Soldiering was not the subject uppermost in the Duc du Maine's mind when he returned to Versailles for the Court season of 1691.

[4] Barbézieux, Louis François Le Tellier, Marquis de, 1668–1701, succeeded his father as Secretary for War, 1691; "his capacity for business, and the quickness with which he worked, were incredible . . . vindictive, unforgiving . . . liable to terrible fits of passion."

In the dragging summer months he had taken counsel with himself, perhaps also with Mme. de Maintenon, on the possibility of a future which every day grew more desirable in his eyes; he was over twenty-one, and his life had been lived on very different lines from those of his cousin, the Duc de Chârtres. He wanted a wife.

But there remained the question, what was he to say to the king? There is one point which nearly all the portraits of Louis XIV have in common, and that is his "terrifying majesty." Even today, it is not perhaps the easiest thing in the world to announce to one's father one's intention of getting married; but in old France it was a piece of presumption that the initiative in such a matter should come from the son at all. It was for him to remain a bachelor, contented or otherwise, until his father announced that he had arranged a suitable marriage for him. To break a universally acknowledged rule of decorum for the benefit of the most formidable father in France was an enterprise beside which a few charges into the enemy ranks at Fleurus seemed trivial. And the prospect cannot have gained in attractiveness with each league which his post horses threw behind them on the long road to Versailles.

We may be sure that, once arrived, he lost no time in entreating Mme. de Maintenon to exert herself as never before in the cause of her *mignon's* happiness.

At this point the modern reader will complain that he, or more especially she, is not being fairly dealt with. Where is the account of the Duc du Maine's first meeting with the girl, and what of the courtship? Why are we thus rushed *in medias res*? There *was* no girl in the case, and, had there been, Mme. de Maintenon would certainly have refused to lend her aid to the impudent proposition that a son should suggest to his father whom he was to marry. It was for the Duc du Maine, if he could summon up enough courage for the task, to ask his father for a wife; it would then be his father's business either to refuse, or else to look about him for a suitable bride. Love matches were material for the poets and romancers, not for real life, where, if not actually improper, they were at least considered in very doubtful taste. Some years before this time, *Mademoiselle* had dismissed a lady from her service, solely for her disgusting conduct in making a love marriage. Turn to St. Simon's account of his own marriage if you will see how matrimonial affairs were transacted in the best families. St. Simon, more fortunate than the Duc du Maine, has no father, and is able to arrange his own business for himself—"Mlle. de Royan (she was a Laval) would have been a noble and rich marriage, but I was alone in the world, and wanted the support of an influential father-in-law and family." After a little search he then pitches on the Duc de Beauvilliers,[5] father of eight daughters; Beauvilliers thinks that the only suitable one would be the eldest, aged fifteen, but adds that she wants to be a nun, and that the last time he saw her, she was more determined than ever. St. Simon replies handsomely that Beauvilliers can hardly suspect him of being in love with a girl he has never seen in his life: that what he desires is an alliance with the Duc and Duchesse de Beauvilliers:[6] and if the eldest girl becomes a nun, why then one of the others will do him just as well. This marriage fell through, and St. Simon next opens negotiations with the Maréchal de Lorges,[7] who has five daughters. The girls are—we can find no other expression—paraded for his inspection, and he chooses the eldest, Mlle. de Lorges, "fair, with a perfect complexion and figure, an amiable face, and a very modest, noble manner; she it was who pleased me most, without comparison, directly I saw them." He married her, and they lived happily ever afterwards. Thus did the ancien régime deal with the problem of marrying and giving in marriage.

Mme. de Maintenon having been won over, she and the Duc du Maine proceeded to lay siege to the king. It proved to be a tougher struggle than either of them had anticipated. Louis was ready enough to promote his favourite son's fortunes, was in fact even then con-

[5] BEAUVILLIERS, Paul de, 2nd Duc de, 1648–1714, son of François, Ist Duke, and Antoinette Servien; Chief of Council of Finance, 1685; Councillor of State, 1691; "entirely occupied with his duty . . . lived like a hermit."

[6] BEAUVILLIERS, Henriette Louise Colbert, 1658–1734, second daughter of "the great Colbert" and Marie Charron; married, 1671, Paul de Beauvilliers, and entered on a life of "unbroken union and mutual confidence"; life-long friend of Fénélon; in disgrace as a Quietist, 1698; much disliked by Mme. de Maintenon.

[7] LORGES, Guy Aldonce de Durfort, Maréchal and 1st Duc de, son of Guy Aldonce, 2nd Marquis de Lorges, and Elizabeth de La Tour d'Auvergne; nephew of Turenne under whom he first served in 1642. "Even the king was cautious how he treated him."

templating their advancement to a point beyond which either Mme. de Maintenon or the duke had anticipated; but for that very reason he was the more alive to the inconveniences and possible danger to the State which might result from allowing the Duc du Maine to found yet another bastard branch of the house of Bourbon. When the duke first made his request, his father told him bluntly that men in his position ought not to leave families; the duke, no doubt swallowing a telling but tactless rejoinder, continued to plead his cause, urging with a sincerity which we have no ground to suspect, that if marriage were forbidden him, his father would be inviting him to live in mortal sin. Mme. de Maintenon used all her eloquence and influence to emphasise the religious aspect of the matter, and late in the winter Louis gave way. The Duc du Maine was promised a wife before the opening of the 1692 campaign, and the king sat down to consider the matter. Suspense and speculation ran high at Court whilst the king's decision was awaited, and even the Duc du Maine must have felt some curiosity, if not anxiety, as to what the decision would be.

Louis, his mind once made up, acted with that innate sense of the fitting (one had almost written, sense of the theatre) which makes so large a part of his charm, and of the perfection with which he played the role of the great king and the great gentleman. Kings of France did not visit, they were visited; and the Prince de Condé[8] must have been considerably startled to hear on the morning of 16th February 1692 that the king was entering his anteroom. He was there, said Louis, not as King of France, but as a father who had come to solicit the hand of one of the prince's daughters for an honest young gentleman, his son. It is hardly necessary to say how Condé received the proposition; and the two fathers concluded the business with the decision to introduce a pretty touch of sentiment into their little comedy by letting Maine himself settle the unimportant detail of which of the girls should become his wife. The duke's choice fell on the second daughter, Anne Louise Benedicte de

[8] CONDÉ, Henri Jules de Bourbon, 5th Prince de, 1643–1709, eldest son of "The Great Conde" and Claire Clémence de Maillé-Brézé; "has not a single virtue; his vices are softened only by his defects, and he would be the most malignant man on earth if he were not the feeblest."

Bourbon, Mlle. de Charolais, now sixteen years of age–"M. le Prince," says a contemporary "had three daughters for him to choose from, and an extra quarter of an inch of stature made him prefer the second. All three were extremely small; the eldest was beautiful, and full of sense and wit. The incredible constraint, to say the least of it, in which the strange temper of M. le Prince kept everyone who was subject to his yoke, made the choice of her sister a cause of bitter heartburning to her." Once the duke had made his selection, no time was lost; the betrothal was celebrated a few days later in the king's private room at Versailles, after which he gave an evening party at Trianon, which included a concert, a lottery, and a supper for eighty guests. And on 19th March, the wedding was celebrated in the chapel at Versailles, Cardinal de Bouillon[9] officiating. The issue of the *Mercure Galant* which describes the ceremony is still in existence, and to the male eye is of no more interest than a similar paragraph in the *Times* today, except for one interesting detail; the bulk of the account is taken up with a description of the men's clothes, and the bride's dress is not even mentioned, though there is a good deal about the groom "in black Tours cloth, trimmed with gold." The king played host at the dinner, reception, and supper which followed the wedding, and then the newly-married couple were bedded in the presence of all the guests, the King of England handing the nightshirt to the duke. On the following morning the new duchess received the visits of the whole Court, in bed, with the Princesse d'Harcourt[10] at her bedside to do the honours. Louis came down handsomely in the matter of wedding presents; the bride was given a hundred thousand francs in cash, with clothes and jewels to the value of two hundred thousand, perhaps £12,500 of 1914 money; and to his son he gave a million francs.

So here is the duke married, and for the moment everyone is

[9] BOUILLON, Emmanuel Théodose de La Tour d'Auvergne, Cardinal de, 1644–1715, second son of 2nd Duc de Bouillon and Eléonore Catherine de Bergh; dean of the Sacred College, 1700; dismissed as Grand Almoner, and degraded from the Order, 1701, exiled 1702; deserted to the allies, 1710; went to Rome to live, 1712.

[10] HARCOURT, Marie Françoise de Brancas, Princesse d', elder daughter of Charles, Cte. de Brancas, and Suzanne Garnier; "one of the prettiest girls at Court"; married 1667, Alphonse Charles de Lorraine, Prince d'Harcourt; she ran to seed in later life, losing her beauty and becoming dirty and untidy. She died in 1715.

pleased, Mme. de Maintenon, the king, the duke himself, and even the bride. "God grant that they will continue as satisfied as I am at the moment of writing," says Mme. de Maintenon. Even our old friend Madame Palatine is delighted, though for a very different reason:

"God be praised, M. du Maine is married, and it is a great weight off my mind. I think someone must have told the king's old excrement what the Paris mob is saying, and that it frightened her. . . . They were saying that if she started to interfere to get my daughter given to M. du Maine, they would strangle him before the wedding day, and that the old woman, as they call her, would not be safe going through the streets."

We may remark in passing that there is not the slightest evidence that the Paris mob entertained the sentiments which *Madame* attributes to it. Let us now see what sort of a family is this house of Condé into whose intimacy the Duc du Maine has so rashly thrust himself.

All the Condés share this characteristic, that they are superficially attractive, and that the better we know them, the less we like them; they were all clever, all eccentric, and some of them were mad. They nearly all were bad-hearted, and the worst and most eccentric of them was Maine's father-in-law; indeed it was only the fact that he was First Prince of the Blood, and that the period was the seventeenth century, that kept him out of a lunatic asylum. When Maine married his daughter, Condé was a man of forty-nine, who had been head of his house since the death of his famous father six years earlier. He was a small, thin, ugly man, who had soldiered with distinguished personal courage, but, in spite of all his ambition, without showing a trace of his father's military genius. Though both mad and wicked, he had done brilliantly at school and college, and under his reign the Condé country house, Chantilly, was a haven for men of letters, with whom the prince could hold his own on any topic, for he had few equals in acquired knowledge of all kinds. It was very unsafe to have any dealings with him, however, for he had the malignant cunning of a monkey, and was never happier than when he could do an unsuspecting friend a bad turn; though if the whim took him, he could be one of the most perfect hosts in

France, and his entertainments were famous both for their lavishness and their exquisite taste. He was greedy, even by Condé standards, and simply did not understand what scruple meant, if anything stood between him and his desires. And yet, a man whom it was very hard to resist when he wanted to make a favourable impression. As time went on, society began to suspect that there was something more serious the matter with *M. le Prince* than an uncontrollable temper; his habits became more and more odd. No one, even in the family, had taken much notice of his having four dinners cooked for him daily at different places, and for the same hour; but people began to be alarmed when the Maréchale de Noailles reported that, on a formal visit, he had come into her bedroom, whilst the maids were making the bed, and with a shout of "*What* a lovely bed!" had plunged into it. At one period of his life he announced that he was dead, and refused all nourishment, until the family doctor agreed with him, but assured him that he was wrong in supposing that the dead did not eat; a party of "dead" men was invited to dine with the prince, and not only did the prince thereafter eat heartily, but had much interesting conversation with his fellow dead on their experiences in a new world. He frequently imagined himself to be a dog, and would prowl about his grounds at night baying the moon, to the terror of his family and the annoyance of the neighbours. Nor were his canine fits all nocturnal; it is a striking illustration of the impression which Louis XIV made on all who came in contact with him that when these dog fits came upon *M. le Prince* in the royal presence, he could sufficiently control his madness to withdraw into a window, from where his barkings, muffled by the end of the curtains which he would stuff in his mouth, would be faintly audible to the company.

In his lucid intervals he was a rather more objectionable neighbour than when he was insane. Rose,[11] the king's secretary, had a country place which adjoined Chantilly, the Condé château, and which was to *M. le Prince* his Naboth's vineyard; he had tried to buy it–at his

[11] ROSE, Toussaint, 1615–1701; successively secretary to Cardinal de Retz, Cardinal Mazarin, and from 1657 to the end of his life, to Louis XIV; "very rich, very miserly, extremely witty: the king could refuse nothing to his secretary, who knew all his secrets."

own price of course – and Rose had refused to sell, so Condé tried to harry him out by a course of calculated annoyances, culminating in the bright plan of loosing five hundred foxes into Rose's preserves. Rose however, making no effort to cope with the foxes, set out for Versailles as fast as horses could draw him, saw Louis, and opened the interview by asking him how many kings there were in France? The upshot of the matter was that Condé had a very unpleasant interview with his master, and was forced to compensate Rose handsomely. His exploit during another lucid interval in 1700 is less high-handed, more amusing, and perhaps more malevolent; he persuaded the Duc de Luxembourg,[12] the foolish son of a clever father, and the husband of one of the most discredited women in France,[13] to attend a fancy dress ball at Court as a stag, and with antlers on his forehead; "the sudden burst of laughter" says St. Simon, "was scandalous . . . Mme. de Luxembourg had known nothing about her husband's masquerade, and lost countenance, notorious though she was . . . even the king could not help laughing." The Duc du Maine was to have ample opportunity of getting to know his amiable father-in-law, who lived for another seventeen years; but we learn, from St. Simon oddly enough, that *M. le Prince* was despised by his son-in-law, who treated him with scant respect. As for the Duchesse du Maine, her first act after the marriage was to throw off her father's yoke for ever – "she laughed at everything the Prince said to her."

The duchess, born Anne Louise Benedicte de Bourbon, Demoiselle de Charolais, was the fourth child of our barking friend and his unhappy wife, Anne of Bavaria. She was already related to her husband, as her brother had some years earlier married Maine's favourite sister, Louise, the young lady who had been in trouble for smoking a pipe in the royal apartments; the second Condé girl had married another Bourbon, the Prince de Conti, and there were two sisters still unmarried. The future Duchesse du Maine's first appear-

[12] LUXEMBOURG, Charles Frederic de Montmorency, 2nd Duc de.

[13] LUXEMBOURG, Marie Gilonne Gillier, Duchesse de, daughter of the Marquis de Clérembault; married, 1696, 2nd Duc de Luxembourg; "a very rich and pretty heiress . . . her mode of living was such that no woman would associate with her." She died at Rouen, 1709, "having always contrived to make her husband believe that she was the best and most devoted of wives."

ance in history shows her in an attractive light, when at the age of four the family doctor reports that she has cried herself ill because her tame bird has been eaten by a cat. As she developed, she showed wit, conversational charm, and an uncommon desire for knowledge, which however got no further than a bright, shallow receptivity, the fruit of a superficial education in a surprising number of subjects. She was a reader of French poetry and romances, with a remarkably retentive memory for dramatic verse, which, when she entered into her kingdom of Sceaux, was to make her, amongst other things, an indefatigable actress in comedies, which she played very badly.

Mme. du Maine and Sceaux are inseparable; Sceaux is more than her house, it is part of the duchess herself, a material extension, as it were, of her own personality. In that delightful château, carefully isolated from the slightest contact with reality, she was to pass the greater part of her life in a world of her own devising, a world of shepherds and shepherdesses, gallantry after the style of Rambouillet, poetizing, philosophizing, play acting, in an incessant, tedious round of elaborate and enormously expensive mock simplicity. At Sceaux everyone had an other-world name which was in current use in this Palace of Armida, and the name which she gave herself gives no bad idea of her character: she was the fairy Ludovise. She was in many respects not unlike a fairy. To begin with, she was a tiny person, tiny even in a Court where to be over five foot six was to be thought rather awkwardly tall; and so diminutive were she and her sister, that at Versailles they were known as the Dolls of the Blood, not the Princesses of the Blood. But in her little face and figure there was something of elfin charm. Like a fairy too, she seemed exempt from the grosser appetites of humanity, for she gave the impression of never wanting food or sleep; night after night the famous *nuits blanches* of Sceaux, the stilted pastoral revels, would continue until the sun rose on the duchess, gay and eager for some fresh diversion with which to greet Phoebus in his glory. For the dark Condé spot on her brain manifested itself in a terror of ever being left alone for a single instant, day or night; even for those few minutes of the day, during which the most gregarious of us prefer to retire behind locked doors, she must be surrounded by a laughing, chattering throng.

But Ludovise was not only queen of the fairies, shepherds, and nymphs of Sceaux, she was the leader of a blue stocking academy. The house was perpetually filled with savants and pedants, to Sceaux gravitated the second-rate in every field of intellectual activity. You could not talk to the duchess, you must sit and listen to her bright, shallow, witty stream of monologue; she prided herself on her understanding of Descartes and on the quality of the disputations which she held with her dear friends on the Cartesian philosophy, but there were in fact no disputations on the Cartesian philosophy or on any other topic; for the slightest disagreement with anything she said or did would at any time throw her into an uncontrollable fit of fury. The dark Condé spot again, inherited from her grandmother, the wife of Condé the Great.

The duchess had too the eternal youthfulness of a fairy; she was a bright, spoilt child, and a bright, spoilt child she remained until the end of her long life. Never for an instant did the spate of childish amusements diminish in pace or volume; fête succeeded fête, opera, opera, and flirtation, flirtation, the latter couched in all the tedious machinery of the *carte du Tendre* and the exaggerated prudery of Rambouillet. Physical age even she could not keep at bay, but in that enchanted world the cold, disillusioning wind of reality never blew; as she grew old, so did her gallant shepherds. When she was over fifty, she was still playing the ingenue shepherdess in a new and exciting love affair with the gentle shepherd La Motte, who was fifty-four, and blind. At all costs the game must be kept going.

In spite of their enormous income, the duchess's life reduced the Maines to embarrassment: or rather, it ruined their tradespeople. For the darkest of Mme. du Maine's fairy-like attributes was her utter lack of heart towards mortals. All the machinery of the most exquisite sensibility of affection she had in abundance, but without a spark of feeling for a single human being. It is significant that at a time when charity was, to put it at its lowest, good form for a great lady, we never hear of her performing a charitable action. To her immediate circle, she could be profuse, because long faces might spoil her pleasure, and no doubt such of the farms and dependencies of Sceaux as came under her eyes daily, were full of plump, nicely dressed stage peasants, for the same reason. But during the terrible years when Marlborough was knocking at the gates of France, when great ladies were selling their jewelry for the poor, when in every province could be found by the roadside, and in Church porches, dead peasants with their mouths full of the grass and leaves which they had been too feeble to masticate, the stream of costly fêtes continued. What was it to her that these horrid, unpicturesque creatures should starve to death? Was there not at that very minute a rehearsal about to begin for tonight's comedy, in which she is to play the lead? And so the senseless, heartless extravagance continued. Louis XIV has been reproached with the extravagance of his entertainments, and Condé at Chantilly had expended vast sums on a single fête; but both men had the good sense and taste to see that fêtes, to be successful, must be rare and perfect. Whereas at Sceaux they were continual, and tediously alike; the ingenuity of the duchess's coterie was not equal to the unceasing demands for new forms of entertainment, and in any case, so long as there were noise, lights, extravagance, bustle, it mattered very little to the mistress of the house that the same thing had been seen ten, twenty, thirty times before. At last hardly a night went by without the wearisomely familiar roar of fireworks, the procession of the Emperor of Hindustan and his Court to pay homage to the incomparable Ludovise, and the emergence from the neighbouring boscage of a troupe of singers brought out from Paris, who, dressed as fauns and nymphs, and led by the Spirit of Sceaux, would sing a fulsome rigmarole to the duchess, comparing her to a compound of all the goddesses of Olympus.

Death, when he visited the château, was an unwelcome guest, especially if his presence was unlooked for, because he could seriously compromise the pleasures of a whole day. A part in the comedy must be recast, a new Great Mogul found at short notice to lead the chorus of adulation from a world under tribute. In her long life Mme. du Maine was to lose many of her dearest friends to whom she was bound by inseparable ties; when the news of the dearest friend's death reached her, there would be a perfunctory exclamation of regret. The friend's name had then been mentioned for the last time, and, after this barely perceptible falter, the merry-go-round would gather speed again, with its blaring reiteration of the maddeningly familiar tune.

In short, the radical defect about the Duchesse du Maine was this: that never for one instant in the whole of her life did a suspicion cross her mind that the world had been created for any other purpose than to serve as a playground for Anne Louise Benedicte de Bourbon, Princess of the Blood, and Duchesse du Maine.

Had you enquired into the nature of her religious beliefs, she would have replied indignantly that she was a Christian. And she no doubt believed herself to be one, but if she ever gave five minutes' thought to God, which is unlikely, she may be imagined as forming an indistinct picture of a deferential old gentleman, whom she must not forget to invite to her first *fête galante* in her heavenly mansion, and in compliment to whom the plot of the opening ballet had better have a Biblical turn.

A contemporary said of her, that not only had she never been out of her own house in her life, but that she had never even put her head out of the window. She was probably wise in not putting it out; what could she have learned from the flood of bitter pamphlets against her extravagance in the years when France was bleeding to death? Even the most weather-wise pilots of the State failed to see in these publications the little cloud on the horizon which was to grow and blacken the whole sky, until the storm burst in 1789.

But this is all for the future; Sceaux still belongs to Colbert at the moment, and at Versailles everything is rose coloured. Three days after the wedding Mme. de Maintenon writes that the duchess is going to spend Holy Week at Maubuisson, where she hopes she will have a good rest.

"They are killing her here with the fatigue and constraint of Court life. She is weighed down with gold and jewelry, and her headdress weighs more than she does. The end of it will be that they will stop her growth and injure her health; she is prettier without her headdress and all her jewels; she hardly eats anything, and I doubt if she gets enough sleep, and I am in a fright in case they have married her too soon. I should like to keep her for a bit at St. Cyr, dressed as a schoolgirl, and running about as carefree as they are, in the garden; for there are no austerities so severe as those of the world."

The tiny bride in all her finery must have looked more like a Madonna from a Spanish cathedral than a human being, one imagines. At first even Mme. de Maintenon is satisfied with the new duchess:

"I am very pleased with her, she has wit, and if she does as she intends doing, she will be worth more than all the other Condés put together; you know that it is not deference that I look for, it is her good alone. I want her to be pleasing to God, to the king, and to her husband: and to all honourable people. All this cannot be done unless she herself wishes it, and puts some constraint on herself."

Let us note in passing, the word "deference" in this letter, as an indication of Mme. de Maintenon's position. What "deference" could a Marquise in an ambiguous position look for from a Princess of the Blood? But a Princess of the Blood might well be expected to show deference to the king's wife.

There were few men, and no women, who could for long continue to throw dust in Mme. de Maintenon's eyes, and she soon began to size up Mme. du Maine; to Mme. de Brinon[14] she writes,

"I have a bone to pick with you. It is about Mme. du Maine. You have deceived me about her in the most essential particular, namely her piety; she does not show the slightest tendency towards it, and wants to follow the crowd. . . . Naturally I do not want her to show the devotion of a professed religious, but I admit I should like to see her live regularly, and adopt a course of life pleasing to God, the king, and her husband; for the latter has enough sense to hope that his wife may be wiser than certain others. I have given her a Lady of Honour who is a saint, but she seems to have no authority over her, and merely follows her about; she is a child, and has more need of a governess than of a Lady-in-Waiting. For the rest, I find her much what you describe, pretty, pleasant, cheerful, witty, and, best of all, in love with her husband, who for his part, loves her passionately, and would sooner spoil her than cause her the least pain. I hope I am able to love her, she being what she is to the man towards whom my heart is tenderest."

Even Madame Palatine, in her joy at not having M. du Maine for a son-in-law is disposed to look quite kindly on the Duchesse du

[14] Ursuline nun, Headmistress of St. Cyr.

Maine–"No beauty," she says, "but she has plenty of wit and knowledge, which gathers the wits and the learned around her."

1692 was for Maine a honeymoon year; the duke availed himself of the privilege of his new status as a husband to absent himself from the army that summer; no royal or ducal privilege this, but one which under the old monarchy was, even in time of war, extended to a private soldier. As in Biblical times, the man who had taken a wife was exempt from serving in the campaign following his marriage.

The summer passed in the solution of that delicate problem which must be solved finally and peremptorily in every marriage, namely who was to rule the new establishment? "If two people ride the same horse," the Great Condé used to remark, "one of them must ride behind." The solution did not long remain in doubt; uxoriousness and timidity, or let us call it tenderness, were poor weapons with which to fight Mme. du Maine. The duke had wanted a wife: he had got what he wanted: and the price which he paid was that before six months had passed, he had taken the rank in society which he was to hold for the rest of his life–he was the husband of Mme. La Duchesse du Maine.

Tu l'as voulu, Georges Dandin, tu l'as voulu!

7. *Smear Campaign*

IN 1693 the Duc du Maine had to put his shoulder to the wheel once more; he had had practically a year of domestic bliss, and his return to the active list was sweetened for him by promotion to the rank of Lieutenant-General, in which capacity he was to command the cavalry of Boufflers' Army of the Meuse, where later in the year the king intended to command in person. General officer though he now was, it is doubtful if Maine was able to appreciate how the strategic situation had worsened for France during his year's absence from the front; and if he could not, it is excusable, for 1693 was to be the year of Landen, Neerwinden, Marsaglia, and the fall of Charleroi, all of them resounding defeats for the allies. But Louis, a far better statesman than he was a general, was not the dupe of his victories; he at least appreciated the consequences of the crushing naval defeat he had sustained at La Hogue in 1692, and saw that it extinguished any hope of putting James II back on his throne. Henceforward William of Orange, firmly in the saddle at London, would be able to come to his continental allies' assistance with the whole strength of England and the Dutch Republic. And even Louis' subjects were beginning to realize the immense strain which was being thrown on the French economy by facing Europe in arms; "France, "wrote Mme. de Sévigné, "is perishing to the sound of Te Deums." More ominous still, generals were beginning to whisper of the poor quality of the recent levies and to complain of the occasional breakdown of their supply and transport services, for, to crown everything, 1692 and 1693 produced exceptionally poor harvests. Louis was ready for peace on his own terms, but unfortunately such a peace could not be had.

Maine was late in getting to the front; it was not until 18th May that he set out in the king's entourage, which was numerous, and included a large number of Court ladies led by Mme. de Maintenon. Amongst these Maine had managed to include his wife, whom we find travelling in *Monseigneur's* coach with him and four other women. Mme. de Maintenon alone travelled with the king.

It would be a mistake to imagine that even for royal ladies, there was anything of the picnic about these summer migrations to the back area of the Flanders front, and as hour after hour the tired, hungry, thirsty women were jolted over the abominable roads, mud-bespattered or powdered with dust from the hoofs of the cavalry escort, they must have asked themselves bitterly, like war-time travellers of a later day, "Is my journey really necessary?" How Mme. du Maine bore it we do not know, but we may imagine that she was by no means the least voluble or loud-voiced in her complaints at the crosses and indignities which she had to bear. As all five young women in the coach were sisters or sisters-in-law, each with a permanent stock of grievances against the other four, one does not envy *Monseigneur* his journey; but that phlegmatic prince, who in virtue of his rank would occupy the least uncomfortable seat, probably shut his eyes and pretended to sleep. Mme. de Maintenon gives us a good idea of the conditions which even she had to put up with when on active service; in the previous year she had lodged in Dinant during the siege of Mons, and here are her impressions of that beautiful place:

"Picture to yourself how yesterday, after a six hours' journey over a fairly good road, we saw a château on top of a rock, in which there seemed no possibility of lodging, even when we had got ourselves hoisted up to it. We were quite close before we saw any road at all, and then at last at the foot of the château, in an abyss, and as if we were looking down into a deep pit, we saw the roofs of some little houses that might have been meant for dolls, surrounded on all sides by rocks, which are perfectly dreadful both by reason of their height and their colour; they seem to be made of iron. One has to get down into this horrible place by a road which is of a roughness of which I can give you no idea, the coach jumping about so as to break all the springs,[1] and the women inside holding on to anything they can catch hold of. After a quarter of an hour of this torture, we found ourselves in a town consisting of a street they call the Grande Rue, in which two carriages cannot pass. There are

[1] Her apprehensions were justified. Her coach had to be left behind with broken springs. I saw it there in 1919.

also small streets in which even two chairs cannot do so. One cannot see anything, the water is bad, and the bakers have orders not to bake except for the army, so that one's servants cannot get bread anywhere. . . . It has not stopped raining since we got here, and they tell me that if it should turn hot, it will be unendurable on account of the refraction of the rocks. . . . So far I have been in only two churches, where, in addition to execrable music, one could not see through a fog of incense which made me giddy. For the rest, the town is so muddy that one cannot drag oneself about it, the pavé so sharp that it cuts into one's feet, and the narrow streets are used as privies by all the inhabitants. My maid Suzon says that she does not know what the king would be at, taking such towns as these, and why cannot he leave them to the enemy?"

Decidedly Mme. de Maintenon would have had little sympathy with the Romantic Movement.

This year she seems to have found things a little better, but not much:

"We wretched vagabonds have had a miserable journey in abominable weather over worse than abominable roads, and with poor lodgings by the way; many coaches stuck, and many ladies had to sleep in chairs, not being able to get their beds, but I have not felt any of these inconveniences, for my servants' affection for me is beyond praise; only, I am so tired in the evenings, and I find that I increase my fatigue by working in the coach; but I must finish the ornament which I have begun for your Church. Here we are at Quesnoy, where we separate from the king . . ."

This was written on 28th May, and on the following day the Duc du Maine took leave of his father and set out for Boufflers' headquarters. The campaign of 1693 is one of the most controversial scenes in Louis XIV's life, and the matter is complicated by the fact that St. Simon was early in the field with a most picturesque and sensational account, which is still too often accepted uncritically.

First the facts: on 2nd June the king assumed command of Boufflers' army, separated by a couple of miles from that of Luxembourg on the 7th when Louis moved to Gembloux. The plan was that the two armies should proceed to cut the enemy communications between Belgium and Germany by capturing Huy and Liège, and thereafter exploit the favourable situation thus created, either by an attack on the Empire or on Holland. William of Orange, strongly posted at the abbey of Park, but inferior in strength to the combined armies of the king and Luxembourg, was covering

Brussels and Liège, having posted Athlone[2] with a strong detachment to observe Boufflers on the Meuse. On 8th June, Louis reviewed his army; and on the 9th, after dinner, he announced that he himself was returning to Versailles, and that *Monseigneur* was leaving to reinforce the army of the Rhine. On the 10th the king left for home, Luxembourg remaining in command of the army of Flanders, and Boufflers in command of that of the Meuse. The whole plan of campaign for the north-eastern front had apparently been abandoned.

Now let us glance hastily at St. Simon's famous interpretation of the matter. He begins by painting the situation of William of Orange:

"He entrenched himself hastily and repented bitterly of allowing himself to be brought to bay in such a situation. It came out afterwards that he wrote several times to his intimate friend the Prince de Vaudemont[3] that he was lost, and could only escape by a miracle."

It is annoying for the historian that only St. Simon has had access to those letters: and, incidentally, how did he get hold of them? The scene now changes to the French camp, the day is 8th June. After depicting the Maréchal de Luxembourg's astonishment at the king's decision, he continues

"But all was useless. The king's mind was made up. Luxembourg, in despair at losing the chance of such an easy and glorious campaign, went down on his knees to him, but could not prevail. Mme. de Maintenon had tried in vain to prevent him from going to the army. His absences made her uneasy; a campaign opened so successfully would have kept him away for long, to gather his laurels in person. Her tears at their separation, and her subsequent letters were arguments to which all considerations of state, all desire for military glory, had to give way."

It is here difficult to acquit St. Simon of a deliberate desire to deceive. The account must give, and is, I maintain, intended to give, the impression that Mme. de Maintenon is at Versailles. St. Simon, then Colonel of the Royal Roussillon Regiment, was spying around the king's headquarters at the time, and must have known perfectly

[2] Athlone, Godart van Ginkel, 1st Earl of, 1640–1703; Dutch soldier; created Earl of Athlone, 1691; his title became extinct in the 9th Earl, 1844.

[3] Vaudemont, Charles Henri de Lorraine, Prince de, bastard of Charles IV, Duc de Lorraine and Beatrix Cantecroix; settled in France, 1707; "one of the handsomest men of his time . . . as anxious to win the affection of the bourgeois and artisan classes as those of persons of higher rank."

well that she was at Namur, within easy riding distance of the king. But let us have a little more St. Simon:

"On the evening of that fatal day M. de Luxembourg, beside himself with grief, confided the secret to Maréchal de Villeroi,[4] to the Prince de Conti, and to his son; they could hardly believe it, and were in despair."

How does St. Simon know it?

"It chanced that I went by myself on duty to M. de Luxembourg's headquarters as I often did, to see what was going on, and to find out what was to happen the next day . . . I found astonishment on all faces, and indignation on a good many . . . the effect produced by this retreat in the army, and even among foreign nations, was incredible. Our enemies could not conceal their surprise and delight. Their comments so far as we heard them, were not more outrageous than those made in our own armies, in Paris, and at the Court; even the courtiers, who are usually glad enough to find themselves back at Versailles, made it a point of honour to be ashamed of their return."

Certainly a deplorable picture of the king, feeble and irresolute as a commander, perhaps even lacking in the common courage of a soldier; but then it happens to be quite untrue. We turn to Dangeau, also a witness of that fatal day, and find that this is what he saw and heard:

"The king held a council with *Monseigneur*, M. Le Prince, Luxembourg, Villeroi, and Boufflers, and announced his decision to send *Monseigneur* into Germany with a large proportion of the troops here. The king had taken this decision at Quesnoy after the news of the capture of Heidelberg, and of the panic which was spreading in Germany. The king prefers conquests in Germany to those which are possible on this front, and he intends himself to return to Versailles."

The news of the unexpected capture of Heidelberg by his army of the Rhine had reached Louis on the 28th May, and he had then decided to exploit that success vigorously in the hope of forcing the Empire out of the war, rather than to employ large forces in gaining a limited strategical objective at the expense of the maritime powers in the north. His strategy may have been unsound, but the picture of Louis, frightened of William of Orange, sneaking off to Versailles,

[4] Villeroi, François de Neufville, 2nd Maréchal and 2nd Duc de, 1641–1730, son of the 1st Maréchal and 1st Duc, and of Madeleine de Créqui; was brought up with Louis XIV, and remained his intimate friend for life. "An abject and clever courtier; beyond that, he had no sort of ability."

is nonsense, for the very good reason that when Louis made his decision, William was not yet at Park, nor had Louis reconnoitered William's position. And, as for his going home, what else was there for him to do? The dynastic principle demanded that the heir to the crown should be given his chance in commanding the army whose prospects were brightest; Louis could not very well supersede Luxembourg the popular hero, and the army of the Meuse, which he had intended for himself, had been reduced to insignificance by the heavy calls made upon it for the reinforcement of the army of the Rhine.

And what of trembling William at Park? Luxembourg, the most dashing general in the French service, with a free hand and 80,000 men set out on 18th June to look into this William problem. His conclusion was that William was so strongly posted as to be unassailable, and it was not until 29th July that Luxembourg manoeuvred him into a position in which he could be attacked.

As for Mme. de Maintenon, whose evil influence was supposed to be at the bottom of the whole business, she is either very innocent or very hypocritical, for all she has to say is, "I am delighted that reasons of state have forced the king to return to Versailles."

With the sudden redistribution of the French forces, the Duc du Maine found himself relegated to a very minor role in 1693. Germany and Flanders were the important theatres, and instead of commanding a cavalry force under the immediate eye of the king, he found himself little more than the commandant of a base reinforcement depot. What was left of the army of the Meuse remained inactive during the rest of the summer, and this must have been particularly galling to Maine, in view of the fact that his cousin, Chârtres serving with the Household Cavalry in Flanders covered himself with glory at Neerwinden. It must have been a welcome moment for Maine when the barren season ended and he was once more able to return to Versailles, where his wife had been living since she got back from Namur on 25th July.

1694 is an important year in the duke's life, for in it occurs a notable step in that "elevation of the bastards" which roused St. Simon to such fury: or, as he prefers to put it, "the peerage received a wound which eventually became its leprosy and cancer." But on this occasion we must not envisage the memoirist as a lone voice crying in the wilderness, for although St. Simon grossly exaggerated the amount of indignation at the new honours bestowed on the bastards, there was undoubtedly a certain amount of subdued murmuring.

Let us be clear as to Maine's status at the beginning of the year. He had been a duke since childhood, but he had never been received as a peer in the Parlement of Paris. We will not endeavour to fight our way into even the outskirts of that terrible jungle, the legislative system of the ancien régime, and it suffices to say that the position roughly was that whilst the king had made Maine a duke *de facto*, he could not be a peer *de jure* until after his reception by the Parlement; or rather, he could exercise none of the judicial or legislative functions of a peer until he had been so received. We saw at the time of Maine's marriage that the king had then the intention of conferring further honours on his son at the first suitable opportunity, and at the beginning of 1694 Louis got his chance. The Duc de Vendôme, son of a bastard of Henri IV, obtained the royal permission to plead in Parlement for precedence over five dukes his seniors, on complicated grounds which, fortunately, we need not investigate. Vendôme's action came so exceedingly apropos for what the king had in mind that one wonders whether Louis had not in fact instigated Vendôme to prefer the claim; he must at any rate have realized that by giving him leave to do so, he made it merely a matter of time until an uproar arose in the peerage which he himself would then have to intervene to quell. The inevitable explosion was not long delayed, and took the form of a loud and angry quarrel between Vendôme and the Duc d'Elboeuf,[5] during a drive with the king from Versailles to Marly; and as this unseemliness was perpetrated almost in the king's hearing, and virtually in the royal presence, it was necessary for Louis to take cognisance of it. The comedy was concluded by Vendôme receiving orders to desist from his precedence claim, with a promise that by way of

[5] Elboeuf, Henri de Lorraine, Duc d', born 1661, son of Charles IV and of Elizabeth de La Tour d'Auvergne.

compensation he would be confirmed in his hitherto unrecognized privileges as a son of a Bastard of France. In the atmosphere thus created, it seemed only right that while the subject was under consideration, a defined position should be secured to the Duc du Maine and his brother, the Cte. de Toulouse, which would settle the status of royal bastards for all time.

The externals of the plot are best followed in Dangeau:

"Monday 3rd May: People say that the king is going to revive in favour of the Duc du Maine, the Countship and Peerage of Eu, one of the oldest titles in the kingdom. . . .

Wednesday 5th May: On Saturday the Duc du Maine will take his seat in Parlement; he will in many ways be recognized as a Prince of the Blood, but in others he will only rank as a Peer, for he will take the ordinary oath. The First President, in asking for his vote, will treat him as Comte d'Eu . . . but he will be treated as a Prince of the Blood in that the First President will address him in the name of the whole Parlement, and will raise his hat to him when asking his advice. . . .

Thursday 6th May: The king has spoken to the Primate about the rank which he wishes M. du Maine to hold in the Parlement. The Archbishop replied that he would consider it an honour to yield precedence to M. du Maine."

Then follows an interesting commentary on St. Simon's picture of the universal indignation at du Maine's new status:

"Some of the dukes complain of the Archbishop, and say that by going to see M. du Maine and promising to yield him precedence, he is trying to usurp with the king the common merit of the peers ready obedience on this occasion.

Saturday 8th May: M. le Duc du Maine was received in Parlement. M. the First President addressed him, and after he had taken the oath, said to him 'M. Le Comte d'Eu, Peer of France, take your seat between Monseigneur the Prince de Conti, and Monseigneur the Archbishop-Duke of Rheims.' "

On 20th May the afterpiece was played; on that date Dangeau tells us

"The affair of M. de Vendôme has been decided, and on those estates which he inherited from his grandfather, Henri IV, he takes rank in Parlement in front of all the Peers, and sits immediately below M. du Maine."

This intermediate rank seems to have been the idea, not of the king, but of Harlay,[6] First President of the Paris Parlement; the original scheme had been that the declaration should merely give the bastards precedence over their seniors in the peerage, but Harlay thought this could be improved upon. He had thoroughly gauged the king's mind, and he knew that where favours for M. du Maine were concerned, there was no risk of over-egging the pudding. And he also saw possibilities for the Parlement in the creation of a new rank in the State, owing its inception to Parlement and its continued existence to the support of that body; but the latter aspect of the matter he probably kept to himself. To the Duc du Maine he urged the importance of having the Princes of the Blood on his side after the king's death, which could not be the case if he attempted to confound his rank with theirs; whilst on the other hand, if he were merely to become senior Duke and Peer, he would irrevocably antagonize those over whom he took precedence, without the prospect of obtaining any compensating advantage. The duke was satisfied with the cogency of the First President's arguments: so was the king: and the famous "intermediate rank" was instituted. Harlay drafted the royal declaration, and as a reward was promised the Chancellorship, the highest prize of the legal profession, on the death of old Boucherat,[7] the present incumbent. A remarkable man this Harlay, but had he valued the opinion of posterity, he would have been less blunt in letting St. Simon see that he did not regard the question of St. Simon's precedence in the Parlement as being the chief preoccupation of the first Court in France: and he has been brilliantly pilloried in consequence. But as usual, St. Simon has let his pen run away with him; Berwick, who had all the professional soldier's contempt for a lawyer, goes out of his way to tell us that Harlay was a man of much wisdom and exceptional probity, whilst Challes, a Parisian law clerk, says that Harlay was universally regretted on account of his uprightness and

[6] HARLAY, Achille III de, 1639–1712, son of Achille II, and Jeanne Marie de Bellièvre; invented the scheme for the legitimization of Louis XIV's bastards without naming the mother; "a man of great capacity and perfect integrity, but with a biting tongue."

[7] BOUCHERAT, Louis, 1616–99, Chancellor of France, 1685; he made his way to the top by pure merit.

fairness. He in fact seems to have been an exceptionally able man, with the appearance of an elderly and dissipated eagle, who made many enemies by his vitriolic tongue and an inability to suffer fools gladly; a famous maker of *bons mots*, which were collected and published after his death under the title of *Harliana*; and with an extremely disconcerting manner. Two provincial lawyers, who had just bought country estates, presented themselves one day at Harlay's lever under their new high-sounding territorial titles; Harlay, who knew them both perfectly well, received them with the ceremonious bow which he reserved for distinguished strangers, turned his back on them, then suddenly whipped round and, putting his face within an inch of theirs, shouted the usual masked fête challenge– "Masks, I know you!" A young lawyer, who was rash enough to call on the First President, dressed not with the sobriety of his profession, but got up as a Court noble, had an even more mortifying experience; Harlay, having transfixed him with a stare, rang for his major-domo, and when that functionary appeared, pointed at a footman and said–"Discharge that rascal at once for having the impertinence to dress like this gentleman."

What was the significance of the rather obscure ritual through which the Duc du Maine had just passed? What the devil was the duke doing in this galley, the modern reader may well ask. The explanation rests on the theory that in the beginning, the peers *had* been the Parlement, and that the lawyers were merely their technical advisers; in proof of which it was advanced that to the present day the official style of a member of the Parlement was "Councillor." However the custom had originated, all peers still had the right to take part in the deliberations of the Grand Chamber as judges, though it was a right seldom exercised, and their attendance was generally limited to seeing a new peer take his seat. But enough for the moment; when we meet the Parlement again, at a crucial moment in the Duc du Maine's life, we shall get some idea of what it was, and what it attempted to do.

During 1694 the Duc du Maine saw little service; he is in fact mentioned only once, when in July he commanded a force sent by Villeroi to oppose a rumoured English descent in the neighbourhood of Dunkirk. But the threat resolved itself into a bombardment by the English fleet, and the duke's force had no other task than to man the defences of the port. Later in the year another honour came to Maine; on 31st August his old general, d'Humières, died at Paris. Amongst other appointments which he held had been the Grand Mastership of the Artillery, and on the 2nd the duke was given the vacant post. It had once been, with the Colonel-Generalships of Cavalry and Infantry, one of the three great military appointments of the Crown after Richelieu had suppressed the office of Constable of France in 1631, but its importance had been systematically sapped by Louvois until now all that remained were certain ceremonial privileges: and of course the large salary. But the salary was perhaps the smaller part of the pickings to be got out of what had become a sinecure, for wherever a captured town had fired in its own defence, all copper and iron articles therein, from the Church bells to the housewives' pots and pans, became the property of the Grand Master, who either sold them for his own profit or allowed the town to redeem them for a fixed sum. It is little wonder that the higher ranks of the French nobility loved war and hated peace, for there were very few posts to which were not attached long-obsolete feudal privileges of this type, which came into force on active service.

1695 was a dangerous year for France. There had been a succession of bad harvests, and every day financial distress was growing, whilst England had definitely emerged as mistress of the seas. There seemed no hope of a speedy end to the war, and every day brought the inevitable Spanish Succession question nearer to a gravely weakened France. But the worst disaster occurred not in the field or at sea, but at Versailles, where on the 4th of January there died Louis' most brilliant soldier, the Maréchal-Duc de Luxembourg. His death could hardly have come at a more unfortunate moment for France; for the day of Villars[8] was not yet, and Luxembourg was the last of the great seventeenth-century generals, as Villars is the first of the eighteenth. There was now to be a sudden and disastrous decline in French leadership. Louis, inferior at sea, threatened

[8] VILLARS, Louis Hector de, son of the Marquis de Villars and of his wife, Marie de Bellefonds, born 1653; his greatest exploit was the command of "the last hope of France" at Malplaquet, 1709; killed whilst commanding in Italy, 1734.

on all his frontiers and in the Mediterranean, his finances badly strained, relapsed everywhere into the defensive, whilst he strove desperately and ultimately successfully to split the undefeatable hostile coalition. Boufflers, with 40,000 men, had spent the winter in constructing lines stretching from the Channel to Namur, and in spite of the crushing burden which had to be shouldered, Louis took the field with five armies: Boufflers on the Meuse, Montal[9] at Furnes, Catinat in Italy, Vendôme in Spain, and Villeroi in command of the crack army of Flanders with instructions that he was at all costs to cover the great fortresses of Ypres, Lille, and Tournai; on his left flank he had Montal, on his right, Boufflers.

Villeroi was no Luxembourg; he was not even a Boufflers or a Catinat, but the most incapable general Louis ever put into a great position; though he had so far been lucky enough to miss any opportunity of disclosing his incapacity to the king. The explanation of Villeroi's employment is as creditable to Louis the man as it is unpardonable in Louis the king; the fact is that he could not bring himself to believe in the inefficiency of the old friend of his schoolroom days. Villeroi was the son of Louis XIV's Governor, the first Maréchal de Villeroi,[10] and was three years younger than Louis; to Villeroi, the king had always been the object of a hero-worship, had been the older boy whom he had so assiduously copied, and whose friendship was a perpetual source of joy and pride to him; to Louis, Villeroi was the boy he had protected and patronized, the youngster to whom he had been an elder brother from the time they did their Caesar together until the time he had given him his marshal's bâton. They had had their quarrels, especially in the days when they were both young men anxious to shine among the women, and indeed Louis had twice banished his old friend from Court; but the underlying friendship was never extinguished, and the only time the word "favourite" ever escaped the king's discreet lips, it was used with reference to Villeroi.

[9] MONTAL, Charles de Montsaulnin, 1st Cte. and maréchal de, son of Adrien de Montsaulnin and his wife, Gabrielle de Rabutin, born 1619; died 1696.

[10] VILLEROI, Nicolas de Neufville, 1st Maréchal and 1st Duc de, son of Charles, 1st Marquis de Villeroi by his wife, Jacqueline de Harlay, born 1598; Governor to Louis XIV, 1646; died 1685.

Villeroi was not entirely unworthy of his place in Louis' affections; he was a handsome man, of extraordinary bodily vigour, magnificent in everything, and with a remarkable air of distinction; with the language and manners of a great nobleman, and entirely devoid of meanness or pettiness. But there was not very much more to be said for him; he had no insight, no real knowledge, and his only qualification for command in the field was the personal bravery of his caste. His fellow-soldiers are unanimous in their condemnation of him; Feuquières[11] calls his tactics "mean and unmasterly," Eugène describes him as "presumptuous and ignorant." Spanheim speaks of him in his secret report with quite unusual animus:

"He knows how to avoid serious engagements, and executes minor ones badly, because he lacks *sangfroid*; not known if he would make a good showing in a general engagement, because he has never given battle. But he appears to be able to get through a campaign pretty well."

Then, after discussing his slowness of decision, his arrogance to his officers and his ambitions, which are beyond his capacity, he goes on to his personal characteristics;

"He is so eager to adopt an easy Court air to everyone that he ends by showing himself lacking in respect. He has not got it in him to hit the happy mean, and by wishing to assert his superiority, he succeeds in behaving like a too familiar dependent."

His portrait in the British Museum corroborates the pen pictures of the man; from under the huge wig, there looks out a stately, very handsome face untroubled by any doubts or perplexities, a great noble satisfied with himself and his surroundings, unperturbed by a lowering sky and the thunder of cannon. Such is the man to whom Louis XIV has entrusted his finest army in the most critical year he has so far experienced, and we have mentioned him at some length because Maine is to be his cavalry commander, and the two men are to be intimately connected in years to come.

Maine is consistently denigrated by St. Simon, whose unrivalled power as an artist in words is apt to blind us to his malice and incorrigible inaccuracy; and nowhere has he played the Duc du

[11] FEUQUIÈRES, Antoine de Pas, 3rd Marquis de, son of the 2nd Marquis by his wife, Anne Louise de Gramont, born 1650; a thoroughly disloyal subordinate, jealous and vindictive; he died 1711.

Maine a sorrier trick than in his account of 1695, when he succeeds in fastening on him charges of cowardice in the field which are in fact wholly unsubstantiated. But before we investigate the matter, it will be necessary to get some idea of the military situation in this year as a whole, and the circumstances on which St. Simon bases his charge.

The allies had in Flanders rather over 100,000 men, and captained by William of Orange, had opened the campaign by simultaneously threatening Ypres, Knocke, and Namur; the investment of Namur on 4th July had disclosed the fact that that fortress was their real objective. Namur was held for France by Boufflers, with 20,000 men, and Villeroi, commanding-in-chief in Flanders, with an army of 80,000, was given orders to relieve Boufflers; William had alloted 70,000 men to the siege, which he conducted himself, covered by Vaudemont, who had 30,000 troops for his task. Villeroi, outnumbering Vaudemont by nearly three to one, and showing an unaccustomed skill in manoeuvre, had by the morning of the 14th forced Vaudemont into a position in which he might have been compelled to accept battle under very disadvantageous circumstances; and, had Villeroi beaten him, William would have been compelled to raise the siege of Namur.

Let us now turn to St. Simon's account of the events of this 14th July, remembering by the way that he was at Versailles during the day he purports to describe:

"As soon as it was light, Maréchal de Villeroi sent word to M. du Maine to begin the attack, and keep the enemy engaged till he could come up with the remainder of the army. Impatient at not hearing the action beginning, he sent repeated orders to the same effect. M. du Maine insisted on reconnoitering, then on confessing himself, then on putting his forces in order for the attack, though they were so already, and eager to begin. While all this was going on, Vaudemont was retreating as rapidly as was consistent with prudence. The generals of our left wing murmured. Montrevel,[12] the senior general present, implored M. du Maine to advance, reminded him of the repeated orders of the Marshal, represented the certainty of an easy victory, the personal glory he would gain, the immense importance of raising the siege of Namur, the defenceless state of the Netherlands after the defeat of Vaudemont's army; he even shed tears.

[12] MONTREVEL, Nicolas Auguste La Baume, Marquis and Maréchal de, 1645–1716, second son of Ferdinand, 12th Cte. de Montrevel, and Marie Olier Nointel; "a born spendthrift, a great pillager, and would have robbed a Church altar."

All was in vain. M. du Maine could not refute his arguments, he did not refuse to advance; but he stammered and hesitated till M. de Vaudemont had effected his escape from the most imminent danger ever incurred by an army. On our side, everyone was furious; even the private soldiers spoke their minds freely. All Marshal de Villeroi could do was to send some cavalry in pursuit, who captured some colours and spread disorder among the rear-guard of the enemy."

Then follows a purely imaginary account of Villeroi, the adroit courtier, dexterously shouldering the blame for the fiasco in an ambiguous despatch, and after that we have the famous portrait of the anxious king, whose suspense gives way to despair as he extracts from a valet the truth that his beloved son "was an object of contempt to the army, and the laughing stock of foreigners;" and lastly we have the scene which all the world knows, of the king losing control of himself after dinner at Marly, and caning a servant for stealing a biscuit as the dessert is removed. What an artist is St. Simon! We see and hear everything: Montrevel's torrent of entreaty, the cowardly duke, determined at all costs not to go into action, the anxiety and rage of his father.

And there is not a word of truth in any of it.

The whole story is uncorroborated, except for a passage in one of Madame's letters, in which she says the king has criticised Villeroi's conduct unjustly, and that the real blame rests on the bastard; but this letter was not written until 21st August, and therefore does not seem to prove much more than that when she wrote, St. Simon's poisonous slanders were beginning to take effect. Neither Berwick nor Villars has any adverse criticism to make on Maine's conduct, and St. Hilaire, who was staff officer of the day to Villeroi, tells a story which directly contradicts St. Simon:

"On 14th July M. de Villeroi, having observed the enemy lines from the church tower, got on his horse and rode over to the left, where M. du Maine's troops were in wooded country, and at a musquet shot from the enemy trenches. I had the honour to follow M. de Villeroi. . . . When the Marshal had reached the high ground on the left, the enemy's entrenched right was very plainly to be seen. . . . A quarter of an hour later he took leave of M. du Maine, saying, 'Monseigneur, be so good as to return to your troops, there is nothing to be done here at the moment; you will remember what we have agreed upon; I am returning to my headquarters at Deinterghen; when the situation alters, I shall let you know.'"

Contrast this with St. Simon's story of Villeroi's repeated orders to du Maine to attack at daybreak. St. Hilaire then goes on,

"After this they separated. It was about 1 p.m. when I and some others advanced on the high ground to see what the enemy were doing, and when I got back to M. du Maine I told him that they had stopped work on the trenches. At 3 p.m. Major-General Bezons[13] arrived with the news that the enemy had begun to retire. The Duc du Maine immediately ordered his horse to mount and the infantry to fall in. The artillery was also got on the move, and M. du Maine sent one of his gentlemen to give the news to the Marshal. The troops then moved forward, M. du Maine at their head, and entered the enemy works without any opposition. They were of sand, and very poorly constructed. The enemy rearguard by this time was at the village of Vinck. M. du Maine there confronted it, without wishing to engage until he had received the Marshal's orders, *as had been agreed upon between them*. People have blamed M. du Maine for not charging the enemy; others have justified him by quoting the rule of the service, that a subordinate must not initiate a manoeuvre without the consent of the general. I record the facts, as a well-informed eyewitness, because the episode subsequently made a good deal of noise. M. du Maine's messenger on his return reported that he had much difficulty in getting an interview with the Marshal, who was resting, and that when he did see him, M. de Villeroi called Puységur[14], who had just come down from the church tower, and who reported that the enemy was *not* retiring. Puységur's report was accepted, and M. du Maine was informed that his report of a retirement was incorrect. On hearing this, M. du Maine exclaimed, 'What! the Marshal does not believe that the enemy is retiring? He is not putting his right wing in motion? Go back to him at once, and tell him that you found me at the head of my troops in the enemy lines, my nose touching his rearguard, and impress upon him that his incredulity will be the cause of our missing a pretty thing.' But, however diligent the gentleman was, three priceless hours were wasted before he returned with the news that the right wing was getting on the move, and orders from the Marshal that the duke *was not to leave the ground which he then occupied, until further orders*. And consequently, that prince remained out of action for the rest of the day, to his great annoyance."

And so, when we come to examine the evidence, we find that, so far from a cowardly refusal to obey orders, the exact opposite was the case. Maine's fault, if fault it be, was a refusal to disobey

[13] Bezons, Jacques Bazin, Maréchal de, 1667–1733, second son of Claude, Seigneur de Bezons, and Marie Targer; "an excellent general, especially of cavalry . . . an honest and straightforward man."

[14] Puységur, Jacques Francois Chastanet, 1655–1753; military tutor to Louis XV, 1721; "of high reputation, and well-known as a writer on military subjects."

orders, a lack of initiative in not assuming control of a situation obviously completely misappreciated by the commander-in-chief. If he had attacked, say the arm-chair critics, he would have routed the army covering the siege, and William, with his communications at Villeroi's mercy, would have been obliged to withdraw from Namur. It all sounds very pretty, as plans made after the event generally do. But what if Vaudemont had been prodded into turning round, and had hit back successfully? It is a ticklish thing for a subordinate to disobey orders at what may prove to be the beginning of a general action; Vaudemont was a better general than Maine, or than Villeroi for that matter. Nothing in war is certain, except the unexpected, and had Vaudemont succeeded in smashing the French left wing while the French centre and right were still unaligned for battle, how would the critics then have viewed Maine's brilliance in disobeying the Marshal's positive and reiterated orders? St. Simon would have led the yelping pack against the arrogant and presumptuous bastard, whose ignorance and self-sufficiency had brought France to the verge of ruin. There is no easier or more enjoyable occupation than refighting a battle on the map, for a general who has lost it on the ground; here is the plan–too often by the way without contours–on which three or four little red bricks face an equal number of black, each with an arrow head to indicate its front. A dotted line or two shows us the movements of each commander, and we pity the loser's stupidity; we would have thrown this brick on the right of the enemy at such and such a moment, and done so and so with the others. But large masses of troops on the ground do not resemble bricks, they are an agglomeration of human beings, on an infinitely graduated scale of intelligence, energy, and initiative; nor does a field of battle often resemble a billiards table. Let the armchair tactician take part but once in even small-scale manoeuvres, preferably in an administrative capacity, and he will learn to his cost something of the extreme complexity of the process which he is so fond of describing as "throwing" an army corps into a battle at a critical place and time.

The remainder of the campaign passed without a French success to offset the initial failure to crush Vaudemont. The allies, heavily reinforced from Germany, pursued the siege of Namur, whilst William of Orange, who showed himself above his usual form, profited by Villeroi's incompetence to entrench himself in such a position that he was at once able to checkmate the relief of Namur, and to refuse battle to the French main army. A final attempt to attack William behind the Mehaigne resolved itself into an indecisive cavalry engagement, in which the Duc du Maine might well have thought that he had cleared his character of the smears put upon it by St. Simon and those of his kind. "M. le Duc du Maine," writes Dangeau on 2nd September, "who commanded our left wing, and gave the order for the charge, had a horse wounded under him, and greatly distinguished himself."

But the mischief was done; a spiteful Court found it much more thrilling to whisper of Maine's cowardice and incapacity at Vinck than to listen to St. Hilaire's defence, or to hear of how he had led a charge on the Mehaigne. In a life which had more than its share of mortifications, one of the bitterest moments must have come when the duke realized how low his name had fallen: so low that such a man as the Duc d'Elboeuf could insult him publicly, and with impunity. Elboeuf, choosing a moment when he had a good audience, asked Maine where he would be serving next year, because, wherever it was, he solicited the honour of serving with him; and, when thanked, and pressed for his reasons for the request, replied with a low bow, that with M. du Maine, a man could be sure of not being killed. It was perhaps his darkest hour.

8. *Ludovise in Fairyland*

THE year 1696 was uneventful in the field; Louis sent out his usual armies, but there was a feeling of suspense in the air, a suspicion even among the junior officers, that the year's chief effort would be diplomatic and not military. And so it proved to be; whilst Maine, once more serving as Lieutenant-General to Boufflers, waited for the battle that never came, Louis achieved a diplomatic victory of the first importance. On 29th August he persuaded the Duke of Savoy to sign the treaty of Turin, whereby, in violation of all his obligations, he made a separate peace with France.

The duke, as usual, drove an excellent bargain, for in addition to securing all Savoy, Nice, Suza, Casal, and Pignerol, he married his daughter, Marie Adelaide, to Louis, Duke of Burgundy, next in succession after *Monseigneur* to the crown of France.

1697 brought the long looked for and sorely needed peace to an exhausted France, but in a form which was for Louis XIV the writing on the wall. It was a peace which his necessities dictated, not one which his ambition desired. The long war had anticipated the resources which he should have husbanded for the dread Spanish Succession struggle, now lowering darker and larger in the European sky than when in 1688 he had plunged into war in order to get elbow room outside the frontiers of France proper. And, after all, he had failed to attain even this objective, for the Peace of Ryswick, signed on October 30th, had virtually restricted him to the position he had gained for himself by the Peace of Nimweguen in 1678. He had bled his country dangerously in order to maintain the status quo, and most galling of all, he had been compelled to recognize William of Orange as King of England. In his cooler moments he must have been seized with a shivering apprehension that his sun was past its meridian.

The Duc du Maine came home to settle down at Court, a half-pay Lieutenant-General of twenty-seven, hoping doubtless for a little of that real domesticity which owing to the war, he had hardly yet tasted. But his Duchess had other ideas, and she was not the woman to let any consideration for her husband stand in the way of the realization of her desires. The intimate life of the king's inner circle bored her beyond endurance, and she made no secret of the fact; it had always bored her, the constraint of the now devout Court, with its solemn inviolable round of religious duties and tedious amusements. But since the coming of the Duchess of Burgundy, it had bored her even more, because the new princess speedily put Mme. du Maine's nose completely out of joint.

The Duchess of Burgundy was adorable, and she still is; we still cannot help loving this plain, witty, graceful, fascinating child; we resent a slur on her character as we would an insult to a living friend, and both critics and historians have dealt very tenderly with her. "Dangeau," says Mme. de Noailles, "makes us love her by talking merely of her smallest actions." The king himself was her first conquest, and she retained her absolute empire over him until the day of her death, because to her alone was it given to discover that Louis XIV was not a demi-god, but an agreeable old gentleman whose society was well worth cultivating for its own sake; and, to the astonishment of the Court, Louis himself was enchanted by her discovery. His own children would as soon have thought of slapping him on the back as of sitting down in his presence; but when he was at his desk in Mme. de Maintenon's room, in would rush the Duchess of Burgundy, sweeping about like a whirlwind, fluttering round him, chattering, perching herself now on the arm of Mme. de Maintenon's chair, now on Louis' knees; throwing her arms around his neck, kissing him, rumpling his clothes, rummaging through his papers and letters, and discussing their contents. Her remarks on the England of Queen Anne have been preserved for us. "Aunt" (so she always addressed Mme. de Maintenon), "it cannot be denied that England is better governed under a queen than under a king, and do you know why? Because under a king, the country is really governed by women, and under a queen, by men." And then she would flash out of the room, first giving Louis an affectionate pull by the ear. As the king turned with a sigh to his interrupted day's work, must he not occasionally have asked himself with a dull wonder whether he was the victim of hallucinations? Could it really be Louis *Le Dieudonné*, by the Grace of God and so forth, whose wig had been knocked sideways and whose features had been maltreated by this engaging chit?

The Duchess was a flirt, a minx, and her conduct lacked decorum, but I, like all her admirers, am convinced that she never gave her husband cause for serious complaint; those who are so ready to accuse a great lady of Versailles of having a lover, forget that, while the thing was quite practicable, it was impossible to keep a liaison secret; and of the Duchess of Burgundy we know nothing which is incompatible with an *honnête galanterie*. A young woman who is generally to be found donkey riding, going to bathing parties, gambling, roaming about Marly garden until four in the morning, will get herself talked about. And her husband can be excused for a certain lack of enthusiasm for her favourite outdoor sport, which was to lie on her back on the grass and get an obliging courtier to pull her round the grounds by her ankles; but real cause for uneasiness I am convinced she never gave him.

The only discordant note in the chorus of admiration came from the other princesses, who, apart from a natural dislike of being put in the shade, complained with some show of reason that while the Duchess of Burgundy could steal a horse, they got into trouble for even looking over a hedge; but for this state of affairs they had only themselves to thank. It is a wonderful tribute to Marie Adelaide's charm that in the spiteful, tale-bearing atmosphere of Versailles, all men, and even all women, instinctively conspired to conceal her improprieties and indecorums, her nocturnal rovings and her flirtations, from the king and from the Duke of Burgundy. Both, until the end of their lives, remained unaware of stories about the Duchess which were known to everyone else at Court, even to Mme. de Maintenon.

The Duke of Burgundy did not so much love, as adore, his young wife, and if, as we are told, she was rather touched by his passion than passionately in love with him, he never discovered the fact. Their union was not a perfect one, for the girl could not always live up to the intensity of his religious convictions and practices, and she found it an effort to return from some gay picnic to listen to him reading a draft essay on the real function of the States-General in the working of the constitution. But they none the less rightly passed for one of the happiest married couples about the Court.

Such being the new state of affairs at Versailles, it is small wonder that the Duchesse du Maine wanted a palace of her own in which she could queen it over a chosen circle of courtiers, and we may imagine the unfortunate duke being nagged in season and out of season to break away from Mme. de Maintenon's leading strings and set up on his own. But at the beginning of 1698 came the illness and death of their infant son, and the duchess's mind was for the moment distracted from the matter of a separate establishment by her joy and pride that in the etiquette of mourning prescribed for the occasion, she had made good her husband's right to be treated as a Prince of the Blood.

We see little more of the Duc du Maine this year, except for a glimpse of him in September, at the Compiègne manoeuvres where he commanded a brigade. The manoeuvres of 1698 stand out for lavishness, indeed prodigality, above most of the other great fêtes of the reign; all, by the king's express command, was to be very magnificent, the troops in new uniforms, the General officer's tables to be maintained with a luxury surpassing that of Versailles. It was a shrewd bit of window dressing, and it attained its object, namely to impress Europe with the unshaken splendour of the French army, and the inexhaustible resources of the kingdom of France; for it is a remarkable fact that Louis, who had recently been borrowing at twelve per cent, was, after the Compiègne bravado, able to borrow at six.

In 1699 the Duc du Maine arrived at a compromise with his peremptory little wife in the matter of a country house; she was expecting another child before the end of the year, and it was agreed that they should accept the invitation of M. Malézieux to spend the summer at his pretty country place, Châtenay. But few women understand the ethics of compromise, least of all such a woman as the Duchesse du Maine, and the duke, whether he knew it or not, had lost the battle; he had allowed his wife to leave Versailles for ever.

We discover with surprise that this is the same M. Malézieux whom we used to meet in the old days in the humble rôle of tutor to the duke. How had he become a man of property, and of such wealth as to be able to entertain this royal couple for a whole summer on his country estates? "He had become rich by the liberalities of the Court," is all that we are told, and with this cryptic explanation we must rest content.

However he had made his position, Nicolas Malézieux was just the man for the duchess; in allegories, impromptus, odes, madrigals, and comedies, his fecundity was inexhaustible. If he never rises above the drawing-room verse level, he at least never falls below it. Fénélon thought him worthy of his friendship, La Bruyère invited his criticisms on the *Characters*, and he has attained the modest immortality of a footnote. He appears to have been an active, astute man of a not uncommon type; one of those who in youth acquire a firm grip of the superficial aspects of several subjects, reach manhood with a set of cut and dried ideas, quotations, and literary opinions which are never added to, but which are employed so dexterously in great houses that the man becomes the oracle of a second-rate intelligentsia. At Sceaux, in years to come, he was to be the ultimate court of appeal on matters of taste and belles lettres—"The Master has said so," was the final verdict; and even those who ought to have known better, were to refer to him as "The Great Malézieux."

To Mme. du Maine he made Châtenay a fairyland that filled her with envy and delight; gallantry, pastoral fêtes, fireworks, a costly and carefully arranged round of artless Arcadian pleasures filled the long days and short nights, and the illusion was completed by the presence of bands of real peasants, dancing and singing. Nymphs, shepherdesses, sighing swains, nothing was forgotten, and as the months slipped by, the duchess's vague dreams of rural bliss resolved themselves into a determination to buy the whole valley of Sceaux, in which stood Châtenay. Indoors, the note of simplicity was maintained, and we find the Duc du Maine, in mock anger, complaining that after a bad night at cards he has lost two whole crowns. It was all very pretty no doubt, but it was the first step on the road which was afterwards to lead the duke into serious trouble. Châtenay was only eighteen miles from Paris, and Maine was still usually at Court, running down into the country for a few days at a time. During the year he made one public appearance which brought him under the lash of the watchful St. Simon. Accustomed as we now are to the vagaries of the seventeenth century, it still seems to us a complete non sequitur that Maine, as Grand Master of the Artillery, should have to take his seat as a peer in the Chamber of Accounts, a sort of Treasury Audit Office. But thus it was, and he was duly installed, not in the seat of the last Grand Master, but between the First and Second Presidents– "a fresh distinction for the bastard," groans St. Simon.

In the summer of 1700, some time after the birth of her son, Louis Auguste, Prince de Dombes, Mme. du Maine entered into her kingdom. It had been obvious to her husband for some time past that his only hope of domestic peace lay in allowing her to set up a country Court of her own, much though he would have preferred to remain at Versailles and draw her into the king's intimate circle, where he himself felt so cosily at home. But the duchess had no intention of remaining any longer one of a crowd at Court; she was shrewd enough to appreciate, firstly that there would be no place for her in the nascent Court of the Duchess of Burgundy, and that secondly a generation had grown up which was increasingly impatient of the yoke of Louis XIV; the king was now a man of sixty-two, who had reigned for fifty-seven years, and already only the elderly could recollect Versailles when it had been the arbitress of fashion to the world. Men and women, especially the latter, complained that it was a monastery in Court dress, which was becoming duller every day. Young courtiers now tended more and more to divide their lives between duty at Versailles and pleasure in the smart great houses of Paris, where everything was in real good taste. At Paris one dined off porcelain and used a fork; at Versailles one still dined off gold plate and used one's fingers. The

Vendômes had succeeded in establishing their own town and country Court at the Temple and Anet, but only those with no reputation to lose could afford to be the guests of the Vendôme brothers. Another Court, more respectable than the Temple, more lively than Versailles, could hardly fail to succeed in the present state of society, thought the duchess, and she found eager collaborators. The duke gave way, and bought her Sceaux.

This lovely estate with its beautiful mansion lay, as we have seen, some eighteen miles to the south of Versailles, in a pretty valley; it had formerly belonged to the great Colbert, who had spent enormous sums there, and from him it had passed to his eldest son, Seignelay,[1] who still lives in Mme. de Sévigné's impromptu epitaph –*c'est la splendeur qui est morte*. For Sceaux, Seignelay's heirs asked a million livres, and the duke, though already somewhat straitened for money, found the price. "Considering the extravagance of Mme. du Maine," says a contemporary, "it may be presumed that her husband could not have made such a purchase if the king had not treated him with his usual kindness." Whether the duchess contributed anything, we do not know, but we may be sure that her father, being a Condé, gave her nothing at all.

But Mme. du Maine's period of unclouded pleasure in her new house was to be a brief one.

On 1st November 1700 there died at Madrid Charles II, King of Spain, King of Naples, King of the Indies, King of half the world, "Charles the Sufferer."[2] His father, Philip IV, had in 1649, when he is described as "a worn-out voluptuary," taken as his second wife his own niece, Mariana of Austria, a girl of sixteen, and of this repulsive union Charles II was the only issue. Charles, says a contemporary, "was not so much a man as a medical curiosity;" feeble-minded, suffering from at least three incurable diseases and several minor ailments, his death had been looked for at any time since his birth, and impatiently awaited in the Chancelleries of

[1] SEIGNELAY, Jean Baptiste Colbert, Marquis de, born 1651; succeeded his father in 1683; Minister of State, 1689; "full of ambition, spirit, and activity . . . eager for every kind of glory"; he died in 1690.

[2] SPAIN, Charles II, King of, son of Philip IV and Mariana of Austria, born 1661; succeeded his father, 1665; died 1700; under him Spain sank to its lowest ebb.

Europe ever since his marriage in 1679, when it had soon become common knowledge that he would never have children. As had been expected, he died childless, the last of the Spanish Hapsburgs, and the great Spanish Succession problem, which had been the cloud on the horizon for twenty years, had at last come up for decision.

Several attempts had been made to arrive at a solution during the lifetime of Charles, notably in 1698, when Louis and William of Orange had negotiated a secret Partition Treaty in which the French king had shown himself unexpectedly moderate: agreeing that the son of the Elector of Bavaria was to have the bulk of the inheritance, but with substantial pickings reserved for the House of Bourbon. But when the terms leaked out, Charles II retorted with a Will in which he left the whole of his vast domains to the Bavarian Prince. However, in 1699 the Bavarian boy died, the whole work was to do over again, and in March 1700 France and England manufactured a second Partition Treaty which, broadly speaking, substituted the Archduke Charles of Austria for the late Prince of Bavaria, and left the other clauses unaltered. But the new treaty was made nugatory by the attitude of the Spaniards, who cared little who ruled them so long as their Empire remained unpartitioned; remorseless domestic pressure was brought to bear on the dying king, and on 2nd October 1700, he signed a new Will, leaving all his crowns to Philippe d'Anjou, second son of *Monseigneur* and grandson of Louis XIV.

Louis' position was a difficult one. He had, as we have seen, only just signed a new Partition Treaty, and was now faced with the question of deciding whether he should stand by it or not. War he could not avoid, whichever course he adopted; for the attitude of Vienna instantly made it clear that Louis' choice was either to fight for the enforcement of the Treaty, or to fight for his inheritance under Charles' Will; for Charles II had added a clause to the document whereby, if France refused the Will, the Spanish Empire in its entirety was to pass to the Archduke Charles of Austria. And Europe could no more afford to see Austria in control at Madrid than France. Louis may well be excused for finding the idea of expending men and money on putting an hereditary enemy of his House on the throne of Spain a distasteful one.

It took the king nearly a fortnight to make his decision, and how he arrived at it we do not know; for his arguments were not committed to paper, and as usual, he said remarkably little. After the meeting of the Council of State on 10th November he observed that there was much to be said on both sides and that he would sleep on it; on the 13th the Duchess of Burgundy wheedled him into saying, "Whatever course I take, I am quite sure that many people will condemn it." This was at Fontainebleau, and on the 15th Louis returned to Versailles with his mind made up. On the morning of the 16th there occurred a famous scene; the folding doors of the king's private room were thrown open and Louis appeared, leading the Duc d'Anjou. Looking round, with an air of majesty, he said, "Gentlemen, I present to you the King of Spain." A magnificent bit of theatre, but one which could not conceal from many present the fact that France had got off to a bad start, and carrying heavy weight, in the race for the prize of the century.

It was a curious war, in that neither of the final protagonists wanted it. Louis foresaw the danger as well as any man, but, rightly or wrongly, had convinced himself that he had no choice but to fight. And across the Channel, William, his life work threatened with ruin, had his hands tied by a blind Parliament and was not able to declare war at all. It looked as if the struggle was to be between Louis and the Emperor, and the issue of that war was in no doubt. The English Parliament would not hear of war, and even Rochester[3] and Godolphin[4] could see in the conflagration nothing except the fact that Spain had the right to choose her own ruler, whilst England had not the means of forcing an arbitration on the interested parties, even if she had been morally entitled to do so.

The position of England in 1700 bears many resemblances to that in the years following 1918. The country had recently emerged

[3] ROCHESTER, Laurence Hyde, 1st Earl of, 1641–1711, second son of 1st Earl of Clarendon.

[4] GODOLPHIN, Sidney, 1st Earl of, 1645–1712, adherent of James II; Lord High Treasurer, and Marlborough's confidential ally, 1702–10; dismissed on Marlborough's fall.

from a long and expensive war in a mood of exuberant and purblind pacifism. A myopic Parliament, which could see no cloud on a horizon black with the coming storm, had enthusiastically proceeded to demobilize the army, and had adopted as its slogan, "No foreign entanglements." William had done what he could to swim against the current, pointing out that France was checked, not beaten, and that English intervention against a France in control of the whole Spanish Empire was sooner or later, inevitable. But his friends regarded him as a Jeremiah, whilst to his many enemies, he was a man who was engineering an impudent plot to expend British blood and treasure on the aggrandisement of his beloved Holland.

To the Duc du Maine and his duchess, the international crisis first presented itself in the guise of an exciting opportunity for the display of the splendours of their new house. On 4th December came to the great entrance doors of the château of Sceaux an apparently endless succession of coaches, enveloped in escorts of Life Guards, and a few moments later, Maine found himself doing the honours to two Crowned Heads; the Most Christian King had escorted His Most Catholic Majesty on the first stage of his long journey to Madrid, and at Sceaux the final parting was to take place. Louis, who appeared profoundly moved, hurried his grandson into a private room where they remained for some time alone; then one by one entered princes and princesses, marshals, dukes, all France in fact, to wish godspeed to the awkward, sullen youth of eighteen on whom such sudden greatness had descended. The Duchess of Burgundy cried bitterly, Louis was greatly moved, the King of Spain less so. If the Duc du Maine was at all affected, we are not told; we know nothing of the parting between the nephew and his left-handed uncle. An hour later Louis escorted Philippe to his coach, kissed him twice, and the two kings parted for ever. The historic scene was over, and Sceaux sank once more into its wonted disquiet.

His mind once made up, Louis lost no time in making the most of his advantages. The Duc du Maine, extracted in mid-winter from the comforts of his new house, found himself posting along the dreary Flanders roads to join Marshal de Boufflers' army as Lieutenant-General. The great military machine, functioning with all its old brilliance, flung itself into the Spanish Netherlands in what proved to be a route march, seasoned with banquets. Louis XIV, it must be understood, was not at war with anyone; he announced blandly to a startled Europe that he was merely the new estate agent, come to take over his grandson's property from the old management. Spanish fortresses welcomed his troops enthusiastically, whilst those which in virtue of the treaty of 1697, were in Dutch hands, surrendered after a token resistance. By the end of February 1701, Namur, Mons, Charleroi, Ath, Oudenarde, Nieuport, and Ostend had for all tactical purposes become part of the kingdom of France. With the single exception of Maestricht, Louis had in two months obtained without bloodshed all that had been wrested from him by Europe in arms in the space of eight years. At Versailles, the season of 1701–2 was an exceptionally brilliant one, in spite of, or rather because of, the inevitable war. The younger men had endured, with more or less patience, the tedium of four consecutive years of peace, and now saw that the best of all pastimes was about to begin once more. They looked forward to pleasant summer months, spent in the congenial occupation of dusting English jackets; William of Orange, who had on the whole shown very poor sport, was said to be dying, and it was hoped that the allies would now find a general who would give France a better run for her money. The game this time was to prove much less amusing than they had anticipated, but for the moment all was joy and expectation, the men's excitement reflected in the faces of the women. Prominent amongst the dance hostesses at Versailles we notice, rather to our surprise, the Duchesse du Maine, who gave several balls in her bedroom, where she was lying in. That she should choose to undergo such an ordeal in the vitiated air of a roomful of fiddlers and dancers is entirely typical of her, but why at Versailles instead of at Sceaux, we wonder? I have an idea that in her presence at Court we see the hand of Mme. de Maintenon. During the summer there had been goings on at Sceaux of various kinds, and none of them to Mme. de Maintenon's taste, or to the king's; Louis had had to give the duke orders to dismiss one of his gentlemen, Longpierre, who had been caught in no less an outrage than endeavouring to make a match between the Cte. de Toulouse and one of the Lorraine girls, Mlle. d'Armagnac.[5] The young lady had been advised by the king to take a country holiday, whilst Longpierre took refuge with the Princesse de Conti.[6] "Longpierre knew a good deal of Greek, and his morals were very similar to those of the ancient Greeks; he produced for Mme. de Conti a very singular play called *Electra*." Then there was the eccentric life which Mme. du Maine was leading down in the country, and the indecorous familiarity she allowed to Malézieux, who was apparently becoming a fixture in the Maine household; as early as April 1701, news of the curious life at Sceaux has reached Madame-Palatine.

"M. du Maine is by way of being very devout these days. He has plenty of wit, and knows how to make himself pleasant when it suits him; but he shuns all society, and one hardly ever sees him. His wife is an oddity; she never goes to bed before four in the morning, and gets up at three in the afternoon. Her dearest friend is one Malézieux. When M. du Maine was told that he makes himself ridiculous by allowing Malézieux to give Mme. du Maine mathematical lessons in his nightcap, he answered, 'Do not say anything against Malézieux; he keeps the peace in my house."

Taking it all round, Mme. de Maintenon may well have persuaded the king that a few months at Court under her own eye would do the Duchesse du Maine no harm.

Amongst the trivial courtesies of that busy season, the Duc du Maine was honoured with a reluctant visit from no less a personage than M. le Duc de St. Simon, compelled by a rigid etiquette to invite the Duc du Maine to witness his taking his seat as a duke and peer. We may doubt St. Simon's assertion that Maine received the visit "with an air of gratification" whilst believing that the host's manner was "tempered with politeness and modesty." St. Simon, in spite of his opinion of Maine, takes care to give us the bastard's reply in full:

[5] ARMAGNAC, Charlotte de Lorraine, Mlle. d', younger of the two daughters of Louis, Cte. d'Armagnac, and Catherine de Neufville de Villeroi; "extremely beautiful."

[6] CONTI, Marie Anne de Bourbon, Princesse de, 1666–1739, bastard of Louis XIV by Mlle. de La Vallière; married Prince de Conti, 1680, who fell in love with her. The Duchesse de Duras said in this year that "she would pay £2,000 and would pawn her shift to sleep the night with the Princess"; for over twenty years, the most beautiful woman at the Court of France; "she is love itself, and they are frightened to let her keep any pages more than ten or twelve years old."

De Larmessin, Sculp.

LOVISE BENEDICTE DE BOVRBON
DVCHESSE DV MAINE; Cÿ deuant Mademoiselle de
Charolois, fille de S.A.S. henrÿ Jules, de Bourbon, Prince de
Condé, Et d'Anne Palatine de Bauierre, Nacquit le 8e. de 9bre 1676,
Elle à Espousé Louis Auguste de Bourbon Duc du Maine, dans la
Chapelle du Chasteau Royal de Versailles, le 19e. Mars 1692, en presence
du Roÿ, de Monseigr. le Dauphin, des Princes, et Princesses du Sang, et
Autres Seigneurs, et Dames de la Cour,

8. LOUISE DE BOURBON, DUCHESSE DU MAINE

9. SCEAUX

From a drawing by Perelle

" 'I will make a point of attending; I am too sensible of the honour you do me in wishing me to be present to miss it.' And with innumerable compliments he reconducted me as far as the garden; for the king was at Marly, and I had been invited for the occasion."

And so, exit the solemn and self-satisfied duke, perhaps forgetting that the man who had shown him such distinguished consideration was half a Mortemart. He does not even draw any inference from the fact that the blunter Vendôme "replied with more simplicity."

The lot of the self-satisfied is indeed an enviable one.

The Duc du Maine may however have felt the nuisance of St. Simon's ostentatious hostility, and have been genuinely anxious to secure his friendship. He was one of those men who like to be liked, even where there is no liking to bestow in return, and he shared the admiration of most of the Court for the popular Mme. de St. Simon. Though we have only St. Simon's account to go by, there seems no reason to doubt that during the course of the year, Maine made further overtures to the spiteful little duke. Mme. du Maine had recently taken a fancy to the Duchesse de Lauzun,[7] the Duchesse de St. Simon's sister:

"Mme. du Maine could not do without her; she was always being asked to Sceaux. M. du Maine was endeavouring to secure the best society for his wife; he tried to get hold of Mme. de St. Simon by means of her sister. She went there; it was one way of pleasing the king; but she did not go very often. I had reason to believe that M. and Mme. du Maine wished to gain my friendship, though they knew how odious their rank was to me. They took to speaking of me in the most flattering way to my wife and her sister: told them how much they wished to see me at Sceaux, and begged them to convey an invitation from them, and bring me with them. I was surprised at receiving such advances from people with whom I had never had any intercourse; but I suspected their motive, and remained on my guard. Their new rank was insufferable to me, and I hoped to see it abolished some day. . . . I adhered steadfastly to my system of complimentary excuses and polite refusals."

If we did not know who the Maines were, would not one imagine from this inimitable account that they were some pushing contractors or financiers, who had so far forgotten themselves as to pester a nobleman with their unwelcome attentions? In the end, St. Simon

[7] LAUZUN, Geneviève Marie de Durfort, daughter of the 1st Duc de Lorges and Geneviève Frémont, born 1679, married the 1st Duc de Lauzun, 1695.

found for his wife "a reasonable excuse for withdrawing from Sceaux, where the company had been for sometime extremely mixed, to say the least of it;" and thenceforward, Louis XIV's son and Condé's daughter had to make their way in society as best they could, without the countenance of the lawyer's grandson, M. le Duc de St. Simon.

We hear little of du Maine for the next year or more, beyond the fact that he served as Lieutenant-General in the Army of Flanders, which at this stage of the war was not engaged in any operation of importance. During 1702, however, he seems to have kept a diary for the first time, and the document, though still unpublished, is of some historical value. Its chief interest lies in the testimony which it affords about the conduct of the Duke of Burgundy, which was so much criticised at the time by a group of malevolent courtiers.

Most of Maine's leisure was passed at Sceaux, whose embellishment, in spite of the prevailing shortage of money, was rapidly making it a show place, rivalling even Versailles. Madame was induced to pay the Maines a visit in the autumn of 1704, and has left us a description of the place which is worth preserving, though we should prefer a description of the circumstances which induced Madame to pay the visit.

"We visited Sceaux, where there is a wonderful garden. In front of the house is a big parterre with a bower; from the bower one passes into a beautiful gallery, full of pictures and busts; from the middle of this gallery there is another way into the garden, into an alley; at the side of the alley is a fine mall, then another alley which runs to the grand canal, much longer than that at Fontainebleau, and which is the source of a large and pretty cascade. In all the parterres are fine fountains and, what I find even prettier, there is near the house a little wood, decorated with springs and fountains. One is in the form of Aeolus chaining a wind, with four other winds at the corners; he threatens them with his sceptre, but the one he is chaining, blows in spite of him. Then there is Scylla, surrounded by dogs, barking and spitting water. There are two fountains of bronze, beautiful workmanship. Next come two fountains of white marble, representing children spitting into the water. . . . All the paths in this wood are decorated with antique marble busts. . . . I then went to see the vegetable garden which M. de Navailles[8] so much admired in Colbert's

[8] Navailles, Philippe de Montaut, Maréchal de, 1619–84, son of Philippe Brevet-duc de Lavedan, and Judith de Gontaut de Biron; Governor to the Duc de Chârtres, 1683; "of the old school, full of honour, courage, and fidelity."

time. They showed him the cascade, the water gallery, the chestnut hall, the bower, in fact everything beautiful which Sceaux had to offer, but he admired nothing at all until, passing through the vegetable garden, he stopped and exclaimed, 'Now that is what I call really good chicory!' When I got back to my room, I heard that Mme. du Maine was at home on the third floor. I climbed up there to call on her, but not without a good deal of puffing and blowing."

It is a pretty picture, infinitely remote from the unburied dead on the field of Blenheim, where less than three weeks ago Louis XIV's hopes had fallen in ruins about him. Blenheim is the death-knell of the Siècle Louis Quatorze; Bourbon armies were to fight brilliantly again, never better indeed than in the years following Blenheim. But at Blenheim something was lost which was never to be recovered. Rocroi in 1643, Blenheim in 1704, mark the beginning and the end of unquestioned French domination in Europe, and never again were Louis XIV's armies to deploy on a battlefield in absolute confidence of victory.

But these world shocks are rarely as violent as historians would have us believe; the Duc du Maine and the Flanders front were not affected for the moment, and at Sceaux, Aeolus and Scylla continued to splash unconcernedly in the autumn sunlight.

By 1705 Mme. du Maine had won her fight against the gloomy and preoccupied king; she had given up regular attendance at Court, and had indeed shaken herself free from all constraint of any kind:

"She cared neither for the king nor for M. le Prince, and the king quite understood M. du Maine's reasons for not contradicting her. If he ventured on the slightest remonstrance, he had to put up with haughty reminders of the honour she had done him in marrying him; and very often, without any reason whatever, she had outbursts of temper which made him fear lest she should go out of her mind. So he resolved to let her do as she pleased, and ruin him with entertainments, balls, fireworks, and comedies, in which she acted in public, dressed like an actress."

This account is strikingly corroborated by Mme. de Caylus:

"Mme. du Maine abused her husband's kindness; she soon threw off the yoke of a too severe education, disdained to pay her court to the king, in order to hold her own at Sceaux, where by her extravagance she ruined her husband who either approved, or did not dare to cross her will. The king spoke to him about it, but it was useless; until at last, seeing that his expostulations had no other effect than to give pain to his beloved son, he decided to keep silent, and let him wallow in his blindness and foolishness."

With all due deference to Mme. de Caylus, we must object to the word blindness, for which we would substitute "refusal to see." The Duc du Maine's was not a strong character; cleverer than his wife, he was much weaker. We may smile at the weight with which he leans on Mme. de Maintenon's strong shoulders, the assiduity with which he sticks to the rôle of favourite son long after he is a husband with children of his own. But there is a bottom of commonsense in him which is utterly lacking in his wife; he had too, some feeling, if not of public responsibility, at least of public decorum, and did not fail to realize the indecency of her extravagance in the existing state of the king's affairs. But what was he to do? We can of course all answer the question for him; he had but to adopt, as his rule of life, firmness tempered with kindness; it is a solution of the problem familiar to every bachelor. The duke is hardly to be blamed if, like so many married men before and since, he accepted the theory and boggled at the practice.

1706 brought with it the darkest hours which Louis XIV had yet known. On 11th May the French were forced to raise the siege of Barcelona; on the following day France lost the Netherlands at Ramillies; in June, the Hapsburg Charles entered Madrid as King of Spain; Louis' armies were driven out of Piedmont in September; and in October the French peace proposals were rejected by the allies.

But Mme. du Maine cared for none of these things;

"She took more and more to acting plays with her servants, and some retired comedians. The whole Court went to them; but no one could understand how she gave herself the fatigue of dressing up like an actress, learning and declaiming the parts of the chief characters, and making a public exhibition of herself on the stage. The Duc du Maine dared not oppose her for fear she should go off her head completely, as he once told *Mme. La Princesse* plainly. . . . He used to stand at the corner of the door, doing the honours. Not to speak of the absurdity of these entertainments, they cost a lot of money."

The thoughts of the retired Lieutenant-General must have been bitter enough as he stood hour after hour in the overheated theatre exchanging meaningless compliments with his wife's guests. How right his father had been in urging him not to marry, he would reflect, as he thought of bygone summer mornings in Flanders, or the music of his hounds through the dew-laden forest in October dawns. And when the last of the throng of guests had departed and the candles guttered in their sockets, rest would still be far off. Instead of peace and quiet would come the noisy supper party, prolonged till sunrise, at which it would fall to him to lead the chorus in praise of his excited, grease-painted little wife.

It is not easy for our generation to imagine the disagreeableness of one of these Sceaux nights, or indeed of any place where a large number of people crowded together by candlclight in the days of Louis XIV. It looks so delightful on the stage or in a film that we are cheated into forgetting the heat, the stench, and such unpleasant details as that these great lords and ladies were very imperfectly house-trained. An evening party must have been bearable only to those educated in the harsh school of Versailles, who had learnt to endure their pleasures uncomplainingly. And we must not assume that because they were living under conditions with which they had been familiar since childhood, they found no discomfort in them. On the contrary, they were perfectly well aware that to cram a room with people on a hot summer night, fill it with candles, and shut all the windows, produced a smell which was objectionable even to their insensitive nostrils; and, short of the desperate expedient of washing, they took all possible measures to eliminate it. The Duchesse du Maine, drenched in aphrodisiacs, would in addition have had sachets of violently perfumed powder buried in her hair, and the duke would be wearing two miniature bolsters of strong smelling herbs strapped into his armpits. The women, though not burdened with wigs, can have been scarcely less uncomfortable than the men, for they were encased in metal corsets as in strait waist-coats; and here again, let us note that in hot weather, wigs and corsets were evidently as uncomfortable to their wearers as they now sound to us. St. Simon quotes it as typical of the Regent's general contempt for decency that in the summer he allowed his gentlemen to appear in public at the Palais-Royal without their wigs: and towards the end of Louis' reign, Mme. de Maintenon is disgusted at the number of women who keep away from Court because if they go there they are obliged to wear a corset under full dress. But one sympathizes more with the men; the women at least had summer frocks, but men made no sartorial concessions to the season. January at Versailles or August at Sceaux, one's ceremonial costume was the same, heavy broadcloth, made heavier by thick embroidery and gold lace.

Whilst we often hear of the Maines' supper parties at Sceaux, no one unfortunately thought it worth while to preserve us a menu; but we may safely assume that in quantity and quality, it did not fall short of the accepted fashionable standards. One might reasonably look forward to working one's way through, say, partridge in cabbage, fillet of duck, galantine of chicken, fillet of beef, roast veal, a dish of rabbits, and a dessert of fruit and cakes. This by the way in addition to casual nibbling in the theatre, for it was an age which indulged in gluttony with the same enthusiasm which it showed for the other deadly sins; in 1710 the Duchesse de Berri at the theatre ate steadily for two hours: caramel peaches, marrons glacés, gooseberry tart, and dried cherries, then, after the performance, a hearty supper. In 1718 this same Duchesse de Berri herself gave a supper party at the Palais-Royal, where she was able to show society how the thing should be done. There were 31 different kinds of soup, 132 of hors d'oeuvres, 132 hot and 60 cold dishes, followed by 234 baskets of fresh, dried, and iced fruit, the whole served up by 332 footmen. Small wonder that the duchess grew stout at a very early age.

It was in the winter of 1707 that Maine struck up a friendship with the Duc de Vendôme. It was at first-sight an odd choice, for not only were the two men of very different character, but Vendôme was Maine's senior by sixteen years. The explanation probably lies in the fact that the Courts of Sceaux and Anet overlapped, rather than in any instinctive personal predilection; such men as St. Aulaire,[9]

[9] St. Aulaire, François Joseph de Beaupoil, 1st Marquis de, born 1643, son of Daniel de Beaupoil, 3rd Baron de St. Aulaire and of his wife, Guyonne de Chavigny-Blot; "his verse is characterized by elegance of a somewhat frivolous kind, and jollity not always free from an ignoble mixture"; he died 1742.

Chaulieu[10] and La Fare[11] were equally welcome guests in either circle and thus the two princes became linked. Politically, they were bound to make common cause, for both were left-handed royalties, holding the same precarious rank, and requiring some more solid support than the mere will of Louis XIV. But we cannot help thinking that Maine, though policy urged him to make a friend of Vendôme, must at times have found his ally's society both uncongenial and embarrassing; for this great-grandson of Henri IV and the beautiful Gabrielle d'Estrées was, in the slang of today, "not everybody's cup of tea." Vendôme, though somewhat hampered in his military career by a succession of obstinate attacks of syphilis, had steadily risen to the front rank of French generals, and in 1705 had wrung from his opponent, Prince Eugène, the handsome compliment that "not to be beaten by Vendôme was more of an honour than to beat some of my other enemies." In August 1706 he had been recalled from Italy to take over the Army of Flanders from Villeroi after the Ramillies disaster–where, according to his preliminary report, he found an army in which "everyone is ready to take off his hat at the mere name of Marlborough." He had restored French morale to such an extent that even Marlborough was unable to exploit his victory, and in the following year, when he again opposed Marlborough, he had maintained a masterly defensive. We get a good idea of the man from St. Simon, once we have excised the palpably untrue, and made that allowance for charity which is so lacking in the Memoirist:

"He was of the middle height, rather stout, but active and vigorous; his countenance very noble, and his bearing haughty. His manners and conversation were easy and graceful; he had much natural, though uncultivated ability. He spoke easily, and his eloquence was sustained by a boldness which eventually developed into effrontery. He had great knowledge of the world and the Court. . . . He took care to be polite when he thought it necessary, but he did not extend his politeness to many people; to those whom he thought might be insulted with impunity, he could be extremely insolent. With the lower orders, his manner was

[10] Chaulieu, Guillaume Amfrie, Abbé de, 1636–1720, "a welcome figure in society," became man of business to the Vendômes, 1675; dismissed by Vendôme in 1699, he then became a habitué of the Sceaux circle; in 1716, "blind, crippled, and eighty years of age," he was in love with Mlle. De Launay.

[11] La Fare, Charles Auguste, Marquis de, 1644–1712. He left very readable memoirs.

familiar and popular. . . . Though the king had formerly been licentious with women, there was one vice which he always looked upon with abhorrence. Yet nobody was more addicted to it than M. de Vendôme; he made no more mystery of it than of the most ordinary gallantry. . . . He could not bear any interference with the daily routine of his life. He was extremely dirty in his person, and proud of it; his foolish flatterers called him a man of simple habits. His bed was always full of bitches, which sometimes produced their puppies by his side. . . . With the army, he rose rather late, and went at once to his *chaise percée*, where he wrote his letters and gave out the morning orders. Anyone who had business with him, even persons of the highest distinction, had to see him then: he had accustomed the army to this infamy. Seated there, he would eat a hearty breakfast . . . many spectators standing round him. He was a great eater, and extraordinarily greedy."

We may feel that Vendôme's skill at, and genuine pleasure in songs, epigrams, and light verse would have to have been of a high order to reconcile us to the drawbacks of his intimacy, but perhaps he was always on his best behaviour with Maine; at any rate Maine seems to have found the society of Anet and the Temple at least as congenial as that of Sceaux.

Life at Sceaux was indeed becoming steadily less attractive, for, as the duchess's slender links with life as it really was became more and more tenuous, her ambitions for her husband grew. The king was visibly ageing: neither of the Maines were on good terms with *Monseigneur*: Mme. du Maine dreamt of a dozen impossible combinations whereby her husband in name, she in fact, could usurp a place in the State after the king's death; "she was enterprising, passionate, audacious to the verge of madness; she sacrificed everything to her object of the moment. She could not tolerate the prudence and caution of her husband, which she called "wretched weakness." The unlucky duke must at times have wondered if even the pleasures of Sceaux were not preferable to its politics. To St. Simon, the Duc du Maine's escape to Versailles in the winter of 1707 is but one more example of the skill with which he trod in dark ways, whereas to us it seems a natural and pathetic attempt to recreate the happy days of the past. For once, Maine does not suffer by our quoting St. Simon without comment, for it is St. Simon's malice and not Maine's craftiness which the passage exposes:

"He had been clever enough to persuade the king that he was absolutely devoid of ambition, an indolent lover of solitude, and the most simple-minded person in the world. Accordingly, he passed his time shut up in his private room, took his meals in solitude, avoided society, and made of this shy and retired existence a merit in the eyes of the king. He saw the king every day in his hours of privacy; he saw him also (for he was a thorough hypocrite) at High Mass, at Vespers, and at the *salut*, which he made a point of attending every Sunday and Feastday. To Mme. de Maintenon, he was the very apple of her eye; he was her oracle, and could do anything he liked with her; and she thought of nothing but how to please him and serve him, no matter at whose expense."

Where St. Simon feels anger at Maine's craftiness, surely the impartial reader must feel sympathy at his escape from Sceaux; with what an "Ah-h!" of relief must the poor man have sunk into his armchair in his empty room at Versailles, savouring the silence and solitude after the hurley-burley of his own home. Let us hope he enjoyed his holiday.

9. *The Sinister Duc du Maine*

THE summer of 1708 saw another crushing defeat inflicted on the Bourbon armies, that of Oudenarde on 11th July; a sorry business, and followed by an even sorrier washing of dirty linen in the publicity of the French headquarters at Versailles. It is irrelevant to our story to attempt to weigh the evidence for and against the Dukes of Burgundy and Vendôme, who between them lost the battle. But we must pause to reject St. Simon's most interesting account of the Duc du Maine as the leader of the cabal at Court which worked so hard by lie and lampoon to discredit the Duke of Burgundy. Burgundy must, in the natural course of events, become king of France in Maine's lifetime; the two men had served together in the earlier stages of the war with mutual liking; they had much in common. What possible advantage could Maine propose to himself by making a mortal enemy of his future master? The story is told simply because in all St. Simon writes, the Duc du Maine must appear in the blackest colours; he must be built up over a period of years as a villain, in order that virtue–and St. Simon–may shine more brightly under the Regency. Let the reader once suspect that Maine did not spend long years in plotting the overthrow of the State, and the big scene, "the degradation of the bastards," falls flat. That the duke exerted his influence to prevent Vendôme from being removed from his command after Oudenarde is very likely; he was enough of a soldier to appreciate Vendôme's professional merits, and he liked the man. But where is the evidence that he wished to prevent his recall because he and his cabal "trusted that before the end of the campaign, Vendôme would complete his task of crushing and discrediting the young prince" (i.e. the Duke of Burgundy). Where, for the matter of that, is the evidence that Vendôme was about to be relieved of his command? St. Simon is our authority for both statements.

But it is not chiefly in military events that St. Simon is interested in 1708, but in the dissolution of the old compact Court, and its reintegration into groups. Louis XIV was not the absolute master that he had been; he was still strong and healthy, but he was seventy years old, and to secure his favour was no longer the first object of an ambitious courtier's energies. Prudent men were already investing for dividends in the future.

St. Simon divides the Court into three cabals; that of Mme. de Maintenon as he calls it, which in fact means no more than those who had grown old with the king, chief amongst whom was Marshal de Villeroi; the second was composed of the group whose centre was the Duke of Burgundy; and the third was formed of the Meudun intimates of *Monseigneur*, the heir to the throne, who was already a man of forty-eight. This picture of Court politics in the winter of 1708 is worth outlining, for the sake of seeing the Duc du Maine as he appears to St. Simon:

"M. du Maine, secure in the affection of the king and Mme. de Maintenon, held aloof from all these cabals . . . nevertheless doing them all as much harm as he could. They knew his character, and all were equally afraid of him."

What then becomes of St. Simon's picture of Maine, the arch-plotter? On St. Simon's showing, the duke has not only no support except the affection of his father and of his morganatic wife, but is engaged in antagonizing all of the possible combinations which may rule France when Louis XIV dies. Odd conduct, to say the least of it, for a wicked man of diabolical cleverness.

1709 came in with three months of unbroken frost, a spring such as Europe had not known for a century; the corn died in the ground, wine froze on the tables at Versailles, and peasants died by scores of cold and starvation. Plenipotentiaries were sent to Holland with abject terms of peace, indeed to get any terms they could beg, but all in vain. Had the matter been left to the soldiers, things might have been different; but the arrogant Dutch tradesmen who represented the allies were determined that Louis XIV should drain his cup to the dregs. As a preliminary to a discussion of peace terms, he was to dethrone his grandson at Madrid with his own army, and at his own expense. "Gentlemen," said Polignac[1], the French negotiator, "it is easy to see that you are unaccustomed to victories." Louis, having heard the terms, remarked that if he must continue fighting, he would sooner fight the Dutch than his own flesh and blood, and nerved himself for a last effort. In June, for the first time in his life, he circularized an appeal to his people; it was a noble and touching piece of prose, which even now stirs the blood, and its effect was electrical. Recruits flocked to the Colours, nobles and bourgeois sold their plate and jewels, the Church taxed its hidden resources, and France took the field once again.

Whether Louis saw the immense significance of his appeal to the people, we do not know; but, consciously or unconsciously, it was a recognition of the fact that a new Europe had sprung to life, that democracy was already struggling to birth, and that not only his sun, but that of all divine kings, was setting. Louis had been born into, and had lived most of his life in a world in which wars were an affair of king versus king, fought by small armies, largely mercenary, for causes which no sovereign condescended to explain to his subjects: cheap wars, comparatively speaking, which affected the common man little and interested him not at all, unless he had the misfortune to live in the cyclone path cut through the countryside by either of the armies. These earlier wars had been fought almost to a set of rules; so many battles won or lost, so many strong places taken or surrendered, and a balance sheet drawn up by the peace negotiators when one or both rulers had had enough of it. And what did it matter to the ordinary citizen whether France or Spain misgoverned Aire or St. Omer? But in the Spanish Succession, we find the first of the modern wars; for the first time, success in the field is dependent, not on who commences the struggle with the better army, but on the war potential of the antagonists; from the Spanish war onwards, wars tend more and more to be clashes in which the whole national resources of each combatant are staked on the issue, until we reach in our own time "total war," the logical outcome of Louis XIV's last struggle, in which the unrealistic

[1] POLIGNAC, Melchior, Cardinal de, son of Louis Armand, Vicomte de Polignac and of his wife, J. de B. du G. de Roure, born 1661; peace plenipotentiary, 1710 and at Utrecht 1712; died 1741.

diplomacy of the allies turned what began as an old time dynastic war into a national struggle for existence.

To Villars was entrusted the terrible task of commanding the last hope of the monarchy, Louis XIV's final stake in what might well prove to be a gamble for his Crown. Villars was told that there were no reserves behind him: he was told that there was no money: he was told that the country must starve in order that the only army which could be mobilized should eat: and with these ill-omened instructions ringing in his ears, he left for Flanders on the mission which was to secure him his place among the great generals of the age.

In this critical year the Duc du Maine did not serve; probably for the same reason which kept the legitimate princes out of the field also, namely that the king could not afford to fit them out in a manner befitting their rank. And, even with his Crown at stake, it would never have occurred to Louis that his family might go into action with a little less pomp than usual, and gain rather than lose in the eyes of the people by so doing. So the Duc du Maine did not serve; he was quietly relegated to the reserve list, and, as it turned out, permanently relegated. He never soldiered again. Sick of his enforced idleness at Sceaux, he keeps up an anxious correspondence with his many old friends in Flanders through this dreadful year. In his not very interesting letters, we can sense his gnawing anxiety for the issue of the campaign, and in the replies, the sympathy of his old comrades for the man who is out of it all. It is pleasant to see that amongst his most familiar correspondents are many obscure officers whose names are otherwise unknown to us, friends of the camp, and not of the Court. Goesbriant is wounded at Malplaquet, and Maine writes in tones of genuine anxiety to enquire into the nature of his hurts; in the following month he is bombarding the War Office with appeals for a pension for his old friend Rosel; he often hears from St. Hilaire of the artillery, who had so fully vindicated Maine's conduct in 1695. Another and a closer link now binds St. Hilaire to Sceaux, for since 1707 he has had as his Chief-of-Staff Pierre Malézieux, son of our literary arbiter and songster-in-chief. Folard is another of Maine's voluminous correspondents at the front; the tastes of the Duc du Maine had always been mildly literary, and we still have Folard's letters, annotated and corrected in his handwriting. He had perhaps some idea of publishing them after the war, for in places he has struck out Folard's hasty phrases and clothed the facts in better prose.

One more glimpse of Maine we get during the closing months of 1709, when we find him at Marly, where he is helping the king to entertain the Elector of Bavaria,[2] his most important German ally; somewhat of a holiday for the duke we guess, for he seems to have been at Marly alone, his wife having probably evaded the party under pretext of being still in mourning for her amiable father, who had died on 31st March.

The death of that madman did nothing to bring the Condés and the Maines closer together; it in fact saddled the Duc du Maine at the beginning of 1710 with an acrimonious lawsuit over the disputed inheritance, in which the opposing party was the new Prince de Condé, who as *M. le Duc* had married the favourite sister of Maine. Of the new Condé, the less said the better; he was jealous, tactless, ferociously ill-tempered, addicted to brutal practical jokes, with a monstrous, disproportioned head, and a bright yellow face; the whole set off by a fixed expression of rage, and a reputation for being the perpetrator of at least one undiscovered murder. "Everyone," says St. Simon, "shunned him as one would a mine which might explode at any moment." But Maine's intercourse with his brother-in-law was to be short, for on 3rd of March 1710 *M. le Duc* died of a tumour on the brain, to the great joy of society in general and of his own family in particular, leaving the lawsuit in abeyance.

But the spring of 1710 had its light as well as shade for the duke, who on 16th March received the gratifying news that Louis XIV had further strengthened Maine's position by granting his children the Prince de Dombes and the Cte. d'Eu the same privileges which had been conferred upon the duke himself.

[2] BAVARIA, Maximilian Emmanuel, 3rd Elector of, son of Ferdinand, 2nd Elector and of his wife, Adelaide Henriette of Savoy, born 1662; secret ally of Louis XIV from 1701; his plan was to get the Imperial Crown and to make Bavaria the leading German state, under French "protection"; died 1726.

We need hardly remark that this outrage does not escape the vigilance of St. Simon, self-appointed watchdog of France; his observations on the subject in fact take up eight pages of print in his best manner, and he is most interesting when he confesses his failure to enlist the Duc d'Orléans as leader of a protest. Philippe d'Orléans is an eighteenth-century prince, not a seventeenth-century one; he is the first Bourbon to give the impression that he does not take the family self-worship seriously, but regards his sacrosanct position of Grandson of France as a very convenient piece of humbug. He was certainly not the man to risk a fall with the king in an effort to forbid the Sceaux princes from indulging in some tedious mummery in the Parlement; "He was perfectly indifferent in such matters," wails St. Simon; "the king saw the impropriety of the proposal submitted to him; he resisted as long as he could, but was finally led to consent against his will." And then we are treated to a scene in which Louis publicly implores *Monseigneur* and the Duke of Burgundy to uphold his decision after his death, and their embarrassed evasions–"The two princes, still bewildered by this extraordinary scene, made some sort of answer, but gave no definite promise. All this was told me word for word by M. de Beauvilliers, who had it next morning from the Duke of Burgundy." So that, even granting St. Simon's honesty, his account is, on his own showing third hand. If the whole incident took place in public, why was not St. Simon himself present? Even more surprising, why was not Dangeau, who never spent a moment out of the royal presence that he could spend in it? And yet the latter, after recording the bare fact of the grant of the new rank, goes on to say, "The king spoke of it in the wisest and tenderest manner to M. du Maine, and those in a position to know what he said have promised me a version of it for insertion at this point."

The conclusion is amusing enough; St. Simon, having fulminated through eight pages, trots off to pay a formal visit of congratulation to the Duc du Maine–"I resolved to drain my cup to the dregs," is how he puts it. It was a busy spring for Maine, who, not content with his lawsuits and his "encroachments," finds time to turn his hand to a bit of matchmaking for his friend Vendôme. Maine's idea that the Marshal should marry his wife's sister, Mlle. d'Enghien[3], was not a new one, but he had made little progress as an ambassador while her mad father was alive. As soon as he was dead however, the duke tackled the king seriously, and towards the end of April he managed to win his consent. Even that unromantic age can show few less romantic marriages; the groom, a chronic sufferer from a disgusting disease, had nothing to offer but his wealth; whilst the bride, aged thirty-three, was an extremely ugly dwarf, fat, apoplectic, and scarred with smallpox. But she was a Princess of the Blood, and that was sufficient for Vendôme. The Duc du Maine, we are told, arranged everything; the marriage contract, the publication of the banns, and the wedding itself. On 15th May Vendôme went from his own house, Anet, to Sceaux, and the same evening he and Mlle. d'Enghien were betrothed, wedded, and bedded. The newly-weds spent the next day at Sceaux, and parted on the 17th–Vendôme going to Anet, and Mme. de Vendôme returning to her mother until the Temple could be made ready for her accommodation.

And so we settle down for the summer at Sceaux, that enchanted oasis where life takes no heed of wars, lawsuits, death, poverty (other people's poverty, that is), or even of the threat of impending national bankruptcy, of which we are already hearing whispers.

We have not yet paid a formal visit to Sceaux, and cannot decently put off doing so any longer; the invitation is after all a semi-royal one, therefore tantamount to an order, and we needs must go when bid, like everyone else. Mme. du Maine is naively confident of the delight which such an invitation affords the lucky recipient, especially if not of the highest social class, and would be stupefied if she knew how her invitations are received in bourgeois circles. A glimpse into the diary of Dr. Galland, Professor of Arabic in Paris University, gives us more real insight into the attractions of Sceaux than do whole volumes devoted to its praise;

[3] Vendôme, Marie Anne de Bourbon, Duchesse de, 1678–1718, fifth daughter of Henri Jules, 5th Prince de Condé, and of Anne of Bavaria; known before her marriage as Mlle. d'Enghien; married the Duc de Vendôme, 1710; died "burnt up by excessive indulgence in alcohol"; "all that could be said of her was that her death left one Princess of the Blood the less."

"Sunday, 20th July: I dined with M. Brue, and gave him the instructions he had asked me for about making me certain purchases when he got back to Constantinople. As we were finishing dinner, a *valet de chambre* of the Duchesse du Maine's came with an invitation for him to go out to Sceaux to see a comedy. He greatly wanted to get out of it, but knows the price one must pay for pleasing the great. The duchess had seen him at Sceaux last Monday, and had been as struck with his good looks as with his wit."

We have seen something of the externals of Sceaux through the eyes of Madame Palatine, its fountains, boskage, parterres and so forth, but we are now entering the salon, where the conversation at once strikes us as being a lightweight version of an evening at the Hôtel de Rambouillet in its palmy days. The tiny little woman in flowered grey, who is doing most of the talking, is our hostess, and we find that the topic is philology; a favourite hare this, and there will be long discussions about the exact shade of meaning of a word, with special attention to its significance in the language of polite gallantry; from there we drift on to the evergreen subject of the niceties of platonic love, perhaps ending with a set debate on the application of the true rules of feminine delicacy in a postulated case. No topic will, however, detain us for long, as the duchess finds logical argument fatiguing; so from here we flit to philosophy, which will lead us, via astronomy, to the immortality of the soul; and after this flight, we descend to earth to hear one of the duchess's tame poets, who has been observed for some time past to be folding and unfolding a manuscript with as much nonchalance as he can assume.

The duchess apart, the most important figure in the room is of course Malézieux, whom we have already met; we gather that since he has been set up as Sceaux's leading light, he has abandoned his own house of Châtenay entirely; his wife is now installed at Sceaux as governess to Mlle. du Maine, his son Pierre, the artillery general, spends his leave here, and in short the whole Malézieux family is indispensable.

Next we notice the seventy-year-old Abbé Genest, whose enormous nose has made his fortune at the Court of Sceaux, for its size, and the chance of a pun, are irresistible; that nose has inspired more epigrams and madrigals than any other object in the Kingdom of Ludovise. Genest has been an Academician since 1698, and a respectable literary figure since 1672, when he had the honour of reading his *Ode on the Conquest of Holland* to the king himself. He is an honest straightforward man, can turn you out a tragedy to order, and five years ago a panegyric of his own writing, to music of his own composing, was encored at Versailles by Louis XIV.

Among the younger set we notice the Abbé de Polignac, tall, handsome, and still under fifty; he is a most amusing story-teller, and has a superficial knowledge of every art, trade, and manufacture; has distinguished himself in the diplomatic line, and is said to be a very favourite friend indeed of the Duchess of Burgundy. He is now engaged in airing his Latinity and his Cartesianism in his much admired poem, *L'Anti-Lucrèce*. For he too is a poet; in fact the only subject of which he is perfectly ignorant is the priestly office, but this will be no bar to his becoming a Cardinal in a year or so. The Marquis de St. Aulaire is a retired soldier, who, when he was over sixty, discovered that he had a talent for writing light verse, and this he has developed so successfully that he has been admitted to the Academy, thereby earning the undying hatred of Boileau, who has no words in which to express his contempt for St. Aulaire's poetic performances: which troubles St. Aulaire not at all.

Anthony Hamilton[4] is a frequent visitor, though nominally resident at St. Germain; in fact he attends St. Germain as a good Jacobite, but is much more often to be met at Anet with the Vendômes, or visiting the Maines at Sceaux. When his prolonged absences from St. Germain are frowned upon, he explains with perfect truth that his talents do not lie in the direction of composing penitential hymns. His fairy tales are held in high esteem by the Duchesse du Maine and her set, and it is a perpetual surprise to recall that this most French of all Frenchmen is in fact an Irish refugee.

Old Chaulieu, who is a Churchman, though one tends to forget the fact, and who has for many years been the factotum of the Vendômes, is here with his inseparable friend, La Fare. Chaulieu is

[4] HAMILTON, Count Anthony, fourth son of Sir George Hamilton by his wife, Lady Mary Butler, born c. 1645; published his *Contes* between 1705 and 1715; his famous *Gramont Memoirs* were published from a stolen MS. in 1713; died unmarried, 1720.

a pleasant old rascal, something of a poet, a freethinker who is to remain an ardent lover of women at eighty, and who draws an income of £1,200 a year from his abbey and his four priories, none of which he has ever seen. His friend La Fare, ten years his junior, is like St. Aulaire, a retired soldier and idler turned poet. Appropriately enough, his two best poems are *Sur La Paresse*, and *La Volupté*. To us, he is better known as the author of some fragmentary, but excellent memoirs, in which he occasionally rises to the height of La Bruyère, and in which, greatly to his credit, and almost alone among his contemporaries, he condemns the revocation of the Edict of Nantes.

The women stand out less clearly, firstly because they are a more shifting population, a rapid succession of "dearest friends" passing into oblivion; and secondly, because Mme. du Maine was no lover of feminine society; she was most at her ease when her salon contained no women but female dependants of the lady-companion order whom she could dismiss without ceremony in the event of their being so presumptuous as to venture into the limelight.

To elegant conversation may succeed a Chapter of the Order, for Mme. du Maine has her own Order of Chivalry, as befits a sovereign—the Order of the Honey Bee as it is called—which has its officers, its decoration, and its motto. It is composed of thirty-nine members, and in this mock Court, admission to its ranks is fought for as keenly as is a blue ribbon at Versailles. The decoration is a gold medal, having on one side a beehive, and on the other a portrait of the Queen Bee, and it is worn on a lemon coloured ribbon by every knight whenever he visits Sceaux; the motto is a line from Tasso, translated by Malézieux—*The bee, though very small, can do great things*. Should there be a vacancy in the Order to be filled, we adjourn to the Chapter House, hung with crimson velvet spangled with silver bees, where we range ourselves round the throne on which sits Mme. du Maine, holding a golden wand. When all is ready, the herald, in a cherry-coloured robe, also sprinkled with silver bees, and wearing a helmet shaped like a beehive, ushers in the candidate, who drops on one knee on the lowest step of the throne. The Queen Bee then administers the oath in seven articles to each of which the postulant swears faith by Mount Hymettus, whilst a concealed choir and orchestra elaborate his responses. And finally the envied favourite has his ribbon and medal hung round his neck by Ludovise.

The Chapter is now ended, and we proceed to the dining room for dinner, only to find that the tiresome ingenuity of Malézieux is not yet exhausted; as we approach the door, we find the way barred by a goddess, holding a glass urn, from which we pick a slip of folded paper. If we are in luck, it proves to be a blank; others however bear the word "song," "madrigal," or "impromptu," and the unfortunate drawer is expected to acquit himself of his task before we rise from the table. Unfortunate at least if he does not know the ways of the house, for those who do are careful never to visit Sceaux without a pocketful of impromptus to cover all normal contingencies. Indeed the impromptu nuisance sometimes gives the hostess more than she bargained for, as on a recent occasion when to make an opportunity for the delivery of an unusually original sample, Genest had been obliged to upset and break a valuable table lamp. Gradually the guests perform their tasks, much wine is drunk, and the conversation begins to take such a gallant turn that Mme. du Maine proposes an adjournment to the gardens, where every tree now sparkles with fairy lanterns, and a hidden orchestra plays selections from the latest musical comedy. Strange figures approaching in the dim light reveal themselves as a set of human ninepins, who, in a cantata for nine voices, complain that their noble game has never been made free of the kingdom of Ludovise; they are officially enrolled among the pastimes of Sceaux, and in gratitude they perform a comic ballet. They have hardly danced themselves off when we become aware of a procession of sledges, drawn by reindeer, which is advancing up the grand avenue. The fur-clad passengers prove to be a deputation of Greenlanders, come to offer their allegiance to Ludovise, and to entreat her to take up her residence in their country. Mme. du Maine objects that Greenland is very far away; but the chief Greenlander has thoughtfully anticipated this difficulty by magical means; he has brought his kingdom with him it appears, for at a signal of his magic wand, the island in the lake bursts into coloured fire. Since sunset it has become an iceberg, on which glitters the palace built for the reception of the new Queen of Greenland, and to which we cross by a specially built bridge for the ceremony of her coronation. When we in due course emerge from the sumptuously furnished palace the bridge has disappeared, but decorated barges are in waiting to re-convey us to the mainland, where we are greeted by the Goddess of Night, accompanied by her Twelve Hours, who welcome us with an Ode specially written for the occasion.

It is now time to go indoors to the card tables, which, with a supper or two, and a good deal of drinking, will occupy us until daybreak. The ninepins, Eskimos, musicians, and all the rest of the pageant get themselves into a convoy of carriages and set out on their long drive to Paris through the moonlight, the rumble of their wheels drowning the howl of the wolves, who get fiercer every night, and the wailing of the starved children in the peasant's huts. As they drive into Paris in the morning sunlight, the dying candles at Sceaux prompt the last impromptu, and we can at length seek our beds. Another of the famous *nuits blanches* of Sceaux is ended.

The year 1711 opened disagreeably enough for the Duc du Maine with a fresh hearing of the Condé inheritance suit, which showed every sign of becoming the cause celèbre of the day; there were dreary consultations to be endured, there were friends and acquaintances to be whipped up for the honour of their attendance at the hearing, and there were the judges to be visited. The last custom deserves a word, for it is that very rare thing, a practice which must have begun as an abuse, but had in process of time turned into an honest formality. If, in the France of those days, you found yourself involved in a lawsuit, it was an indispensable social duty to call on each judge before the hearing, bespeak his good offices in the politest terms you could devise, and make him a small present, known as *les épices*. So universal was the custom that Alceste's refusal to comply with it is the opening stroke with which Molière calls attention to the singularity of his character in the *Misanthrope*; "Aucun juge par vous sera visité?" exclaims Philante in astonishment. It is sufficiently obvious that such a custom can only have begun as an open attempt to bribe or overawe the Bench: it may still have had that effect in petty country courts: but it remains an incontrovertible fact that in the superior courts of Paris, it was accepted both by judges and litigants as a formality, and there is no evidence that a visit or a present swayed any judge in his verdict. In this particular case, owing to the importance of the contending parties, the king had forbidden either side to solicit, but in fact both did so, though each refrained from bringing a small army of friends and supporters to the actual hearing.

Society showed itself fair-minded to the duke, whom it recognized as being driven by his wife into a battle in which he was not primarily concerned; but this did not save him from being roughly handled in the preliminary skirmish of lampoons. His life at Sceaux, his queer guests and intimates, his wife's fêtes and theatricals, were plastered with ridicule, and for many weeks the unfortunate man found himself an object of pity and derision in the taverns of Paris.

On 17th April the Dauphin, better known by his Court title of *Monseigneur*, died at Meudun after a brief illness; he had been a figure of secondary importance all his life, and even in the hour of death was not permitted to occupy the centre of the stage. For on the same day, in distant Vienna, died a far more important man, namely the Emperor. In England the Emperor's death meant the removal of the last Whig argument for a continuance of the war, and to France it meant salvation: for the new Emperor was the Allied candidate for the Throne of Spain. England had entered the war to prevent the house of Bourbon from ruling two great kingdoms; if she continued to fight, it could only be to make the Hapsburgs predominant on the continent. That Spain should be governed from Vienna was only a degree less dangerous than that she should be governed from Versailles, the balance of power called for an English volte-face, and Louis XIV's government was quick to establish further contacts with the willing Tories.

The Duc du Maine has been accused of feeling little sorrow for the death of *Monseigneur*, though it is difficult to discover the evidence on which the charge is based. True, the Dauphin had not much liked him, for Joseph is rarely popular with his brethren, especially when Joseph's mother is a bondwoman; and it is probable, that had *Monseigneur* come to the throne, there would have been no place for Maine under the new régime. But not even his enemies suggest that he showed any indecent rejoicing at his half-brother's death, and that is surely as much as we have a right to expect. Nor need we linger over St. Simon's denunciation of his crime in accepting visits of condolence from the nobility on the death of the heir to the Crown: except to remark the significance of the fact that this insult to the legitimate Princes of the Blood was resented by none of their own number: by no one indeed except St. Simon.

It was not long before the Duc du Maine himself came within an ace of death. On 6th June the Court was at Marly, and on that evening everyone noticed the duke's high spirits; until nearly two in the morning he had been the life and soul of the king's private circle, keeping his father amused with his jokes and stories. But he had hardly gone to bed when his valet, who slept in his room, heard him gasping for breath and in a few moments realized that his master had lost consciousness. To the fact that the valet was a light sleeper Maine probably owed his life; the servant ran for Maréschal, the king's surgeon, who arrived in his slippers, bled the patient, who was now in convulsions, and proceeded to administer, rather at random one feels, a variety of emetics and "English drops." Three hours of unconsciousness was followed by delirium, and it was not until seven in the morning that Maine was in a state to make his confession; after which he spent the day in a tranquil sleep. By the 9th, his health was completely restored. The duchess, by the way, was at Sceaux at the time, and when summoned to Marly, contented herself with sending a message that "it would kill her to see M. du Maine in such a state." The subsequent squabble between the distinguished practitioners to whom fell the task of drafting a bulletin on the duke's illness, is worthy of Molière, and throws a vivid light on contemporary diagnosis; Fagon, the leading physician of France, diagnosed indigestion: another voted for apoplexy: a third suspected a meal of Marly mushrooms: and there was a further group which insisted that the disease had plainly been epilepsy.

Indigestion won the day, rather on Fagon's personal merits than through any faith in his diagnosis.

The Duc du Maine is now forty-one, and we have watched his development from the night of his birth; we have had the opinions of friends and enemies, we have reluctantly been driven to admit that the brilliant promise of his earlier years has failed to mature. But we must remember that our very intimacy with him prevents us from seeing the man objectively, we can no more so look at him than we can at one whom we have known all our lives. It is therefore fortunate that there now appears a shrewd, detached observer who saw him for the first time this year, and was to have the opportunity of studying him for the rest of his life.

In September 1711 Mme. du Maine took into her employ one Mlle. de Launay, who has left interesting memoirs of Sceaux and its inhabitants between 1711 and 1736. Her story is a tragic one; brought up in luxury, she was left friendless and penniless at the age of seventeen, and the rest of her life was to be devoted to finding out, as she herself puts it, how steep are other people's staircases. But there was a rare spirit in Mlle. de Launay; she hides nothing of the bitterness of her lot, yet she never loses her courage or the cool ironic gift of seeing people and things as they are, and making the best of them. She is neither overawed by, nor contemptuous of the great; finds them, on the whole, much like other people, only a little more ridiculous. There is no malice in her pitiless dissection of the Fairy Ludovise, whom indeed she finds more considerate to her women than many other great ladies, though she is under no illusions as to her character. The post of chamber-woman to Mme. du Maine was found for her by the Duchesse de La Ferté[5] in mid-September, after, to quote Mlle. de Launay again, "she had seen herself taken round Paris from house to house, like a monkey at a fair." As a waiting woman she was not a success, as she candidly admits, having bad eyesight, and being given to the absent-minded inversion of basins of water and powder boxes over her mistress, who

[5] La Ferté, Marie Gabrielle Angélique de La Motte-Houdancourt, Duchesse de, ob. 1726, third daughter of Philippe, Maréchal de La Motte-Houdancourt, and of Louise de Prie; in 1680 she attempted to seduce Louis XIV, who had to exile her; widowed, 1705; "an outrageous woman."

showed an unexpected gentleness and patience under the treatment. But, very luckily for Mlle. de Launay, Fontenelle was one of her correspondents, and, her letters to him being shown around in society, Mme. du Maine realized that here was just the tame lioness that Sceaux needed. From chamber-woman she was promoted to reader, and from reader to mistress of the revels; or perhaps we should say to producer and stage manager. To her fell the business of engaging Spirits of Sceaux, human ninepins, Laplanders, clowns, and singers, and arranging the nightly revue; when talent ran short in the theatre, she could knock up a play and act a minor part. Two of the comedies written by her indeed still survive, though both are second-rate.

Here are Mlle. de Launay's impressions of the master of Sceaux, or, if you prefer it, of the husband of the mistress:

"M. du Maine had an enlightened understanding, subtle and cultivated; *savoir monde* in perfection; a noble and serious character. Religion rather than nature made him virtuous and kept him so. He loved order, justice, decorum. His natural inclination was for solitude and study. Gifted with all the qualities necessary for success in society, he mixed in it with reluctance. But when compelled to do so, he appeared gay, easy, obliging, and equable. His solid, but at the same time lively, conversation was full of charms, and of a peculiar light and easy turn; his stories were amusing; his manners noble, polished, and easy. Though his air was candid enough, one could not see into his mind; his diffidence kept one at arm's length, and prevented him from opening his heart."

Much the best portrait we have had of the duke so far, and from which we recognize one of those men in whose intimacy we make rapid strides up to a certain point, after which there is no getting to know him any better; a man who never seeks our society, but who, when we seek his, is always good company; who, even when we are most at our ease with him, gives us the feeling that he has no need for us, that we remain for ever outside his real life. It could hardly have been otherwise; such a reticence is the protective crust grown by every solitary child who emerges into adolescence to find himself a square peg in a round hole; the superficial social charm itself is but another envelope to bear the inner life unbruised through its inevitable contacts with an alien world. And if, as in Maine's case, marriage fails to establish a union of souls, the crust will remain unbroken, the man will be alone and secret to the end of his days.

While Mlle. de Launay was peering about her at Sceaux with those short-sighted eyes which saw so much, France was climbing out of the morass of war which had so nearly overwhelmed her. In September, Prior arrived in Paris, where the poet proved himself a match for Torcy, and had the honour of an interview with Louis XIV; in October the English government heard of the failure of its expedition against Canada, and announced publicly its intention of opening peace talks; Marlborough fell in December; and on the penultimate day of the year, Anne created twelve Tory peers. On 12th January 1712 the Congress of Utrecht opened, and just a month later there fell upon the old king at Versailles a series of domestic catastrophes which completed the work of the war in hastening his end.

On 6th February, the Duchess of Burgundy, or the Dauphine as she now was, went to bed with a feverish chill; she appeared to be better on the following day until six in the evening, when she was attacked by excruciating pain in the temples; snuff, opium, pipe tobacco, and bleeding were resorted to, by which, or in spite of which, the pain disappeared, but throughout the 8th and 9th the princess was drowsy, in a high fever, and wandering in her mind. Red marks appeared on her skin, giving hopes of measles, an epidemic of which was raging in Paris. But by the 11th the baffled doctors had to admit that the Dauphine's case was desperate, and on the 12th she died.

That charming modesty which the king had praised in her on the first day he met her, remained until the end; "Goodbye, dear Duchess," she said to Mme. de Gramont, "today I am Dauphine of France, and tomorrow nothing;" and a little later she bid farewell to her doctor in words which show how much the thought dwelt in her mind: "Today I am still a well-loved princess, tomorrow nothing, and the day after that, forgotten." She did herself, her contemporaries, and posterity an injustice. As Louis XIV left her deathbed he knew that the last lingering gleam of twilight had faded from his own life, and that the night was upon him, whilst for her husband, the parting was, in literal truth, his own death sentence.

He was not with her at the end; he had been dragged from her bedside in a high fever, which he could no longer conceal, and when she died he had already started on the same journey as his duchess. The day following her death he had himself taken to Marly, where the king, on seeing him with his haggard face covered by livid blotches, instantly ordered him to bed. This was on Saturday 13th February; at half past eight on the morning of the 18th, he too was dead.

The result of the deaths was a poisoning panic such as France had not known for thirty years, and when on 20th February the late Dauphin's infant son died too, after exhibiting the same symptoms as his parents, society's hysteria rose to a point approaching madness. Who was the poisoner, was the question on everybody's lips, and a scapegoat was soon found. It was the Duc d'Orléans, who was systematically killing off all of the royal family who stood between himself and the Throne. No evidence, no weighing of probabilities, shook the popular opinion, no consideration of the obvious fact that the last thing Orléans would have wanted was the Crown of France; he believed nothing in particular, not even in the divinity of the Bourbons, and he had long ago realized that the steps of the Throne made a more comfortable lounging place than the Throne itself. Exactly what proved the depths of his villainy, hissed society, this long built up parade of indifference towards the secret object of his ambition. And then, was he not a chemist? In vain the horrified Orléans protested that he was in fact engaged in experimental pneumatics. Quite so, said society: see the diabolical cleverness of the man in having all this apparatus prepared in advance to conceal his manufacture of poison to kill the Dauphin. To St. Simon, Orléans' lifelong friend, the duke was a victim of a deliberately planned attack, and planned by whom? The reader will by this time know his St. Simon well enough to guess the answer: the Duc du Maine of course. Dearly as St. Simon would like to say outright that the Duc du Maine himself was the poisoner, even he feels that this simply will not do. But he can at least give a hint which will sow a suspicion in our minds; in the following sentence he shows that he has nothing to learn from the dirtiest school of modern biography in the gentle art of damning a man by professing disbelief in a charge which no one has thought of preferring–

"To the Duc du Maine, the news of their deaths came as a most welcome deliverance; his spirits revived amidst the general lamentation; but, being a past master in the most treacherous practices–*I will not say the most criminal, for no hint to that effect ever reached me*–he thought it would be to his advantage to cast suspicion on somebody, and more particularly on the Duc d'Orléans."

This goes far beyond anything that even Madame Palatine has to say, who confines herself to generalities about Maine's ambition, whilst categorically asserting that it is "old Maintenon" who has tried to persuade the king that Orléans is a poisoner. As St. Simon warms to his work, the hint about Maine becomes an assertion; having pointed out, perfectly correctly, that Orléans has nothing to gain by the death of the Dauphin, he slips in the startling deduction that because Orléans has nothing to gain, the Duc du Maine has everything.

"The Duc d'Orléans had an assured position, which nothing could disturb, and which must descend to his children; let his position be compared with that of M. du Maine–and then ask ourselves which of the two was more likely to be the poisoner."

Stripped of the tumultuous prose which for a moment throws us off our balance, St. Simon's case comes simply to this: the Dauphin was poisoned: if the Duc d'Orléans did not do it, we cannot definitely say that the Duc du Maine did: but it is at least obvious that the commission of the crime gratified him, and that he at once proceeded to throw suspicion on the Duc d'Orléans. Even now it is not clear how the Duc du Maine was supposed to have benefited by the calumny of which he is accused, and as for the hint that he committed the poisonings himself, I have completely failed in my efforts to paint the man if any reader thinks him capable of such a crime; to say nothing of the fact that, at this stage in his career, no number of deaths in the royal family could have brought him an inch nearer the Crown. And yet St. Simon's smear has had a long lease of life; in the spurious memoirs of Cardinal Dubois, which were not published until 1829, the Cardinal, in discussing these deaths, is made to say, "It seems to me that the Duc d'Orléans had everything to lose by their deaths, and the Duc du Maine everything to gain."

10. *Brittle Splendour*

The year ended for the Duc du Maine with a Christmas present over which a needy prince with an expensive wife might well smack his lips; on his way to Mass one morning, the king told him that he had conferred the government of Guyenne on Maine's second son, the Cte. d'Eu. As the new governor was about eight years old, we may surmise that his share of the windfall was a scanty one; so indeed we may suspect was the Duc du Maine's, for doubtless most of the emoluments of that handsome sinecure were speedily converted into fireworks and Palaces of the Moon. We must for once agree with St. Simon when he says sourly that the Maine children "were now tolerably provided for," as between them they held, in fact or in reversion, the governments of Guyenne and Languedoc, the command of the Swiss Guards, and the command of the artillery. It must have been a contented Duc du Maine who returned to his rooms after Mass to add a touch or two to his newly begun undertaking, a French version of his friend Polignac's *Anti-Lucrèce*. In passing, one regrets to find that the duke's literary activities did not bring him any closer to his wife, who preferred that she, and not her husband, should dazzle Sceaux with fresh outpourings of the poetic fire; his one recorded effort to read his translation to his duchess met with a damping response - "One of these mornings," she snapped, "you will wake to find yourself a member of the Academy, and the Duc d'Orléans Regent of France." For already her quick, shallow brain was at work on the advantages which might be drawn from the contempt and ostracism which was now the portion of the unlucky Philippe d'Orléans at Court; why should not Maine be Regent after the king's death, or, to put it more plainly, why should not Mme. du Maine be in effect Queen of France during a long minority?

As we turn over St. Simon's pages for 1713, we are surprised to see the Duc du Maine referred to in almost a friendly tone, and stop to investigate the mystery. Alas for that noble Roman spirit which has so often spurned the overtures of the abhorred bastard. St. Simon we find has been wounded in his tenderest spot, his ceremonial privileges are threatened, and only Maine can help him; so he pockets his pride, and trots off to appeal for our duke's help and countenance. Maine is, as we know, governor of Guyenne, and Marshal de Montrevel is his deputy; St. Simon is governor of Blaye, a town situated in the government of Guyenne. Now the great principle of subordination has no more fanatical supporter than St. Simon, in theory; but when it comes to practice, and he is the subordinate, he dislikes the position as much as any man in France. Montrevel's "encroachments" as he calls them, have become intolerable, and St. Simon's petition is that Maine shall arbitrate between them in the matter of their respective rights:

"M. du Maine, who had never ceased to make advances to me, in spite of the coldness with which I had received them, was extremely polite on this occasion; he expressed himself much gratified by my proposal, and undertook to do what I had asked."

He went further, for when Montrevel arrived post haste at Court to plead his case, and St. Simon at once observed that the Marshal saluted him "with marked negligence," it was Maine who nipped the matter in the bud by reminding these two crowing cocks of the respect due to the king's house. The whole affair would be too trivial to detain us, were it not for the light thrown on Maine's forbearance and kindliness; if there was anyone at Court towards whom he could be fairly expected to show his dislike, it was St. Simon; yet, so far from taking the opportunity to snub him, he goes to considerable trouble to oblige his enemy:

"M. du Maine ordered La Vrillière[1] to draw up a report; it contained twenty-five clauses, for I had particularly asked him that it should be full and complete, so as to leave no loophole for future disputes. M. du Maine

[1] Vrillière, Louis Phélypéaux, 1st Marquis de La, 1672–1725, elder son of the Marquis de Châteauneuf and of Marie Fourcy; "generally liked, because he was always ready to do anyone a good turn."

was very willing to oblige me in a question of importance to myself, for he knew that it mattered little to his son, who was not likely to exercise the functions of governor of Guyenne in person.

But, lest we should suspect St. Simon of any unmanly display of gratitude, he hastens to undeceive us:

"moreover he (Maine) was not sorry to have an opportunity of showing his impartiality, and so diminish the ill-feeling caused by the new favours bestowed upon him."

It is all, you see, merely a new display of cunning on the part of the false-hearted Duc du Maine.

And after all, there was a crumpled rose leaf in St. Simon's bed; when the famous treaty came to be ratified by the king on 19th March, it was found that Montrevel has been confirmed in his right of having his guards "in greatcoats and bandoliers" when he visits the citadel of Blaye.

Three weeks later Louis XIV put his signature to a treaty of almost equal importance, namely that of Utrecht, the contracting parties to which were France, England, Holland, Prussia, Savoy and Portugal. Louis had, thanks to Queen Anne and the Tories, not only escaped destruction, but could, in a sense, describe himself as the victor; he had entered the war to put his grandson on the Spanish Throne, and Philippe V was recognized by the allies as king of Spain; he had recovered Lille, Aire, Béthune, St. Venant, and Orange; and if he had lost most of Canada, he had at least retained Cape Breton and the fishery rights. But the price he had had to pay left him ruined, and on the long term view it ruined the Monarchy; he himself was to pass the short remainder of his life in peace, but the bill had to be settled. As a modern historian puts it, Louis XVI had to meet the creditors, but it was Louis XIV who overdrew the account.

One more domestic blow was to fall upon the old king before the day came when he too must go to his rest; on 11th May 1714 his youngest grandson, the Duc de Berri, died from the results of a hunting accident:

"Never was M. du Maine so beaming and cheerful as at this time. He secluded himself even more than usual; but, when he did appear, it was evident, in spite of all his efforts to conceal it, that he was beside himself with joy."

Evident to St. Simon, that is, for no one else remarked on it, and his knowledge of the Duc du Maine's feelings seems to be inferred from the fact that at Sceaux the duchess took no notice of the catastrophe, being immersed in her usual round of festivities, "M. du Maine sitting near the door, doing the honours more often than he liked, and seeming rather ashamed of himself." And he might indeed have felt ashamed of himself had these festivities at which he did the honours followed immediately on the Duc de Berri's death; but when we come to look into the matter, we find that Maine was then at Versailles with the king.

On Sunday morning, 29th July, St. Simon, returning after a stroll to his room at Marly, found there a footman of the President de Maisons;[2] he was the bearer of a note begging St. Simon to cancel all his other engagements in order to call on him at once on business of the highest importance. When St. Simon got to Maisons' house, he found with him the Duc de Noailles.[3] Both men were in a state of considerable perturbation:

"They told me . . . that the king had decided to declare his bastard sons and their posterity for ever, not only Princes of the Blood in every respect, but also capable of succeeding to the Crown in the event of the other branches of the royal family becoming extinct."

Here was pretty news, for St. Simon of all men, for no hint of this astounding decision had leaked out beforehand; and we are not surprised that "his arms dropped helplessly to his sides." Could not something be done, he asked feebly? His friends, who were "stamping about the room, using very violent language, and making the house ring with noise," answered with considerable heat, that it was just because nothing could be done that they were so angry; it was not merely that the matter was under discussion, or even that a decision had been come to; the thing was actually done, the declara-

[2] Maisons, Claude de Longeuil, 4th Marquis de, 1668–1715, son of Jean, 3rd Marquis, "a tall man, of rather imposing appearance, with a great deal of sense and ability, though his professional knowledge was very superficial."

[3] Noailles, Adrien Maurice, 3rd Duc de, 1678–1766, son of Anne Jules, 2nd Duc and M. F. de Bournonville; married, 1698, Françoise Aimable d'Aubigné, niece of Mme. de Maintenon; Marshal of France, 1734.

tion was even then in the hands of the Parlement for registration; and no opposition was possible, for the Princes of the Blood were children, and Orléans on no terms to speak to the king; whilst the Parlement was a mere tool for registering the king's will. St. Simon was the first to rally under the blow, remarking, very surprisingly, that he would rather have the bastards capable of succeding to the Crown than in their present intermediate rank; and after some general hopeful remarks about no one knowing what the future might bring forth, St. Simon took his leave and hurried back to Marly "lest my absence should give rise to talk." Having arrived at Marly, and having seen the king sit down to supper, he then went to see Maine, though it was a highly unusual hour for making calls:

"I found him as delighted at my visit as astonished; lame though he was, he seemed rather to fly than to walk as he advanced to meet me. I told him that this time I had come to congratulate him very sincerely; we did not pretend to any rivalry with the Princes of the Blood, but claimed only that no one should stand between the Princes and the Dukes; and that now that he and his sons were really Princes of the Blood, we could only rejoice over the disappearance of that intermediate rank which I must honestly confess I had always found intolerable. M. du Maine's delight at being congratulated in this fashion was indescribable; I cannot repeat all he said to me, with the politeness, and even the deferential airs a man finds it easy to adopt in his hour of triumph."

So runs the most vivid and enduring account of Louis' much discussed edict, which successive historians have represented as being extorted from his weakness by the joint efforts of Mme. de Maintenon and the Duc du Maine.

But if we are to accept this verdict, we may surely demand the production of some better evidence than St. Simon's assertion that the Duc du Maine was ambitious of the Throne of France? The duchess perhaps, indeed probably, but outside St. Simon it is difficult to find a hint that Maine entertained any such desire. Nor can we blindly accept St. Simon's assertions about the universal indignation which the edict roused all over France, and that the public reaction to it was carefully kept from the king; "M. du Maine took care not to tell him (the king) of the gloomy, constrained air with which a servile Court brought him its forced congratulations." But what of

St. Simon's own congratulations, which he has told us of on the same page? Can they be described as "forced," or alternatively, are we to believe that he alone in all France took this view of the matter? Throughout the Duc du Maine's life we have been on the watch for any signs of popular dissatisfaction at his elevation, from the day of that spontaneous welcome given him at Bordeaux, thirty odd years ago. We have not found them, and we do not find them now at the moment of his great triumph. Turn from St. Simon to Mlle. de Launay, and what do we find? She is of the Sceaux household it is true, but her memoirs were obviously secret during her time there, and she was in a position to digest the considered opinion of society. This is all she has to say: "The sudden death of so many princes of the royal house both motivated and facilitated the decree, which was accepted without any opposition."

On Sunday 2nd August the duke and his brother, the Cte. de Toulouse were formally received in Parlement in their new rank, in the presence of a distinguished audience, including St. Simon, who "witnessed the shudder which passed through the crowd when the two bastards appeared;"

"and heard the stifled murmur which arose as they crossed the floor of the Chamber. Hypocrisy was depicted on the countenance and in the whole bearing of M. du Maine . . . bending over his stick with studied humility, stopping at every step so that his bows . . . might be deeper; sometimes with a marked pause before he raised himself again. His face, composed to an expression of mild gravity, seemed to say *non sum dignus* from the depths of his soul; but the joy which sparkled in his eyes as he darted furtive glances over the assembly gave the lie to his assumed humility. When he reached his place, he again bowed repeatedly before sitting down; and it was delightful to watch him during and after the proceedings."

Buvat records the whole ceremony with tedious minuteness, but there is in his account no trace of the ill-concealed dissatisfaction which St. Simon tells us was visible on every face.

But we must not dismiss St. Simon's account as unimportant. Dissatisfaction there must have been, dissatisfaction both deep and justifiable, which was to break out as soon as Louis was dead. Buvat gives us the royal speech in full, the burden of which is that the king is impelled so to act, not out of any undue affection for the Duc du Maine, but through anxiety for his people, whom he is eager to save from the anarchy of a disputed succession; and he several times emphasizes the fact that the edict becomes operative only after the death of the last surviving legitimate successor to the Crown. It would be unfair to dismiss the king's arguments as a piece of hypocrisy perpetrated in the interests of his favourite son. Who knows his own heart, much less that of another? We easily persuade ourselves that that which we desire is by a fortunate coincidence also that which is good. France had just had a terrible lesson that all princely flesh is grass, and the series of deaths had left the succession ill-provided for. If the legitimate line was doomed to extinction, was it not better for the nation that the illegitimate should reign rather than that Europe should tear the kingdom in pieces to provide it with a new royal line? But this argument is a specious one, and cannot justify Louis' decree, for which indeed no defence is possible. France was not Louis XIV's property, it was, even on his own view of kingship, an estate which was strictly entailed. On no conceivable theory of the Monarchy could a reigning King of France choose his own successors, even under the pretext of safeguarding the realm from serious danger. It is very doubtful if even the States-General possessed the power of ratifying such a decision, still more so if any such right rested with the Parlement of Paris. The edict struck at the very roots of even such a shadowy constitution as that of monarchical France. True, the rights of the legitimate successors appeared to be rigorously guarded, but what did that amount to when once it had been admitted that the king could nominate his own successor? Edicts had been reversed before, even by their authors, and if Louis lived, what guarantee was there that a new edict might not appear, conferring rights of succession on Maine and his children to the prejudice of the legitimate heir? Whether intentionally or not, Louis XIV had taken the first step towards converting the house of Bourbon into a dynasty on the Asiatic model, in which the succession depends on the caprice of the ruler; and, had his edict become effective, French history might have run into an Oriental mould. Maine was a weak man, and had he come to the Throne, a Grand Vizier would soon have emerged behind it; why should not Maine have been terrorized into leaving the Crown to the Grand Vizier, and why should not the Grand Vizier have anticipated his inheritance? Instead of a French Revolution, we might have had a French Partition when the anarchic state of an orientalized France had become intolerable to the rest of Europe.

Louis XIV was now an old man, the demi-god was ageing visibly like any mere mortal; the stately, inexorable routine of Versailles showed no slackening, but the iron constitution, indifferent to the demands of pain and pleasure, and which had worked so hard, was noticeably failing. The old actor still played his part as no one else was ever to play it, but with a fatigue which was apparent to the spectators. It was noticed that he had begun to dislike being stared at while he dined; in the seclusion of his private room, only Mme. de Maintenon could lay the ghost of the Duchess of Burgundy which was ever behind the weary, disillusioned old man's chair. More and more he dwelt in the past; his stories now were all of the old days, "when I was king" as he himself would say;

"The king abandoned himself more and more to Mme. de Maintenon and M. du Maine, on whose devotion he thought he could rely. They had brought him to believe that M. du Maine, with all his ability, was absolutely devoid of ambition: a simple, honest, straightforward sort of person; attentive, like a good father, to the interests of his children, but otherwise caring nothing for rank or high position; devoted to the king personally, whom he tried to distract by his cheerfulness and natural wit, after working hard all day in the faithful discharge of his various functions. . . . . All this was very pleasant to the king and he felt quite at his ease with his well-beloved son. M. du Maine amused him exceedingly by his jokes and funny stories, which he told better than anyone I ever met; he had such a charming, easy way of putting things that he made all his hearers think that they could have said as much themselves."

We need not reject this pleasant picture because it is St. Simon's artful introduction to what he asserts to have been a conspiracy to extort a Will from Louis that would reduce Orléans to a figurehead Regent. That the king endeavoured by every means in his power to tie Orléans' hands when he himself was gone is undeniable. But we need invent no conspiracy to explain his actions. If the king did not believe Orléans to be a poisoner, a large number of influential people did; and Louis was at least sure, for it was unfortunately notorious, that his nephew was an irreligious man of the worst possible morals. He must be Regent, but his claws must be clipped by every available method. Mme. de Maintenon disliked and distrusted Orléans; but she does not seem to have been consulted about the king's Will; and we know that Maine was for a long time ignorant of its contents. The extent to which the king was influenced by their opinions is of course imponderable, but that there was any formal or tacit agreement between the two to sway his decision, is highly improbable, if only for the reason that his Will would probably have been in the same terms if neither of them had ever mentioned the subject to him. Even from the point of view of Orléans himself it was highly desirable that he should not be left in absolute control of the young Louis XV; the child was delicate, and if he died there would not be wanting a formidable body of opinion to assert that the Regent had at last succeeded in removing the only life between himself and the Crown. Separating St. Simon's facts from his suppositions, then throwing into the balance what we know of the characters of M. du Maine and Mme. de Maintenon, there is not only no weight of evidence for the conspiracy story, but the facts are all consistent with the theory that the Will was Louis' own act.

St. Simon is too popular a dramatist not to feel the need of a rascally attorney in this scene, so the Chancellor Voysin[4] is cast for the part: "the two Consuls and their Lictor took counsel together and agreed upon the rôle each was to play in the sinister tragedy." So runs the stage direction. It is unfortunate for St. Simon that historical accuracy compels him to make use of Voysin, for he is miscast in the part of the venal lawyer; Voysin, a man nearing sixty, had had the good fortune to entertain Mme. de Maintenon in his house at Dinant in 1692 whilst the king was besieging Namur, and Mme. de Maintenon had taken a great liking to Mme. Voysin. Since he had thus got his foot on the upper rung of the ladder, there had been about him no trace of the intriguing Court lawyer what-

[4] VOYSIN, Daniel François, 1655–1717, son of Jean Baptiste Voysin, and of Marie Talon; Intendant of Maubeuge, 1692, where he lodged Mme. de Maintenon; "never was there such a personification of the bureaucratic spirit . . . he was an official from head to foot."

soever; indeed even St. Simon, not then foreseeing the base usage to which he would subsequently have to put Voysin, describes him earlier in his memoirs as a shy, stiff man, who shunned society and hated to be seen, an excellent and indefatigable official, with whom it was next to impossible to obtain an interview. A portrait corroborated by Berwick, who says that Voysin had no interests of any kind, outside his official duties. In fact, about the last man in France, we should say, to lend himself to a femininely engineered *coup d'Etat* to extort a will from his most important client, and who in fact comes into the picture merely because as Chancellor of France, it fell to him to advise on the technical aspects of the instrument, and on its safe custody when drawn.

But Voysin plays a minor part in the plot, whose tempo is now accelerated by a new technique on the part of the leading conspirators, Maine and his old governess:

"Up to this time, their one object had been to please and amuse the king, ... finding that Voysin was unable to bring him to the desired point, they now began to show themselves in a different light. They became grave, taciturn, and melancholy; not only did they never start a topic of conversation themselves, but if the king made an effort to do so, they quickly let it drop; sometimes they would not so much as notice what he said, unless he put a direct question. This had the effect of discouraging the few ladies who were admitted to Mme. de Maintenon's sanctuary; they always took their cue from her, and their fear of giving offence made them even duller and less entertaining than usual. When the king was in his own room, he had nothing to entertain him but tiresome stories which the Comte de Toulouse told him about his hunting and shooting; the Comte knew nothing about the plot, and he was not entertaining naturally; if one of the confidential valets began talking, he soon dropped it when he saw that M. du Maine did not pick up the topic and carry it on . . . time went on, and the gloom which overshadowed the king's private life became darker and darker."

From this private life, be it remembered, St. Simon had always been entirely excluded, and the fact seems to strike him at this point, for with an aplomb which takes our breath away, he continues,

"I should merely be romancing if I attempted to describe scenes which occurred during this long period. Regard for the truth compels me not only to relate what I know, but also to confess when I am in ignorance. One thing however is certain; cheerfulness revived all of a sudden; and those who witnessed the revival were as much puzzled as they had been by the preceding period of gloom, because the secret cause was equally unknown."

So history is written. Let the king and his family spend a few melancholy evenings, and some consequential valet will step out to the mob of courtiers, whispering in some ducal ear, "The King . . . ." And at the magic word, the throng falls upon him like a swarm of bees to hear his interpretation of the royal ennui. If there be a St. Simon present, the valet's gossip becomes history.

But the Will was at last drawn, and the large packet, sealed with the apocalyptic seven seals, was handed over to the First President and the Procurer-General for safe keeping. "Gentlemen," said Louis XIV, "this is my Will; its contents are unknown to anybody except myself. I give it to you to be placed in the custody of the Parlement of Paris." An elaborate repository was constructed for the document in the wall of the Parlement buildings, closed with an iron door behind an iron grille, with three keys for each, in the keeping of the great officers of the Parlement; and Louis, reflecting dourly on the fate of his own father's will, and with no illusions as to the fate of this, sat down to write to the Duc du Maine:

"You know that however great I make you, you will be nothing after me, and it will be your business to turn all that I have done for you to account–if you can."

There is no remark which shows more clearly his profound knowledge of France, and of his own son.

Louis would have done better, one thinks, either to have left no will, or else to have published the details of the form of government which he wished to come into force after his death. The method which he adopted satisfied no one, but fomented an unhealthy excitement and speculation which was to continue for the short remainder of the reign. The fact that the Regent designate was to be shorn of much of his power, either in favour of the Duc du Maine or of a Council of Regency, was made public by the mere knowledge that a will had been made; and the result was that France was split into two camps which maintained an uneasy and malevolent equilibrium. The country grew feverish in what was recognized as a transitional state, and the tension released on the king's death made the inauguration of the new régime unnecessarily stormy.

The Duc du Maine's position was at least as uncomfortable as that of the Duc d'Orléans;

> "He told his friends candidly, in that quaint way in which he often talked of serious matters, that his position was that of a louse between two fingernails (meaning the Peers and the Princes of the Blood), and that, if he was not very careful, he must inevitably be crushed."

He was afraid of the Princes of the Blood, he feared the Parlement, he even feared the dukes. But if Maine was, as usual, for caution and circumspection, he had a grey mare at Sceaux who viewed the situation very differently; it was a situation which few women could have endured with patience, and which was utterly beyond Mme. du Maine's powers of self-control. What was in the king's will was the question which she asked herself and her husband, day and night. They *must* know. The duke *must* insist on old Maintenon's insisting on finding out from the king. Day after day made it abundantly clear to the duke that no relaxation of the domestic torture to which he was subjected was obtainable, except at the price of making an endeavour to penetrate the secret. With much reluctance and many misgivings he set about the task of badgering Mme. de Maintenon.

His ex-governess was now a remarkably shrewd and non-committal old lady of seventy-eight, whose knitting needles had clicked to the history of France for nearly thirty years; during that time she had, to use her own phrase, been torn in pieces by princes, the objects of whose honied visits she had generally known before they were announced. She had acquired the wisdom of the serpent, and could in her later years be very deaf and very dense when conversing with importunate minor royalties. No, she said at length, she could not help her dear duke in this matter, any mention of the Will would greatly annoy the king. And she was right, as usual. Louis was a great egoist and a great actor, and the universal interest in his will annoyed him in both capacities. That the limelight should already be turning on his successor was intolerable to the egoist, whilst the actor felt the need of a quiet period in which to prepare himself for that final scene which must be played in a manner worthy of his European reputation. Was it not whispered in Paris that a few days ago he had said to the Queen of England in Mme. de Maintenon's presence,

"Madame, I have made my will; I have been worried into it, but I trust that I shall now be left in peace; but I well know what an impotent and useless thing it is. So long as we are alive, we can do anything we please; but as regards arrangements for the future, we are more powerless than any private gentleman; we have only to see what became of my father's will, and the will of many other kings. I know all that well enough; but they gave me no peace until I had made a will. Well, now I have made one; I care little what becomes of it, but at any rate I shall be teased no longer."

It was decidedly not the moment to re-open the delicate question with the old king, who about this time had the additional annoyance of finding himself involved in the momentous business of the cap, the *affaire du bonnet*: important to us only because the Maines, rebuffed in the matter of the will, saw in it an opportunity of acquiring the support of the peers for the maintenance of their position after the king's death.

The great matter was this: when the peers were judicially present in the Parlement, custom prescribed that the First President should remove his cap before asking each peer for his vote; but in process of time, and by imperceptible degrees, a stage had been reached at which the president in fact addressed the peer covered; and St. Simon was now the leader of a movement to force Parlement to revert to the ancient custom. The Duc du Maine, anxious to conciliate the peers, offered his intercession on their behalf with the king, and, after some discussion, a meeting of the dukes was held at the house of the Duc d'Harcourt,[5] to consider the matter. D'Antin,[6] one of the dukes, and, by the way, the only legitimate son of our old friend Mme. de Montespan, was the bearer of a message from the king, who said that if the matter could be settled by mutual

[5] HARCOURT, Henri de Beuvron, 1st Duc and Maréchal d', 1654–1717, son of François, 4th Marquis de Beuvron, and of – de Tourneville; "an able and an honest man."

[6] ANTIN, Louis Antoine de Pardaillan de Gondrin, 1st Duc d', 1665–1736, son of Louis Henri, 4th Marquis, and of Françoise Athenais de Rochechouart-Mortemart.

agreement, he would be glad to hear the last of it; and d'Antin further reported that he had seen the First President, and found him "all sugar and honey." Then, after a preliminary interchange of compliments, both sides settled down to fight the battle with a steadily increasing acrimony, regardless of Louis' attempts to bring both or either to reason. Within a few days, Parlement and peers were at open war, and the delighted Mme. du Maine, who was quite likely at the bottom of the whole commotion, suggested that a deputation of peers should meet her at Sceaux to discuss the matter. The peers received the suggestion with long faces; what Mme. du Maine wanted, the duke would do, but the question was, what did she want of the peers? It would almost certainly prove to be something compromising, but how was compliance with her wishes to be evaded, without giving offence to her husband, and, through him, to the king?

Ultimately two of their number, the Ducs de La Force[7] and d'Aumont[8], were appointed ambassadors. To these noblemen Mme. de Maine, after a little beating about the bush, disclosed the Sceaux terms; if M. du Maine carried the day for the dukes, it would only be in return for their written pledge that they would undertake to uphold Maine's right of succession to the Crown. Neither La Force nor d'Aumont were men to be particular about what they signed, but they were not prepared to put their names to such a dangerous piece of paper as this; Mme. du Maine, who had so far kept her temper with obvious difficulty, blazed out upon their polite evasions:

"She and M. du Maine would know how to protect themselves; and, that there might be no mistake, she would tell them plainly that when a man had once been declared capable of succeeding to the Crown, he did not allow that privilege to be wrested from him; sooner than that, he would set the kingdom in a blaze from one end to the other."

[7] La Force, Henri Jacques Nompar de Caumont, 5th Duc de, 1675–1726, son of Jacques, 4th Duc, and of Suzanne de Beringhen; "very clever and ready with his tongue."

[8] Aumont, Louis de Villequier, 3rd Duc d', 1667–1723, eldest son of Louis Marie Victor, 2nd Duc, and of Madeleine Le Tellier; Ambassador Extraordinary to London, 1712; suspected of setting the London Embassy on fire, 1713, to conceal his contraband trade; "a spendthrift, who had lived by his wits all his life."

And having said her say, she rose abruptly and flounced out of the room. The famous conference was over, and at this stage the exasperated king announced that so was the *affaire du bonnet*; he declined to hear any more about it. And the matter closed with the infuriated St. Simon waiting on the Duc du Maine to tell him that the day would come when he would regret having deliberately tricked all the greatest noblemen in the kingdom. It would be useless to discuss St. Simon's "proofs" that the *affaire du bonnet* was deliberately engineered by the Duc du Maine to embroil the peers with the Parlement; that pot was permanently simmering, and boiled over from time to time without any poking of the fire. That the duchess did what mischief she could, we may well believe, and with what futile results we have seen. If the episode has any significance, it is in showing that the duchess's incapacity for power was at least equal to the duke's dislike of it.

On 19th February 1715 the king gave a State audience to the Persian Ambassador; it was the setting splendour of the Sun-King, the last time he was to appear in public with his well-loved son in all his new dignity by his throne, the last of the stately pageants in which Louis XIV had so delighted. And it would seem that he himself had some premonition of the fact, for contrary to his habit of recent years, he expressed a wish that the Court should be as magnificent as possible for the ceremony; and he himself set the example. At the end of the vast suite of apartments, a magnificent throne was erected, round which stood the princes and peers, Maine one of the foremost, wearing pearls and diamonds lent him by his father. Louis, departing from his usual sober brown suit, was in black and gold, with the blue ribbon and star of his Order, wearing jewelry to the value of about £50,000. His splendour emphasized his ill-health; he was almost sinking under the weight, thin and broken, and his face looked very ill. But all agreed that in spite of the ravages of diseases, the king had played his part in a manner worthy of his best days.

It was a gallant ending to a long journey.

11. *Humpty Dumpty*

THE Duchesse du Maine, snubbed in her attempt to enlist the support of the peerage, returned with increased energy to the fascinating topic of the king's Will; once more the screw was applied to her husband, and once more he proceeded to lay siege to Mme. de Maintenon. The dripping finally wore away the stone: at least to the extent that Mme. de Maintenon persuaded the king to communicate the contents of the document to the Duc du Maine. But Louis had not observed life for sixty years for nothing; he knew all there was to know about Court intrigue, and he knew his son, and his son's wife, as neither of them knew themselves. He made it a condition that Maine should swear that he would not divulge the information to a third party, then learnt with bland surprise a day or two later from his stuttering and embarrassed son that he was not prepared to learn the contents of the Will on these terms. "This was a capital blunder," observes the indignant and loyal Mlle. de Launay, now completely identified with the fortunes of Sceaux. When Mme. du Maine was brought to realize that, but for her stupidity in insisting on knowing the great secret, it would have been given to her husband, whose subsequent actions would have given her the key to the riddle, her fury was alarming. But even she understood that she had been outwitted, and that it was hopeless to attempt to reopen the subject. But the Maines' joint investigation had not been entirely fruitless, for somehow they had discovered this much, that the King of Spain was not in any circumstances to be called to the succession in France; which meant that, either as regent or king, the Duc d'Orléans must exercise the supreme authority for many years after the death of Louis XIV. Mme. du Maine was, deservedly, in as deep disfavour with the Duc d'Orléans as it was possible for anyone to be with such an easy-going prince, but if there was one thing of which

Mme. du Maine was certain, it was the irresistible quality of her own charm, and now, thoroughly alarmed for the future, she came up to Court to try its influence on Orléans and Mme. de Maintenon.

Both attempts failed completely; revenge was a passion utterly lacking in the makeup of the Duc d'Orléans, but he had all the genial sinner's contempt for a pious and henpecked husband. And, which was worse from Mme. du Maine's point of view, the Fairy Ludovise was the type of woman that bored him beyond all others. The mere thought of being drawn into the Sceaux circle conjured up such a yawn as might overcome a dissipated stockbroker of our own day, let in for a week-end of modern poetry readings, relieved by charades and platonic flirtation. With Mme. de Maintenon, Mme. du Maine's failure was immediate and final; the old lady had probably resisted more blandishments than any woman in France, she had known Mme. du Maine from her cradle, and she had for many years regarded her as does a fond mother a detested daughter-in-law. It was soon apparent, even to Mme. du Maine, that there was nothing to be hoped for in that quarter.

But though Mme. du Maine had been rebuffed by the Duc d'Orléans, her husband had his own plan of campaign, and hoped to succeed where she had failed; Maine's eldest son, the Prince de Dombes, was now a youth of fifteen, and Orléans' third daughter, Mlle. de Chârtres,[1] was seventeen. If, thought Maine, a marriage could be arranged between the two, the Duc d'Orléans would then be bound by family ties to afford him that support of which he stood in such need if his position was to be made secure after the king's death. The fact that Mlle. de Chârtres was determined to be a nun, and that she disliked the Prince de Dombes personally, weighed not at all with the Duc du Maine; and he felt sure that he need fear no refusal from Orléans, eccentric though he was, on the score of the young lady's disinclination. What the Prince de Dombes thought

[1] CHARTRES, Louise Adelaide de Bourbon, Mlle. de, third daughter of Philippe, Duc d'Orléans and of his wife, Françoise Marie de Bourbon, born 1698; professed nun 1718; subsequently became Abbess of Chelles; became a fervent Jansenist, 1720; resigned the Abbey, 1734, and retired to the Paris Benedictines; died of smallpox, 1743.

about it we do not know; probably he had not been informed of the fate in store for him. But if he had heard the subject discussed in society, he can hardly have welcomed the prospect of marrying a girl two years his senior who regarded him with unconcealed dislike. It is at first sight surprising that Maine, whose offers of friendship to Orléans had been so coldly received, should contemplate the possibility of a more intimate alliance with him; but he had his secret supporter in the Palais Royal in no less a person than the Duchesse d'Orléans, Philippe's wife and Maine's sister.

We have so far seen little of this lady, who we may remember was the first-fruit of that reconciliation between Louis XIV and Mme. de Montespan on the famous day when the king and his mistress retired into Mme. de Montespan's bedroom, after making a profound bow to the company of matrons assembled to certify the propriety of the interview. We may also remember that Mme. de Maintenon had flatly refused to bring up the children of this second liaison, with the result that Mlle. de Blois, as she then was, had received a very indifferent upbringing from one Mme. de Jussac. At the age of fifteen she had been married to Philippe, then Duc de Chârtres, and had borne him a son and six daughters. She was a drawling lackadaisical, rather good-looking woman, whose chief characteristic was her insane pride, which she carried to such heights that she actually believed she had conferred an honour on her husband by marrying him. Had she married a Condé instead of an Orléans, this delusion would probably have been dispelled with a cane; but Philippe, secure in his own rank, and in any case rather uninterested in the whole matter, merely christened her *Madame Lucifer*, and by that name she was usually known in society. Next to her pride, her most noticeable trait was a devout terror of Louis XIV, which had been in no way diminished by the fact that she had received official and formal rebukes from him on at least two occasions–once for keeping her father-in-law awake all night by letting off fireworks under his bedroom windows, and once for joining her sister's pipe-smoking club at Versailles. But it was only rarely that she was on sufficiently good terms with her sister to join her in the perpetration of such outrages, though both women would occasionally combine to annoy their half-sister, the Princesse de Conti. The Duchesse d'Orléans' mother-in-law, Madame Palatine, who hated bastards on principle, and who never recovered from the affront of having one foisted on her as a daughter-in-law, disliked her cordially. Her many references to her son's wife make amusing reading, but they cannot be accepted without corroboration; we know for instance from other sources that the Duchesse d'Orléans spoke with a curious drawl, but it is left for Madame to tell us that she always talked as if her mouth were full of thick soup. Nor can I find any corroboration for Madame's assertion that the younger duchess was in the habit of "getting as drunk as a bellringer three or four times a week."

To conclude, the Duchesse d'Orléans was a woman who "never forgot that she was a Daughter of France, even on her *chaise percée*:" a woman capable, by virtue of both her position and her intellect, of being a tower of strength to her brother as soon as her husband became Regent.

For her relations with the Duc du Maine we have no authority but St. Simon, who, if only we could trust him, would be a witness of the first importance on the interior of the Palais Royal; he had been educated with the Duc d'Orléans, and the continued intimacy between the two men is a fact, not a figment of St. Simon's imagination: an intimacy, let us note, which was official rather than social, for Orléans, like our own Charles II, tended to divide his life into two watertight compartments. His mistresses and his *roués were* mere companions in debauchery, and from this side of the Regent's life St. Simon held steadily aloof. As for the duchess, she and St. Simon may definitely be described as cronies; they were about the same age, Mme. de St. Simon was lady-in-waiting to the duchess's daughter, the Duchesse de Berri, and a lot of St. Simon's time was spent at the side of the sofa on which Mme. d'Orléans passed most of her life. That he knew her real feelings towards the Duc du Maine seems certain: whether he has given them truthfully to posterity is another matter.

According to him, the Duchesse d'Orléans did not like her brother; but she felt that Maine, as a son of Louis XIV, should reach

10. PHILIPPE D'ORLÉANS, REGENT OF FRANCE

From the portrait by Santerre

II. VERSAILLES: THE GARDEN FRONT

From a drawing by Perelle

an elevation to which it was indecent that her husband, a mere Grandson of France, should aspire:

"M. du Maine's interests preponderated in her heart to such an extent that no bliss in the other world would have equalled her felicity in this one, could she have seen him established on the Throne of France at the expense of her husband and her own son, much more if she could have contributed to his elevation. And yet she knew M. du Maine thoroughly; she neither loved nor respected him; she saw through his wiles and his artifices, and resented them. She told me so herself, speaking without the slightest anger, calmly and argumentatively."

Well, it may be so; the Duchesse d'Orléans was an original, for she was half a Mortemart. But I find it very difficult to believe that she carried her complaisance for a brother whom she disliked to the point of wishing to see him elevated to the prejudice of her own husband. She was not called *Madame Lucifer* for nothing; are we to believe that if the little Dauphin died–which might happen at any moment–she wished to see Ludovise usurping her own rightful position of Queen of France? If so, all I can say is that her husband's nickname for her was a gross slander on a woman whose power of self-effacement was almost saintly.

She was however certainly eager for the proposed marriage, which she urged with all her eloquence both on St. Simon and on her husband. But Orléans was strongly opposed to the scheme for a variety of reasons, one of which is as rare in the period as it is creditable to him. He was a very indulgent father, and had no intention of forcing his daughter into a distasteful marriage. On the other side, he could not reject his wife's proposal out of hand, for what if she appeared some fine morning with a royal order that the marriage was to take place? The duke temporized, with all a lazy man's ingenuity–"We are marching through a dark wood, and we cannot advance too warily," as he said to St. Simon. And further, observing that St. Simon was, as usual, eager to meddle with what was none of his business, he adroitly entrenched himself behind his friend:

"I had some attacks to sustain from the Duchesse d'Orléans; sometimes the duke was present on these occasions, and he was good enough to leave all the talking to me, for which I took the liberty of scolding him well in private; but my scolding did no good, for it suited his indolence better to listen to what I said and applaud, than to argue the point himself."

St. Simon, needless to remark, was strongly opposed to the suggested alliance, and got more than he had bargained for in setting up as the man behind the Throne at the Palais Royal: "The duke could evade (his wife's) enquiries by running away; but for me there was no escape." However, it turned out in the finish that Mlle. de Chârtres was more than a match for her mother and the Duc du Maine combined; being unable to secure her parents' consent to her entering religion, she dispensed with it. One evening she drove off to the convent of Chelles, where she was admitted as a boarder, and from where the united efforts of the family failed to dislodge her. In 1718 she at last extorted permission to take the veil, and a year later she became Abbess.

At the beginning of August 1715 watchful courtiers noticed that the king's appetite was failing, and on the 10th he had a violent attack of indigestion at Marly: but recovered sufficiently to go round the gardens in a bath chair to give directions about the siting of a collection of statuary which had just arrived from Italy. At six that evening he set out for Versailles, having seen his beloved Marly for the last time.

On 11th August, after a bad night, he succeeded in getting through the routine of his day until the hour of the afternoon drive, which he cancelled, feeling too tired to face the jolting, and at his supper it was noticed that he looked worn out. On the following day he heard Mass, and dined in bed, but got up in the afternoon.

So far no one, and least of all the royal doctors, had taken the king's illness seriously, but by the 14th he was suffering intense pain in his left leg, and on the 19th he shut himself up in his private suite, which he was never to leave again.

Wednesday 21st had been fixed for the review of the Life Guard, but Louis was too weak to take the salute, even from his balcony, and the Duc du Maine acted as his deputy. By this time, there was no doubt at Court what was happening; the king was dying, the old oak was about to fall at last, and men looked at each other in bewilderment. Louis had often reminded them that he was mortal, but no one had realized the fact. The king was part of the fixed order of things, *was* in fact the fixed order of things in that thronged Versailles where there were not half a dozen people who could remember his predecessor. The incredible, often discussed but never wholly believed in, was happening at last; the longest reign in European history was drawing swiftly and terribly to its close.

But not even the onset of death could deter Louis from playing out his part to the end; to modify his plans to accommodate that grisly intruder would be an act unworthy of a man of quality, and on the morning of the 22nd, the dying king began his day by choosing a coat to wear when he came out of mourning for Prince François de Lorraine; and after that held his usual meeting of the Council of State. Dying he was, but the world should see that he was still King of France. Nor did he so act in ignorance of his state, for on this day he refused rather abruptly to fill some vacant benefices, saying that in his condition he could not take it upon his conscience to meddle with a business which could be settled at leisure by his successor.

On the 24th, black patches appeared on his leg, and he spent the day in great pain, but by sheer will-power kept the engine of State running. He dined and supped in bed in the presence of the Court, presided at a meeting of the Council of Finance, and saw his Chancellor on business.

Sunday 25th was his Feast-day, the Feast of St. Louis, and by the king's express command the usual ceremonial was observed. The drums and hautboys played beneath his window as soon as he was awake, and at his dinner he insisted on having his four and twenty violins, so as not to disappoint the musicians. Later in the day he did a little business, amongst other things adding a codicil to his Will, whereby the command of the civil and military Household was entrusted to the Duc du Maine. His wife and her ladies were with him in the evening until seven o'clock, when he fell asleep. He woke with his mind wandering, recovered himself almost immediately, and, with apologies to the ladies, sent for Cardinal de

Rohan[2] to administer the Sacrament to him; after which, the Duc d'Orléans was summoned, the room cleared, and a long private conversation took place. His concluding words to the Regent must dispel any lingering idea that he suspected his nephew of the horrible crime imputed to him, or that he deliberately deceived him as to the tenor of the Will:

"My dear nephew, remember me. I have made such arrangements as I thought fairest and most prudent for the good of the State, but one cannot foresee everything, and if there is anything that needs altering or amending, you will do whatever you think best."

Compare this with St. Simon's version:

"Awful to relate, at this moment when the Body of Our Lord had only just passed his lips, he assured him (the Regent) that he would find nothing in his will to displease him."

The first account, and a great many other interesting details of the last hours of Louis XIV, we owe to one Anthoine, the king's gun carrier, a servant so humble that he was apparently overlooked, or considered too unimportant to be excluded from the dying man's room, and whose journal deserves to be better known than it appears to be.

On the morning of the 26th, Louis rallied himself for the last effort; he had done with life, it only remained for him to say his farewells and be gone. For the last time, the whole Court assembled to hear its king:

"Gentlemen, I have to ask your pardon for setting you so bad an example. I thank you for the manner in which you have served me, and for the loyal attachment which you have always shown. I am sorry it has not been in my power to do as much for you as I could have wished; the bad times must be my excuse. I ask you to continue to serve my great-grandson with as much zeal and fidelity as you have shown me. He is a child, and may have many unpleasantnesses in store for him. I hope you will set an example which will be followed by all my subjects. Obey the commands which my nephew will give you. He is about to govern the

[2] Strasbourg, Armand Gaston Maximilien de Rohan, Cardinal-Prince-Archbishop of, 1674–1749, fourth son of François de Rohan, Prince de Soubise, and of Anne de Rohan; but strongly suspected of being a son of Louis XIV; "a man of much natural ability set off . . . by the charm of his manners . . . gentle and obliging . . . polite and considerate to everybody."

kingdom; I trust he will govern it well. I trust you will all do your best to preserve unity, and, if you see anyone attempting to disturb it, you will bring him back into the right way. I feel that my emotions are becoming too strong for me: and I perceive that you also are moved. I am sorry if what I have said has been too much for your feelings. Farewell gentlemen, I hope you will sometimes think of me when I am gone."

It was then the turn of the servants, to all of whom, even the humblest as Anthoine tells us, he said goodbye, asking their prayers for his soul, and their pardon for any annoyance or pain he had ever caused them: a request which touched them the more, because, says Anthoine, there never was any gentleman more considerate towards servants. He then told them that he had given them the best of characters to the Duc d'Orléans, who would take care of them, warned the upper servants to treat those under them kindly, "as I have always done myself, to the best of my ability," and wound up by saying, "Goodbye, my good folk, this is all I have to say before I leave you."

Then came the turn of old Villeroi, followed by the princesses, for each of whom there was a kindly word: even for Mme. du Maine, who had been persuaded–with difficulty–to come up to Versailles to receive her father-in-law's last blessing.

Finally came Louis XIV's farewell to his natural sons, Maine and Toulouse, and of this interview we know nothing, except that it lasted a long time, behind closed doors. Never have we succeeded in penetrating the king's relations with his beloved sons or with his second wife; we say that Louis lived all his life in public. But not quite all. Even for the Grand Monarque there was a final locked door, guarding an inner privacy, that ultimate circle of intimacy without which life ceases to be human. We can but speculate on the tender outpouring of love with which that wise old brain endeavoured to forearm his sons, so alone in their perilous elevation and whose dangers he saw so clearly. According to Mlle. de Launay, the king told Maine the contents of his Will; "but," she adds, "it was too late for M. du Maine to profit by the knowledge, and he could only represent to the king the inconveniences which were in store for him." But we must remember that Mlle. de Launay's only source of information would be Mme. du Maine, and that

Mme. du Maine knew no more of the interview than her husband chose to tell her.

As Mme. de Maintenon sat by Louis' bed that night, the dying man said suddenly, "One always hears it said that it is difficult to make up one's mind to die; I don't find anything difficult about it." And a little later, hearing her crying, he said "Come, Madame, are you allowing yourself to be upset at seeing me about to die? Haven't I lived long enough? I have thought of this for a long time, and prepared myself for it, knowing well that there is a King of Kings, whose orders must be obeyed."

On the morning of the 28th, when all hope had been abandoned, there arrived at Versailles a peasant from Marseilles; after the manner of the ancien régime, he found no difficulty in making his way to the king's bedside, where he explained that, hearing of His Majesty's illness, he had come to persuade him to try some of his elixir. The king was now in such a state that his futile and flustered physicians were prepared to let anyone try any remedy upon him. Fagon, First Physician of France, did indeed demur, but "was answered so roughly and rudely by the peasant, that he was left speechless with astonishment." "Life or death, God's will be done," said the king as he drained the draft; and, whether it was the elixir, or merely the last flare of the sinking candle, there was on the morning of the 29th some little improvement in his condition. But during the day, the transient hope was extinguished, and Louis himself dismissed the subject from his mind; to the Curé of Versailles, who came to tell him that prayers were going up all over France for his recovery, he said that the time had come to pray for his soul, not for his life. And the few people he saw during the day noticed that he no longer spoke of "The Dauphin," but of "The young king."

On the 30th the royal suite was shut to everyone except Mme. de Maintenon, the Duc du Maine, and the doctors; the innermost shrine of France, the central cell of the Versailles beehive, had ceased to function, and in the vast outer rooms the dazed courtiers buzzed to and fro, a swarm without a leader. Throughout the night the king was conscious, able to speak, but usually silent, and with his eyes shut. Who can say what thoughts passed through that weary old brain before the night paled into the dawn of his last day on earth? Further, ever further back would memory lead him, to the day when he had stood by the deathbed of a King of France, a solemn little boy in tight jerkin and embroidered breeches, and how the dying man, whose darkened eyes could no longer recognize his son, had asked, "Who is it?" and his own triumphant answer, "Louis XIV." And the long troubled years of the Regency; now there was another Regency, beginning tomorrow as like as not, and when he was gone, who was left who would remember his own minority? Dead, all dead, the silky, insinuating Mazarin, his beautiful mother with her slow smile, and her soft Spanish accent, behind whose ample skirts he used to hide from his tutors, and whose comfit box he and *Monsieur* used to rifle. *Monsieur* too was gone, how long ago, with his scents and his sulks; gone too *Monsieur's* bewitching wife, and her royal scamp of a brother, who, like himself, had been an unconscionable time in dying; how he envied Charles II that apology. And Marie Mancini, with the dark bright eyes and the imperious charm, and Beaufort and his Frondeurs, where were they all tonight? And that dreadful evening when he had lain in his State bed, pretending to sleep, as he did now, while the Paris mob had tiptoed to his bedside to assure itself that he was really there, and had not been smuggled out of Paris. But he would dismiss this nightmare with an uneasy sigh, and let his thoughts rest on the glorious years which had followed, sinking again into a restless doze before the kaleidescope of that France whose splendour had dazzled the world, his great Captains, his Guards, the blood beating against his ears in the hour of victory, the triumphant return to savour the incense of that bright flowerbed, the youthful Court of France; flowers, flowers, great red roses, the heavy scented summer night at Fontainebleau, and La Vallière waiting for him in some secret arbour. But such thoughts would be dismissed as he started into wakefulness once more: *Mea culpa, mea culpa* the sad-faced watchers heard him murmur more than once, and also the single word, *Confiteor*.

On 31st August, the last day of his life, he was mostly unconscious. Mortification was running swiftly upwards from his gangrened leg, and all pretence at remedial treatment was at an end, though the king complaisantly swallowed whatever was presented to him, including a sovereign remedy sent by Mme. du Maine. At eleven in the evening the prayers for the dying were offered, Louis himself repeating them in a loud voice. To Cardinal de Rohan he said, "This is the Church's last favour." He never again spoke to a mortal, but at intervals during the night, he was heard to say "*Nunc et in hora mortis*," and "Help me, O my God, haste Thee to help me."

At a quarter past eight on the morning of Sunday, the 1st of September 1715, he died, aged seventy-seven years less three days, and having reigned for seventy-two years, three months, and eighteen days.

"Thus passed the glory of the world, *sic transit gloria mundi*." So writes Anthoine, and yet we say that no man is a hero to his valet. "The glory of the world" sounds excessive to modern ears; but we cannot quarrel with the epitaph written for Louis XIV by a French man of letters of the Third Republic—"He walked into eternity with the same tranquil majesty with which he used to cross the Hall of Mirrors."

* * *

The wave of emotion which had carried the mob to Versailles to pray for the king ebbed with Gallic swiftness; his corpse was hardly cold before France discovered that she was sick of her Grand Monarque, sick of the Grand Siècle. Louis XIV had contributed a great chapter to the history of France; he had done much good, which was to be interred with his bones. None but the old attempted to weigh it against the evil, and the elderly were an unpopular minority. Away with them, let them disappear like old Maintenon, who had gone into hiding at St. Cyr, there to finish her too prolonged life. Hustle what was left of the fourteenth Louis off to St. Denis. After the rather grisly custom of the Royal House, his heart was handed over to the Jesuits, his embalmed entrails sent to Nôtre Dâme:

> "À St. Denis, comme â Versailles,
> Il est sans coeur et sans entrailles,"

sang the mob joyously. The hypocrite threw his Mass Book into the fire with a great sigh of relief, the fast lady and her maid disinterred the long neglected rouge pot and hare's foot, babbling excitedly about change in fashion when the Court came out of mourning. The Parlement smacked its lips over the prospect of a long minority and suppled its toes for the congenial task of kicking the dead lion. Everything must be different in the brave new world, was the cry of St. Simon and his like. The eighteenth century, held at bay by Louis XIV for fifteen years, came in with a rush. The Regency had arrived, the eight hectic, bankrupt, debauched years of frenzied reaction against the gloom and rigid etiquette of old Versailles. Versailles ceased to exist in a social sense with the coming of the Regency, and was never to recover its old splendour. The Duc d'Orléans, a Parisian to his finger-tips, had always hated the place, and never visited it if he could help it; witty, lazy, clever, and dissipated, he settled down cozily in his own home, where such time as he could spare from brandy cocktails and the front row of the chorus he devoted to the neglect of his duties. His habits were as irregular as his morals: though now over forty, with a wife and family, he was still the fast young man about town, a frequenter of brothels and gaming houses, a seeker of adventures in dark streets, and a constant anxiety to the Paris police. His days and nights present a startling contrast to those of Louis, who even in his salad days, never forgot in his amorous adventures that he was King of France. The Regent, if he happened to have gone to bed at all, was an early riser; not out of any eagerness to welcome a new day, but because he "awoke so heavy with the fumes of the night's debauch" that it took him a couple of hours and several restoratives before he could be said to be fully conscious. Having pulled himself together, he would first pay his daily visit to the little king, generally bringing with him a present of toys; not in any sycophantic spirit, but because he liked children and liked to make them happy. After that came the Royal Mass, from which even Orléans dare not absent himself, but whose tedium he alleviated with the aid of his Rabelais, which he had bound in an old Prayer Book cover. Then would come the dreary business of governing France, council meetings, despatches, and, worst of all, interviews; for he made a point of being accessible to all comers. Though, if you struck him on a bad morning, your reception was apt to be somewhat different from that which Louis XIV gave his petitioners, as witness a little chat he had with de Mesmes,[3] who has evidently been unlucky in his choice of days:

"The First President, being at the Palais Royal, where he was very roughly handled by M. le Duc d'Orléans, who called him *gros cochon* and *vieux b . . .* with other outrageous insults, replied, 'Monseigneur, when the late King did me the honour to ask my opinion, he was always good enough to listen with his usual moderation. I am a gentleman, and First President of the Parlement, two titles which require a different treatment to that which I have received.' Whereupon the Prince replied brusquely, 'The late King did as he pleased and so shall I. Get to hell out of this!' "

For a man with a bad headache, mornings so passed could not fail to be exhausting, and his afternoons the Regent tried to keep to himself. His eyesight debarred him from hunting, but there were always drawing rooms where he was welcome; for though society in the usual sense of the word bored and embarrassed him, he had inherited from his father, *Monsieur*, a keen relish for witty and malicious gossip. With all his talent, he had few resources when left to himself. Chemistry he had given up at the time of the poisoning panic in favour of painting, at which he achieved some success; and he had executed a nude portrait of his favourite daughter, the Duchesse de Berri,[4] a performance which scandalized even that lax age. At some time during the afternoon he would invariably pay a visit to his mother, old Madame Palatine, to whom he was an affectionate son, and with whom he lived on the best of terms.

But even the longest day has an end, and at nine o'clock came supper time. At nine the Regent disappeared for the night. It was the only inviolable rule of his Court, if Court it can be called, and

[3] Mesmes, Jean Antoine III, of an old legal family, son of Jean Jacques II by his wife Marie de La Bazinière, born 1662; aped the courtier, and shunned legal society; died 1723; "his great ambition was to pass himself off as a man of quality."

[4] Berri, Marie Louise Elizabeth de Bourbon, Duchesse de, second daughter of Philippe, Duc d'Orléans, and of his wife, Françoise Marie de Bourbon, born 1695; had an illegitimate daughter, 1719, by one Riom or Rion; died 1719; known (and detested) in society under the name of *Messalina*; "she was a model of all the vices, except avarice."

the only one about which he was inflexible. Catastrophic despatches might arrive after that hour, Paris might be on fire, a province in revolt, it made no matter. Under no circumstances was there any access to the Regent between nine in the evening and his lever the following morning, for the night was sacred to debauch with his roués. And a very odd collection these chosen spirits were; Nocé,[5] of whom his friends could find nothing better to say than that he was "fairly honourable, for a man of the world:" Simiane, who owed his place in the select circle to the fact that he was the hardest drinker in France: Broglie,[6] who had been admitted because of his talent for saying the filthiest things in the grossest possible language: and Brancas,[7] a famous manufacturer of *bons mots*, were the leading spirits in a dozen or so men forming the group. With them there were a few soiled butterflies like the Duchesse de Gesvres, Mme. de Sabran, and Mme. de Mouchy, together with occasional visitors, such as chorus girls, debauched foreigners of distinction visiting Paris, and street walkers. For rank ceased to exist at these supper parties, wit and debauchery being the only qualities which conferred a claim to admittance. As the bottles were emptied the fun grew fast and furious, even the perfunctory initial pretence of decorum being abandoned; on one occasion the Regent had all the lights extinguished, and, after a suitable interval, threw open a number of cupboards in which he had previously placed lighted candles: with results which proved embarrassing even to that brazen company. In the early hours of the morning the party would stagger out for a drunken stroll round Paris, and in the places they visited the Regent, who rarely lost his head in drink, would pick up a surprising and intimate knowledge of what was afoot in the capital; not that he made any use of the information thus gained, but it helped to wile away the tedium of his daily interview with the Chief of Police to listen to that officer's laborious deductions and surmises about some outrage of which the Regent knew every detail. Altogether a

[5] NOCÉ, Marquis de, son of Claude de Nocé, Seigneur de Fontenay, born c. 1664; presented Voltaire to the Regent, 1718.

[6] BROGLIE, Charles Guillaume, Marquis de, son of the first Maréchal de Broglie by his wife, Marie de Lamoignon.

[7] BRANCAS, Louis, 3rd Duc de, son of Louis François, 2nd Duc, born 1663; died 1739.

deplorable ruler this Regent, but one can understand that to a generation kept on a tight curb by Louis XIV, his supper parties must have been attractive.

The Duc du Maine emerges into the Regency a disconsolate and uncomfortable figure; he had realized at last how much and how heavily he had been accustomed to lean on the king and Mme. de Maintenon, and now both his supports were withdrawn. We can all drive the car while the watchful expert sits beside us, but it is quite another thing to take it out alone for the first time. In the early days of September, his father's words, "It will be your business to turn all I have done for you to account–if you can," must have sounded often in his ears. Had he been a Guise, or even the shadow of one, he had the ball at his feet; Orléans was easy-going and had not a united body of public opinion behind him. Maine had charge of the young king's education and the command of the Household Troops. The struggle for power between the cousins should have been at least on equal terms, and we can understand, if not sympathize with Mme. du Maine's exasperation at the feebleness of the denouement.

On the morning of 7th September the young king was brought to the Parlement to hold a *Lit de Justice*, at which the late king's Will would be read, and the Regency formally inaugurated. Needless to say, all France was there, but, which was unusual, so were the French Guards, who had quietly occupied all the approaches, with officers and picked soldiers about the interior of the building. It is a little difficult to understand this precaution, for the Regent can hardly have supposed that Maine was about to attempt a coup d'etât in the king's presence. Perhaps–and it would have been very like him–it was to force the Duc de Gramont, commanding the French Guards, into a public acknowledgement of his shame; for the duke[8] had hitherto been reckoned a firm supporter of the Duc du Maine, until a gratuity of £25,000 had persuaded him to reconsider his views, and he had now convinced himself that the welfare of the State summoned all honest men to rally round the Regent. Society

[8] GRAMONT, Antoine, 3rd Duc de, 1671–1725, only son of Antoine Charles, 2nd duke, and of Charlotte de Castelnau; Marshal of France, 1724.

has, we perceive already adopted the principles of the age of enlightenment, which are so rapidly sweeping away the obscurantism of the old Court.

The Parlement, having listened with what patience it could to a speech by St. Simon on the *affaire du bonnet*, proceeded to the business of the opening of the King's Will. It was a long document, of which the crucial provisions were that the Regent was to be bound by a majority vote of the Council of Regency, whose members were named in the Will: and that the Duc du Maine was to be superintendent of Louis XV's education. Whilst it was being read Maine, according to St. Simon,

"was obviously ill at ease; he was like a man when the moment has arrived for him to undergo a severe operation . . . his eyes were fixed intently on people's countenances; he turned pale, and kept glancing at the Duc d'Orléans to see how he took it."

The reading finished, Orléans took the floor, and speaking with the Bourbon majesty which he could assume when it suited him, protested the provisions of the Will as regards the Council of Regency; the council had such ample powers, he said, that he was left with no shred of authority, which was not only an infringement of his birthright, but a personal slight on his honour to which he would not submit; he called upon the assembly to give him those untrammelled rights which were his due; and whilst admitting the necessity for a Council of Regency, he insisted upon having the appointment of its members, who moreover must sit in an advisory, not an executive capacity. As regards the king's education, he approved the late king's choice. The codicil was a matter which he proposed to deal with separately.

The decision of the assembly was unanimously in the Regent's favour; the Will was set aside, as Louis XIV had all along known it would be, and the Duc d'Orléans then proceeded to deal with the codicil; he was astonished, he said, to find that by this instrument he, the Court, the Parlement and the city of Paris, were placed completely in the power of the superintendent of the king's education, in virtue of his control of the Military and Civil Households; the young king could thereby be completely isolated from the nominal Regent, who would indeed hold even the appearance of power only during the pleasure of the real master of France; he more than suspected that the late king was not in possession of his full faculties when he signed; and it would be apparent to the company that no Regent could rule under such conditions. He demanded the annulment of the codicil.

Maine spoke in reply; the king's education must include the care of his person, and without a complete control of both the Civil and Military Households, the superintendent would be unable either to be responsible for the king's safety, or for the enforcement of obedience; there could be no question of the state of Louis XIV's mind when he signed the codicil which had been dictated, not by dying weakness, but by the speaker's well-known devotion to the late king's person.

To the insinuation contained in the concluding sentence of this speech, the Duc d'Orléans took the strongest exception; the Duc du Maine replied with equal warmth; and the assembly was deprived of the spectacle of a good set-to, only by the disputants adjourning into another room, to continue the argument in private. But privacy was a luxury not easily to be obtained if St. Simon happened to be on the premises, and the two princes were soon favoured with his company–"I drew near to the Duc d'Orléans with the air of a man who has something to say. 'What is the matter now?' he said very impatiently." After so much that is dubious, we recognize for once the unmistakable ring of truth in this ingenuous recital. Well might Orléans be impatient, for he had had the benefit of St. Simon's almost continuous advice since within an hour of the king's death, when St. Simon had rushed from his bed to the Palais Royal to point out that a more favourable moment for reopening the portentous matter of the *bonnet* would never come again. But nevertheless, St. Simon's intervention lost the battle for the Duc du Maine; the exasperated Regent adjourned the house until after dinner.

At four o'clock the Parlement reassembled; Orléans announced with regret that he had been unable to reach agreement with M. du Maine on the matter of the codicil; he recapitulated his arguments against its provisions, and demanded its annulment, which was immediately granted without a vote. The unfortunate Maine was beginning to understand the value of those lavish promises of parliamentary support which had been so freely offered to him whilst his father was alive; he became flustered, and took up a line which was masterly in its ineptitude. If, he said, he was deprived of the authority conferred upon him by the codicil, he could no longer hold himself responsible for the king's safety; he must ask to be relieved of all responsibility other than that of superintending the king's education. "Nothing could be more reasonable," replied Orléans blandly, and in a matter of minutes the unfortunate Maine saw himself dispossessed of the command of the Household Troops; the man who had got up that morning with good prospects of becoming the unofficial king of France, went to bed the supervisor of the tutors of a five-year-old child. It was a sorry eclipse, if Maine were indeed the ambitious upstart of St. Simon's imagining; but then he was not. Left to himself, he probably would not have made even such a fight as he did. Such aggressiveness as he showed was supplied by no innate ambition, but by those terrible machine guns of Sceaux, trained on his back. We may believe as much as we please of the only extant account of his reception by his duchess on his return to Sceaux that evening; it rests on shaky authority, but it is at least *bien trouvé*:

"When Mme. du Maine saw the Duc arrive, all sighs and silence, she suspected what had happened.

'Well, Monsieur,' she said severely, 'what has taken place?'

'The king's Will is ignored, repudiated, annulled. . . .'

'And you endured this, Monsieur?'

'What would you have me do, Madame? I was surrounded by swords, pistols, even cannon.'

'It were better never to return than to return dishonoured.'

'What good would it be, pray, to get myself killed by the Orléans faction?'

'You are a coward, Monsieur; if I had been in your place I would not have given in so cheaply. Leave my presence, or my indignation may carry me to excesses which will dishonour us both.'

She uttered the last words in a voice so charged, and with such a resolute gesture, that the Duc du Maine hobbled away, much put out of countenance."

But even as things were, Maine had made Orléans pay a long price for his victory. The only real victor of that 7th of September was the Parlement. Not only was its right of remonstrance restored, but it had stood forth once more as the arbitress of France, had annulled a king's will, and had seen a Regent plead to it for confirmation of his authority; a very few days have taken us a long way from the old maxim, *L'Etat c'est moi*. But if Maine had found the Parlement a broken reed and the dukes hostile, there was still another considerable body in the State on which he, or rather his wife, built great hopes, which were not to go entirely unfulfilled.

That body was the nobility.

Now the peers were in a sense nothing more than a standing committee of the nobles, and a committee is both the delegate and the scapegoat of those from whom its authority derives. It is at the outset of the Regency that St. Simon, in virtue of being a peer, achieves a real political importance, strengthened by his personal friendship with the Duc d'Orléans. In season and out of season, his best efforts were devoted to urging a return to what he imagined to have been the ancient constitution of France, the rule of an hereditary oligarchy of peers under a *roi fainéant*; it is obvious that, had St. Simon been able to turn his dreams into reality, the peers would soon have ceased to stand in that relation to the rest of the nobility which the noblesse held to be the traditional one; patrons they perhaps would have been, delegates certainly not. The noblesse had a much clearer idea of the peers than the peers had of the noblesse. There were few untitled, that is non-ducal, nobles, who needed to go beyond the written or traditional records of their own houses to appreciate just what it would mean to revert to the good old days, so much regretted by St. Simon, when an irresponsible peer held sovereign power over his feudal inferiors.

Nor must we ignore the powerful irritant of St. Simon's personality; we have now seen a good deal of him, and can form a very vivid impression of the fury which his ducal self-satisfaction might well produce in some count or marquis, better born than the duke himself; for this intolerable St. Simon would open a political

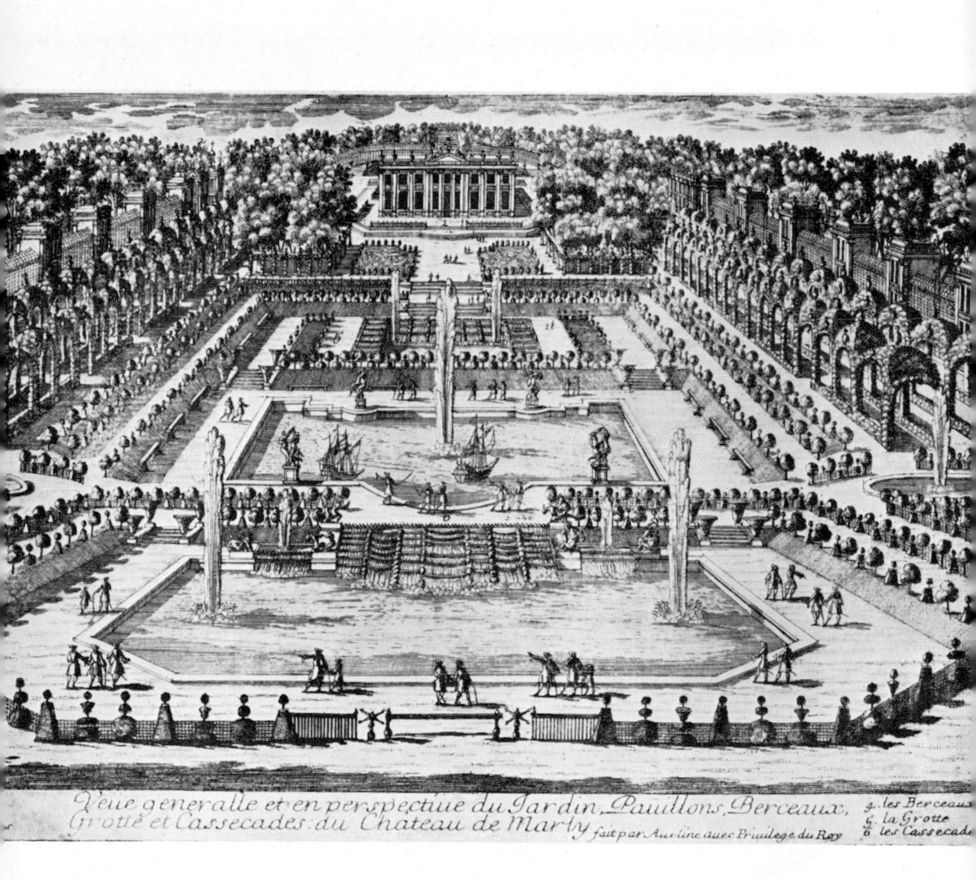

12. THE CHATEAU DE MARLY: GARDENS AND CASCADES

After Aveline

13. THE DUC DU MAINE

By Croixier after F. de Troy

discussion with such a man on the naif basïs that all men, the marquis included, were agreed that the non-ducal nobility was an inferior social caste. There was a considerable, if unorganized resentment amongst such families at the peers' new pretensions as voiced by St. Simon, and it was in these troubled waters that the Maines are accused of fishing.

This, be it understood, is only one version of a situation which St. Simon sees rather differently. This is how it appears to him:

"There existed at this time among the untitled nobility[9] a great deal of jealousy and ill-feeling against the dukes, originating partly in the mesalliances contracted by some of their number. Many untitled noblemen of the first quality had, it is true, married very much beneath them; but as their wives did not enjoy the special privileges granted to duchesses, these mesalliances did not cause so much ill-feeling. It was galling to the pride of ladies of quality to see a duchess of low birth exalted above them. . . . This jealousy was sedulously fomented by M. and Mme. du Maine; their emissaries went about among the nobility, dropping hints and insinuations, and gradually stirred up a number of proud, ignorant fools, who served as decoy ducks to attract others. The object was to induce persons of good birth to combine against the dukes; so that the latter, far from being able to attack the bastards, might be reduced to the defensive in order to protect their own privileges."

And he goes on, at great length, to draw a picture of a peace-loving, duke-worshipping nobility stirred up to act against its true interests by the wicked Duc du Maine. The significance of St. Simon's anger emerges when, in the course of the narrative, he admits that Maine was successful in preventing an alliance between the dukes and the rest of the nobility: "He fomented the quarrel between them, and artfully contrived to throw the dukes on the defensive."

One rather doubts the capacity for artful contrivance in the man who had been so easily routed in the affair of the King's Will, but it may have been so; though more probable that he saw in the dissatisfied nobility a plank to cling to in his shipwreck, whilst they

[9] By *untitled nobility* St. Simon does not mean those who were not counts, marquises, or barons, but those who were not dukes; *gens titrés* was the official Court designation of the dukes and their wives only.

on their part saw in the Duc du Maine a useful rallying point in an agitation which would still have arisen even had the Duc du Maine not existed. But however the thing came about, Maine, who after the fiasco of 7th September had stood perilously alone, now found himself at the head of a party.

12. *Humpty Dumpty Falls Farther*

IT IS difficult to see how the Duc du Maine could have played his hand worse than he did in the closing months of 1715; knowing himself, as he must have done, to be lacking in any of the qualities essential for a successful struggle with the Regent, he would have done better to capitulate gracefully. If, when once he had sensed the Parlement's reaction to the King's Will, he had then and there resigned all claim to the position conferred upon him by Louis XIV, had given his adherence to the newly constituted Regency, and had publicly offered his services to the government in any capacity, he might have saved a good deal from the wreck. There would have been in such conduct a touch of chivalry and modesty which would have caught the public fancy, and which would have put Orléans in the position of either having to respond generously to Maine's surrender, or else appearing in the light of a vindictive opponent. Instead of which as we have seen, he simply dithered—"He did not know how either to retain or surrender his authority, but simply let himself be deprived of it," as a contemporary observes.

However, what was done was done, and 1716 found Maine settling down to make what he could of his position as Superintendent of the King's Education and informal leader of the discontented element of the nobility. Of the superintendence there was little to be made so long as the king was a mere child, and the establishment allotted to him does not suggest a post of a very extended scope; at the Tuileries he was given two rooms for the accommodation of his official suite, a sorry come-down from his palmy days at Versailles; in fact, stripped of the command of the Household, the post proved a liability and not an asset, for he was both powerless yet constantly in the public eye, where he served as a scapegoat both for those who were genuinely concerned about the king's education, and for those in search of a stick with which to beat the Duc du Maine.

But worse troubles than these were in store for him; by July, even Buvat, a mere clerk in the Royal Library, knows that

"a great quarrel has arisen between the Duc de Bourbon[1] and the Duc du Maine. The former wants the cancellation of the edict given by the late king in 1714 by which M. du Maine was given rights of succession to the Crown."

The storm had not broken on Maine unexpectedly. The Regent and Bourbon were allies, perhaps not very wholeheartedly, but still agreeing in their dislike of Maine's pretensions to the Throne; and it is highly characteristic of Orléans that, in spite of his views, he could not bring himself to leave Maine in ignorance of the danger which threatened him. He sent for him, gave him private notice that the Duc du Bourbon was about to make an attack on his position, and advised him to defer the Cte. d'Eu's reception as a peer so as not to arouse the sleeping dog; to which Maine agreed, having indeed no option in the matter. Whether Orléans expected any result other than being able to announce Maine's compliance to Bourbon as a proof of his anxiety to please, we do not know. He had known Bourbon for some time, and would I should think have realized that he was not a man who would be easily turned from his plans. This, by the way, is not that Duc de Bourbon whom we have already met, the animated land-mine with a head the same width as his shoulders and the bright yellow face, but his eldest son, a nephew of Mme. du Maine's. This duke is perhaps the least attractive member of an unattractive family; his insensibility at the time of his father's death had given offence to a society not prone to a strict outlook in such matters, and his greed disgusted even those who admitted the avarice of the House of Condé to be a sort of family heirloom. He not only was but looked a singularly brutal man, and

[1] Bourbon, Louis Henri de Bourbon, 7th Prince de Condé, 1692–1740, eldest son of Louis III, 6th Prince, and of Louise Françoise de France, Mlle. de Nantes; succeeded his father, 1710; made an enormous fortune on stock exchange, 1719; responsible for Louis XV's Polish marriage, 1725; died in exile; "every act of his government reflected his brutality and his stupidity."

his appearance had not been improved by having an eye shot out in 1712 by the Duc de Berri;[2] he disliked nearly everybody, hated most people, and detested his uncle by marriage, the Duc du Maine. Not at all the sort of enemy for poor Maine to have on his hands in addition to all his other troubles, but one with whom it was absolutely necessary that he should attempt to establish some form of *modus vivendi*; and accordingly Maine determined in the early part of 1716 to see what could be done.

In that year the great Condé lawsuit showed signs of being about to come to its third or fourth hearing, the matter now lying between the Duc de Bourbon and his aunt, Mme. du Maine; the latter had the better case, and this she and her husband decided to use as a bargaining counter with their dangerous opponent. But before doing so, it was determined that a final attempt should be made to win over the dukes, which as things now were meant St. Simon. To win St. Simon would not only be to win the dukes, but probably the Regent as well, and distasteful as the attempt was to both husband and wife it was decided to make it; with what success, let us leave St. Simon himself to relate:

"One morning I was much astonished to see M. du Maine come into my room with an easy air, intended to conceal his embarrassment; and he began at once to converse in the most engaging manner, as if there had never been any unpleasantness between us, and without the slightest allusion to the past. Nobody could talk more delightfully than he did; and he displayed his talent to its full extent, doing his utmost to make himself agreeable, but without touching on any subject of importance. I was in my own house, and could not do less than meet him halfway . . . but I got out of it pretty well, taking care not to be behind-hand in politeness, yet careful at the same time not to overdo it. His visit lasted more than half an hour."

After which St. Simon went off to a meeting of the Council of Regency, where he reported the whole conversation to the Duc d'Orléans; Orléans, with all the lazy man's dislike of scenes and unpleasantness, "begged me to return the visit, and since M. du

[2] Berri, Charles de France, Duc de, third son of *Monseigneur* by his wife, Anne Marie Christine of Bavaria, born 1686; died as a result of a fall out hunting, 1714; "good-humoured, generous, honourable, and well-meaning, but a little stupid and quite childish."

Maine had made the first advances, to treat him less stiffly and coldly." Unpalatable advice, but advice which St. Simon did not see his way to disregard:

"I purposely went to return his visit in the morning, so as to avoid seeing Mme. du Maine. But my precaution was of no avail; he received me most graciously, even going so far as to thank me for coming; but when I was about to take leave, he said that Mme. du Maine would never forgive him if he let me go without seeing her. So he insisted on taking me up to her room, and made me sit in an arm chair at the head of the bed while he sat opposite to me. My reception was most gracious, for the wife was as good an actress as the husband, and had her tongue completely under control; nobody could make herself pleasanter when she chose. I thought I should at any rate get off with a display of politeness, but not a bit of it. . . . She began to talk of more serious things, to my great surprise, but not at all to my embarrassment. There were seven or eight men and ladies of the household present. . . . She took the lead in the conversation, M. du Maine only putting in a word now and then. She brought up the topic of the First President, but I told her that respect for her closed my mouth . . . but she went on teasing me until at last I gave her my opinion in terms which completely satisfied her, and myself too. She burst out laughing, and M. du Maine, who was a capital hand at that sort of thing, kept up the joke some time longer. At last I tried to take my leave, but they both exclaimed that it was such a pleasure to them to see me that they could not let me go yet. . . . She then began talking about a dispute between the Duc de Bourbon and them which had been fermenting for some time, though as yet not much had been heard of it. I tried to avoid talking on this subject; but she kept on asking me questions till I found myself undergoing a regular cross-examination, watched and listened to attentively by the little group who were present. I told her she must know my sentiments, for I had expressed them more than once to M. du Maine. She was not content with this, and reproached him in a joking way with keeping things back from her, and urged me to speak out more plainly. This made me rather angry; I replied that . . . I was quite content that they should be Princes of the Blood . . . because in that position there was nothing to dispute between them and the Peers; but I would tell her plainly that if by any chance they lost that position, we would not tolerate a rank intermediate between us and the Princes of the Blood, and would do all in our power to prevent their having it. . . . 'But,' said Mme. du Maine, 'will not the Peers try to set the Princes of the Blood against us?' 'Madame' said I, 'the Princes of the Blood are quite capable of looking after their own affairs; they do not require advice from us, and have not asked for it.' In this way I danced on the tightrope over this delicate question; they professed to be satisfied with what I had said, and I was content with having got out of it without yielding on any question of principle. Their polite speeches began again. At last I left them after a visit of more than an hour, which seemed to me a good deal longer. I never saw Mme. du Maine again in private."

So that was that, reflected Mme. du Maine, recapitulating the heads of the conversation, from which it was only too clear that the overture was a failure and that, so far as it lay in St. Simon's power, the dukes could be counted upon to oppose them in a body, if and when Bourbon made a formal complaint against the King's Edict of 1714. She could only see the future darkly, but dark enough it looked, and she was deprived of the one satisfaction which foreknowledge would have given her, namely that she had had her last conversation with St. Simon. It now only remained to be seen what the Duc du Maine could extract by way of negotiation with the Duc de Bourbon. There was no difficulty about opening a discussion with Bourbon; where there was any prospect of making money, he was not only accessible, he could even be almost polite, and the one eye in the big-boned, sullen face must have lit up as, after some preliminary skirmishes of compliment, Maine disclosed his offer. His proposal was a simple one; if the Duc de Bourbon would give his word to abstain from any formal or informal attack on the Maines' rank, Mme. du Maine for her part would undertake that half the Condé inheritance should be made over to the Duc de Bourbon. After some further discussion Bourbon accepted the offer. He pledged his word to respect Maine's rights as a Prince of the Blood, and Maine set to work to give legal effect to his wife's promise.

It is paradoxical enough that whenever the Regent appears in the sordid story of the Regency, we feel that we have judged the period too harshly; things cannot have been as bad as they appear to have been, with this likeable scoundrel at the helm. The fact is that Orléans, though a blackguard, was not a cad; the steel frame which keeps his ramshackle character from collapse is his unvarying good nature, coupled with an almost modern instinct for the things which can, and cannot be done. He was lucky in inheriting from his German mother a preponderating strain of honest blood, which went far to counteract the weak viciousness which was his birthgift from his worthless father. He thoroughly understood the Duc de Bourbon's character, and unlike the more ingenuous Maine, attached no importance whatever to his pledged word. And though he had no particular reason to befriend Maine, he disliked the idea of letting him be robbed. So he sent for him and told him plainly that Bourbon would first take his money, and then proceed to attack his position, just as he had all along intended to do. What the Duc du Maine thought of the warning we do not know; what he did was what we might have expected him to do–he did nothing. And Bourbon, as soon as his plunder was secured, submitted a memorial to the Regent, demanding the degradation of the Duc du Maine and his brother, which he caused to be signed also by his cadet, the Cte. de Charolais,[3] and by the Prince de Conti, his brother-in-law. This was submitted on the 2nd of August.

While the Regent hummed, hawed, and procrastinated over the petition, the Maines were not inactive; in February 1717 the duke's position was strengthened by his getting real control over the young king, for until then Louis XV had been in the hands of the women, and the superintendent's position was largely honorary. The 15th of February was the king's birthday, and was celebrated in the traditional manner:

"The Regent, all the Princes, Princesses, ladies, and seigneurs of the Court came in the morning to the Tuileries, all magnificently dressed, for the ceremony of stripping the King naked, in order that all might bear witness that the child was a male, well-nourished, and without blemish. Having been inspected, the King was re-dressed and formally taken out of the hands of his women, and entrusted to those of the Duc du Maine and the Maréchal de Villeroi."

After which the newly-appointed officers of his household were presented to him, beginning I suppose with Maine, and ending with a uniformed Swiss, complete with halbert, for his personal guard; this warrior, son of one of Maréchal de Villeroi's Swiss, was six and a half years old. The ceremony finished with a presentation to

[3] CHAROLAIS, Charles de Bourbon, Cte. de, second son of 6th Prince de Condé, by his wife, Louise Françoise de Bourbon, born 1700; "a half-crazy prince of ferocious depravity."

the king's governess, the Duchesse de Ventadour[4], of his cast-off clothing and his nursery furniture.

Troubles continued to fall thick and fast on the poor Duc du Maine's head; Bourbon's petition was still under consideration when, on the the 22nd of February, the dukes, egged on by St. Simon, presented one of their own which struck at the bastards more deeply. If, said the peers, M. du Maine could not make good his title to succeed to the Crown, then he was nothing but his late father's bastard on whom a dukedom had been conferred. If his claim under the Edict of 1714 was annulled, on what logical basis could the edicts of 1674 and 1711 remain in force? All or nothing is the peers' argument; and the petition closed with a hypocritical wish that the merits which the peers recognize in M. du Maine were sustained by legitimacy; but this is something God alone can confer. Black days for Maine, black days for poor old Mme. de Maintenon amongst her girls over at St. Cyr.

Meanwhile let us turn to the party of the nobility, or as St. Simon puts it, "the people who arrogated to themselves the name of the nobility." So far, their discontent had been a potential rather than an actual trump in the Duc du Maine's hand, but at last things were stirring in that quarter. The matter came to a head in April, when on the 18th of that month a deputation waited on the Regent with a formal protest against the honours and privileges accorded to dukes and duchesses: presented too by a respectable-sounding deputation of six, MM. de Châtillon,[5] Rieux,[6] Laval,[7] Pons,[8] Beauffremont,[9] and Clermont.[10] But alas, the business proved to

[4] Ventadour, Charlotte Madeleine Eléonore de La Motte-Houdancourt, Duchesse de, second daughter of Philippe, Maréchal de La Motte-Houdancourt and of his wife, Louise de Prie; Assistant-Governess to Louis XV; Louis was still calling her "chère maman" in 1739; "kind hearted, but far from clever."

[5] Châtillon, M. de, First Gentleman of the Chamber to *Monsieur*, and afterwards to the Duc d'Orléans; "had nothing to recommend him but courage and a handsome face."

[6] Rieux, M. de, "a very clever man, proud, miserly, and designing."

[7] Laval, M. de, "had served with some distinction . . . dangerously ambitious."

[8] Pons, Renaud Constant, Marquis de, "though the chief of an ancient and distinguished family, was extremely poor."

[9] Beauffremont, M. de, a rich spendthrift, married a Courtenay "even prouder and sillier than himself."

[10] Clermont, M. de, "a good-looking fop, absolutely devoid of common sense, who had arrived from Mans by the public coach to push his fortunes at Court."

be the merest flash in the pan, for the Regent, tardily seeing the danger of such a movement–or, if not quite danger, at least endless bother for himself–"declined to receive the petition, expressed his displeasure in a few sharp words, turned his back on them, and left the room." So far from the Maines deriving any benefit from this operation, it was actually damaging to their cause; for the Regent, who had so far hung in the wind over the Duc de Bourbon's memorial, now told Bourbon that he proposed to deal with his complaint without delay and as soon as he received the report of the committee appointed to investigate the matter. Needless to say, this alarming decision soon reached the Duc du Maine's ears, who thereupon presented a counter-petition in which he stated that the only judge he would recognize in the matter would be the king when he should have attained his majority, or alternatively, the States-General. This was somewhat of a facer for the Regent; even he realized the difficulty of either convoking a body which had not met for over a hundred years, or else letting the question fester until the king came of age, six years hence. D'Effiat,[11] who was now acting on Maine's behalf in the Regent's entourage, used his best endeavours to have the States-General assembled, for reasons which were obvious to everybody. Who could say what might or might not happen if that formidable unknown could be resuscitated? What might not be accomplished for the Maine interest by the judicious flattery of a turbulent and ignorant assembly, whose very rules of procedure were known only to antiquaries? Something not unlike the days of the League might come again, with Mme. du Maine in the part of the great Duc de Guise.

D'Effiat might have carried the day for the Duc du Maine had not the duchess seen fit to put in her oar. She had from the outset dashed into the business with her usual self-confident impetuosity; a cursory glance into the Duc de Bourbon's memorial convinced her that constitutional law and historical research came as naturally to her as philosophy or belles lettres, and she was soon deep in the

[11] EFFIAT, Antoine Coffier de Ruzé, 3rd Marquis d', 1638–1719, son of Martin, 2nd Marquis; suspected by his contemporaries of having poisoned *Madame*, 1670; Equerry to *Monsieur*, whose perversion he shared; "a thorough rascal, the more dangerous because he had a good deal of sense and ability."

great civilians and the Merovingian chronicles. Mlle. de Launay has left us an ironic, but not unkindly picture of whole nights passed by the bed from which the excited little duchess, quilted in folios, dictated thesis after thesis asserting, with a wealth of inaccurate precedent, her husband's claim to the Throne.

This would have done no particular harm had she not insisted on an interview with the Regent, whom she proposed to dazzle with the unassailable brilliance of her legal arguments. No one appears to have discovered what took place at the meeting, but it was evident that the Duc d'Orléans made up his mind that at least he would not endure another lecture on constitutional history from Mme. du Maine; as soon as he had got rid of her he issued orders to the Princes of the Blood and to the Bastards to submit their final pleadings for consideration within the next forty-eight hours. And, as if all this were not enough, a tiresome domestic annoyance befell the Duc du Maine early in May.

France had now been at peace for nearly five years, and a generation was growing up to whom that fact was the chief count in the indictment against the Regent's government; things had come to a pretty pass when a French gentleman, anxious to stop a bullet, had to travel all the way from Versailles to East Hungary to gratify his fancy. Fathers too were irritated by a state of affairs which rendered the satisfaction of their son's quite reasonable desires so uncommonly expensive; among them the Duc du Maine, who had had to allow his seventeen-year-old Prince de Dombes to join the spring exodus to Vienna. What between bribes, lawyer's fees, and the duchess, he was already hard put to it when, at the end of May, he received the exasperating news that the Prince de Dombes had got no further than Châlons, where,

"his grooms, having got drunk, and smoking in the stables, set fire to them after falling asleep, thus burning sixteen or seventeen of the prince's horses, the whole of the 'Crown of France' Inn, and some neighbouring houses; which has obliged the owners of these properties to come to Paris to obtain recompense from Monseigneur le Duc du Maine."

The Prince de Dombes seems to have been quite innocent in the matter, but one does not envy him his reception at Sceaux: probably bringing with him an unpaid bill for post horses from Châlons as the final straw. An angry, anxious, and embarrassed father of the ancien or any other régime is hardly to be trusted for a dispassionate appraisal of an expensive accident, and we may be sure that, to the young prince, the duke affected to regard the matter as deliberately devised to add to his father's troubles. At any rate it seems for the moment to have closed the question of his winning his spurs under the Emperor, for he was still at Sceaux in May, when his father and mother had the honour of entertaining Peter the Great. The duke must however have relented subsequently, for during the following winter we are told of a present of Turkish arrows and quivers made to the king by the Prince de Dombes on his return from the Hungarian front.

In the meantime the affair of the petition trailed on, commissioners were appointed to report to the Council of Regency not later than the 20th of June, and the nobility, whether instigated by Maine or not, were preparing to take a hand in the game once more. Early in the summer thirty-nine of their number presented a petition to Parlement, demanding that the dispute about the Duc du Maine's rank be referred to the States-General, on the ground that only that assembly was competent to decide on a matter affecting the succession to the Crown. It was not only, as St. Simon remarks, "an unexampled piece of impudence," it is also a striking illustration of the nobility's lack of political astuteness. To expect the Parlement, of its own free will, to resign to an unknown body the power of arbitration in matters of state, wrested so recently from the Regent, argued not only an utter ignorance of the Parlement but even of human nature. The result was what might have been foreseen; the Parlement refused to accept the petition, and referred the matter to the Regent. Even that easy-going prince was roused, for hardly a month had passed since he had issued formal and stringent orders forbidding the nobility to hold any political meetings whatsoever: to say nothing of the fact that the petition was a tacit declaration that the authority of the Parlement overrode the Regent's. The petitioners promptly found themselves in the Bastille, and though their detention was a short one, it was longer than anyone had expected, seeing the incurable good-nature of Orléans. And short though it was, it effectually quashed any further attempts on the part of the nobility to acquire a collective status in the government.

On 5th July 1717 the affair of the petition against the bastards at last came to a hearing; on the preliminary question of deferring the decision until the king had attained his majority, the Duc du Maine lost the day by 70 votes to 113. The loss of this question settled, as everyone understood, that of the major point, and the Parlement's subsequent declaration that the bastards were incapable of succeeding to the Crown was scarcely more than a formality. But once more the Regent intervened generously to break the fall of the Duc du Maine and his family; whilst allowing the ruling of the Parlement to stand, he caused the king, as an act of grace, to bestow afresh on Maine and his brother the rank of legitimated Princes of the Blood, but for their own lives only. The Prince de Dombes and the Cte. d'Eu were at the same time given the style of "dear and well-beloved cousins," whilst Maine and Toulouse were to be referred to in all official documents as "dear and well-beloved uncles"– a considerable concession by the ideas of the time, considering that their real status was that of not particularly well-beloved great-uncles on the wrong side of the blanket.

It would be pleasant to be able to record that Mme. du Maine was touched by the Regent's chivalry and generosity: Mme. La Duchesse d'Orléans too. But such was not the case. Mme. du Maine, we are told, "shrieked like a madwoman" whilst the Regent's wife "wept day and night for two months, during which she would not see anybody except two or three of her most intimate friends." In fact no one was satisfied, for on the other side, the Duc de Bourbon was indignant that so little hurt had been done to the man he had injured, and almost immediately began to make trouble about Maine's continued exercise of the "honours of the Louvre," conferred upon him in 1711. These honours, so eagerly fought for in old France, seem trifling enough to us in proportion to the bitterness which their grant created; they consisted in the inestimable privilege of being eligible to hand the king his shirt whilst he was dressing, and a damp towel on which to wipe the royal face. Such as they were, however, the Duc du Maine clung to them passionately while the Duc de Bourbon was equally passionate in his determination that he should be stripped of them; and, in addition, was already talking of the necessity of appointing another superintendent of the king's education. In the latter demand he found an ally in Madame Palatine, who was only too ready to see the Duc du Maine deprived of this, or indeed anything else that could be taken away from him:

" 'The young king has round him' she writes about this time, 'a number of people who are very ill-intentioned towards my son (i.e. the Regent), especially the Duc du Maine, the falsest of hypocrites; he looks as if he would like to eat the images of the saints, but is in fact as wicked a man as there is on earth.' "

Poor Maine, he might well say like Louis XV half a century later, and with considerably greater justification, "What have I done that they should hate me so?"

1718 brought no slackening in the attack on the bastards, but it disclosed a serious difference of opinion amongst the attackers; Bourbon persisted in his demand that Maine should be deprived of the superintendence of the king's education, on the ground that the post belonged of right to a Prince of the Blood and that by the Edict of 1717 Maine no longer held that rank. With all the swindler's fear of his victim, he harped on the fact that as the king grew older M. du Maine must necessarily grow greater; he continued to assert that to leave Maine in his present position was to hand over the princes to his mercy as soon as the king was of an age to be prejudiced against them; and so eager was he to carry his point that he even let slip the most important motive underlying his zeal for the State; his young brother, the Cte. de Charolais, was ill-provided for, and Bourbon thought, in his own words, that "the spoils of M. du Maine" would set him up nicely.

The Regent was in an awkward position; Bourbon was next in seniority to himself in the royal family, and could be a nasty enemy. It was impossible to give a blunt refusal to his demands, yet Orléans was beginning to wonder if he really desired Maine to be removed in order to make way for Bourbon; and the whole matter was complicated by the fact that Bourbon and his allies, mistrusting the

Regent's promises, were anxious that Maine should be despoiled at the forthcoming *Lit de Justice*, summoned for a very different matter, namely to crush the Parlement's attempt to intervene in the financial crisis which had followed on the failure of Law's Bank.[12]

Bourbon and St. Simon, who up to this time had been hunting in couples, split on the question of the *Lit de Justice*; to Bourbon the important matter was to create a situation from which the Regent could not escape; to St. Simon it was the crushing of the Parlement. For, much as he hated the Duc du Maine, he hated the Parlement even more, and he saw clearly the danger of attacking the two enemies simultaneously. With that exaggerated estimate of Maine's cunning which he seems genuinely to have held, he pictured Maine and the Parlement posing jointly as victims in the struggle for the amelioration of the condition of the people, for which indeed a plausible case could have been made out, had Maine been the adroit politician St. Simon imagined him to be.

Acting as Orléans' spokesman, St. Simon had many long conversations with Bourbon, whom he urged with all his eloquence to leave the degradation of the bastards to the Regent, rather than confound the matter with the pending constitutional struggle; he even drew an alarming picture of a possible civil war; he called repeated attention to his own altruism in foregoing an opportunity for immediate revenge on the Duc du Maine; and he wound up by offering Bourbon a signed promise from the Regent that Maine should be deprived of the superintendence. It was all in vain; Bourbon continued to represent the danger in which they all stood so long as Maine held the king in his hand; he did not believe in the threatened civil war; and as for Orléans' written promise, he regarded it, not unjustly, as of no more value than his verbal one.

We must do St. Simon the justice to admit that he had honestly striven to avert the attack on Maine at the forthcoming *Lit de Justice* until he found Bourbon's obstinacy invincible. Nor, holding the

[12] LAW, John, of Lauriston, born Edinburgh, 1671; migrated to London, from where he fled to the continent in 1694, after killing a man in a duel; established the first French Bank, 1716; founded Mississippi Company, 1717, out of which enormous gambling fortunes were made; Comptroller-General of Finance, 1720, but had to fly the country when the Mississippi bubble burst in the same year; went to Venice, where he died in 1729.

views which he did, can we complain of the really ingenious expedient which he now found for gratifying his own spite, and re-uniting Bourbon with Orléans. The scheme, accepted instantly by Bourbon, and with some misgiving by Orléans, was this: let the bastards be deprived of the status of princes at the *Lit de Justice*, and be reduced to peers, taking rank with their fellows from the date of creation of their peerages: the superintendence would then automatically be vacant, by reason of the Duc du Maine's incompetence to act in that capacity, he not being a Prince of the Blood. And with his scheme St. Simon also delivered something very like an ultimatum; the Duc de Bourbon could choose–if he would propose this measure, he would make the peers his grateful supporters for life: if not, they would regard him as a man who had betrayed their order, and he could in future look to them for nothing more than the minimum of deference due to his rank. We give the merest outline of St. Simon's harangue, which he himself gives in great detail, with the characteristic conclusion, "After this vigorous address I stopped short, regretting that owing to the darkness, M. Le Duc was unable to see the fire which flashed from my eyes."

The matter did not quite end there, for in a subsequent conversation it emerged that the amiable Duc de Bourbon understood to be included in their compact, the stripping of Maine not only of the superintendence, but of all official posts and pensions, for the benefit of the house of Condé; and here, not even St. Simon, much less Orléans, would follow him: the former protesting that there was such a thing as justice, while the latter had no desire to see his enormously wealthy cousin become still wealthier. So with what pickings he could extract from the superintendence the Duc de Bourbon had to be content. After a final discussion between the conspirators it was agreed that Maine's isolation should be rendered complete by a concluding motion to be brought before the Parlement for registration; after both bastards had been stripped of their princely rank, the younger brother, the Cte. de Toulouse, would immediately be reinstated, for his own life only, with no descent to any children he might have.

And so at last, towards the end of August, all parties got themselves agreed, the ground was prepared, and nothing remained but to open the attack. It is perhaps unnecessary to say that, although the secret had been well kept, there were too many people in it for Bourbon and St. Simon to bring off a complete surprise; Orléans must of necessity know all, and Orléans' wife was Maine's sister. That something ominous was in the wind was known at Sceaux for some time ahead, but neither Maine nor his duchess seem to have known the exact nature of the blow, or when it would fall. Still, they had begun to take general defensive action before this, though it will be convenient to see how the attack fared before we examine the defence.

The evening of Thursday, 25th August saw the final touches put to the government's plans, and the great attack mounted, ready for launching on the morning of the 26th: at the Tuileries, for as an additional safeguard it had been decided to hold the *Lit de Justice*, not in the Parlement house but in the royal palace. St. Simon returned home on the evening of the 25th, where

"freed from anxiety about more important matters, I gave myself up to the delicious thought that I was the means of obtaining for the Peers of France a restitution of rank which their united efforts had been unable to procure."

These "delightful meditations," which occupied him "for nearly two hours," were interrupted by the arrival of one Millain, messenger of the Duc d'Orléans, to let him know that the last technicalities had been completed;

"A cordial embrace was my reply, and no kiss by a lover to a beautiful mistress was ever sweeter than that which I implanted on the fat old cheek of this charming messenger."

There were other visitors during the evening, including the Duc de Bourbon, whose call is worth mentioning for the odd sidelight thrown on the curious lack of amenities in even a ducal house in 1718; St. Simon hears the duke's speech for the morrow, and suggests some alterations, to which Bourbon agrees:

"He inserted a passage from my dictation, writing on a dog kennel, which I brought him for lack of a portable writing table."

At one o'clock on the morning of the 26th orders were sent to the French and Swiss Guards to stand to: a touch of irony being added to the proceeding by the fact that it was the Duc du Maine who had to be roused to issue the orders to the Swiss. He had just returned to his rooms, having slipped away from a great entertainment which his wife was giving at the Arsenal, and was not unnaturally somewhat startled at being wakened for such a purpose. However, all unsuspecting, he signed the orders, and at five the roll of drums was heard in the dusty Paris streets as the troops took post round the Tuileries. At six, members of the Parlement received orders to assemble at the palace as soon as possible; and by eight, all concerned, except the Parlement, were at their posts. Including St. Simon, who was rather shocked to find the sensible d'Argenson,[13] Keeper of the Seals, in full regalia, standing eating a crust of bread, as much at his ease as if the occasion had been an ordinary one: St. Simon having apparently marked the solemnity of the day by having no breakfast. It must here be understood that it is not for the *Lit de Justice* that we are assembling, but for the preliminary meeting of the Council of Regency, at which the real business will take place, after which the Parlement, at the *Lit de Justice*, is to be put in its place by being told to register the decisions of the Council without comment.

One by one the leading figures in France drifted into the hall, the Duc du Maine arriving rather late, and wearing a mantle:

"He was always lavish of his bows; but he never made so many, or so low ones as on this occasion. He stood leaning on his stick by the side of the table, looking intently at everyone; while he stood there I made him, with keenest pleasure, the most smiling bow I ever made him in my life. He returned it graciously, and continued to watch the scene with an agitated countenance, muttering to himself continuously."

Maine's arrival had created something of a stir in government circles, true, he was a member of the Council of Regency, and had a full right to be present, but he had not been warned of the meeting. What did his arrival portend? How much did he know, and what

[13] ARGENSON, Marc Réné Voyer de Paulnay, Marquis d', 1652–1721; put Voltaire in the Bastille, 1716; Chancellor of France, 1718; "a finished student of the weaknesses of French mankind."

were his plans? He was followed soon after by his brother, the Cte. de Toulouse, who saluted the company in a grave, preoccupied manner, extorting from the good-natured Regent the hurried whisper, "It cuts me to the heart to see that man; I should very much like to explain matters to him." But while he hesitated, Toulouse went over to speak to his brother "who was standing at the foot of Marshal de Villeroi's bed;" this by the way being the first hint we have had that the room which had swiftly been converted into a debating chamber in the small hours of the morning was that unfortunate old gentleman's bedroom: which, as much as the business in hand, may have accounted for Villeroi's "angry and dejected look."

In the meantime the Regent had made an opportunity to confide in the Cte. de Toulouse, and was now justifying himself to St. Simon: "I have just told him everything. I could not help it; he is a worthy, honourable man, and I could not bear my situation with him." Probably Orléans did not tell St. Simon that he had also advised the brothers to spare themselves the pain of being present at the *Lit de Justice*, which was evidently his main object in confiding the secret to Toulouse. At any rate, when the Regent invited those present to take their seats at the Council the two bastards left the room, the Duc du Maine "deadly pale, and almost fainting." They having withdrawn, the twenty odd members of the Council, St. Simon amongst them, got down to business, after a bow to the empty armchair at the head of the table, which was deemed to contain Louis XV.

Orléans opened the proceedings by ordering d'Argenson to read the decrees which were about to be presented for registration to the Parlement; adding that he had summoned that body to the Tuileries because he feared that the excessive heat might have an ill effect on the young king's health if he were forced to go to the Parlement building: an explanation so remote from the truth that many members of the Council must have had much ado to keep a straight face.

Let us here give St. Simon another innings; we have often had occasion to desparage him as a historian. Not to him can we safely go for facts, but what a star reporter he makes! What a colourist the man is! The meeting of the Council is a specimen piece displaying all those qualities on which his true reputation rests:

"While the letters were being read, I enjoyed myself in scrutinizing people's faces. The Duc d'Orléans bore himself with an air of gravity and authority so new to me that I was quite struck with astonishment. M. le Duc looked cheerful and confident. The Prince de Conti[14] seemed dazed, and appeared to take no interest in the proceedings. The Keeper of the Seals, grave and thoughtful, seemed rather oppressed. And it is true he had a good many things to think about, especially as it was his first appearance in that capacity; nevertheless, as he rose and opened his bag, he had the appearance of a clear-headed, resolute man. The Duc de La Force, with sidelong glances, was studying people's faces. Marshals de Villeroi and Villars occasionally whispered to each other; their eyes looked angry, and their countenances dejected. No one had more command of himself than Marshal Tallard,[15] but he could not altogether repress the emotions that agitated him; Marshal d'Estrées[16] seemed stupefied, as if he did not know where he was; Marshal Bezons, his face hidden more than usual under his great wig, watched the proceedings intently with angry, lowering eyes. Pelletier looked on with the air of an indifferent, yet inquisitive spectator; Torcy, three times stiffer than he usually was, furtively kept his eyes open to everything; d'Effiat, hot-tempered and angry, sat with knotted brows, ready to burst out, glancing with haggard eyes in all directions. Those on my side of the table I could not see so well; I did occasionally lean forward and look down the rank, but these glances were very brief. I have already mentioned the inquisitive vexation of the Duc de Noailles. D'Antin, usually so free and careless in his manner, seemed stiff and ill at ease; Marshal d'Huxelles[17] tried to put a good face on the business, but could not altogether disguise the vexation which he really felt; the old Bishop of Troyes, quite bewildered, showed nothing but surprise and perplexity."

[14] Conti, Louis Armand de Bourbon, 5th Prince de, born 1695, son of François Louis, 4th Prince, and Marie Thérèse de Bourbon; detested by his father; commanded Berwick's cavalry in Spain, 1719; there "his name was a byeword," and he was sent home in disgrace; a loathsome and semi-insane brute, insatiably greedy and mean, a coward, a homosexual, held in contempt by all classes.

[15] Tallard, Camille d'Hostun, Maréchal and Duc de, 1652–1728, son of Roger, 1st Marquis de La Baume, and of Mlle. Catherine Bonne d'Auriac; Marshal of France, 1703; beaten and taken prisoner, Blenheim, 1704; "witty, acute, a clever intriguer . . . though nobody trusted him, everyone was delighted to be in his company."

[16] Estrées, Victor Marie, 5th Duc d', 1660–1737, son of Jean, Cte. d'Estrées and M. M. Morin.

[17] Huxelles, Nicolas du Blé, 4th Marquis and Maréchal d', 1652–1730, second son of the 2nd Marquis and of Marie de Bailleul; refused the Order, 1688, on the ground that it would prevent him from haunting taverns "and other places"; Marshal of France, 1703; "a frigid, taciturn kind of man, of a judicious cast of mind, rather than exalted or fearless."

There we have them, the rulers of France at a critical moment, over two hundred years ago, all unconscious that they were sitting for their portraits for the benefit of posterity.

D'Argenson, having explained the constitutional limits of the powers of remonstrance possessed by the Parlement and the steps proposed to prevent its abuse, gave place once more to the Regent, who,

"assuming an air and tone of authority which no one had ever noticed in him before, and which put the finishing touch to the astonishment of his hearers, said 'On this occasion, Gentlemen, I intend to depart from my usual method of taking the opinion of the Council, and I shall continue to do so for the remainder of the sitting.' "

There was a silence says St. Simon, during which "the noise of an insect walking would have been audible." It was a critical moment; but though there were looks of dejection on the part of those who were for various reasons averse to seeing the power of the Parlement abased, the Regent had carried his point, and immediately passed on to the real business of the day. He had, he said, some time ago received a petition from the peers, requesting the reduction of the bastards of the late king to their proper rank in the peerage. Though the persons concerned were nearly related to him, he had seen their elevation with displeasure; there was no precedent for such an intermediate rank being granted to bastards of France; he had communicated the peers' petition to the bastards, who had not been able to put forward any valid arguments for their retention of a status differing from that of the peers; and he had instructed the Keeper of the Seals to embody his ruling in a declaration which would now be read to the meeting. According to St. Simon,

"A profound silence followed this very unexpected declaration. Anger was to be seen on the faces of d'Effiat, Bezons, and Villars. Tallard looked stupefied, and Villeroi as though he were about to lose self-control altogether."

The declaration having been read, the Regent summed up; it was, he said, very unpleasant for him to make a proposal so deeply affecting his brother-in-law; but he was bound to render equal justice to the demands of the Princes of the Blood, and the peers.

Members were then called upon for their votes, beginning with the Keeper of the Seals, who spoke in favour of the bastards' degradation, "but in a manner which put me in mind of a dog running over hot embers." And the motion was carried.

Then came the business of the Cte. de Toulouse, and again the Council approved the Regent's decision to reinstate him in his honours for his own lifetime; after which the Council, which had thought that the surprises of this most surprising morning were at an end, was astonished to see the Duc de Bourbon rise; the Duc du Maine, he said, had been given the superintendence of the king's education at a time when he was a Prince of the Blood; by that morning's work he had ceased to hold such a rank and was now a duke and peer, junior to Marshal de Villeroi who had, until today, been his subordinate in the king's household. He, the speaker, was now of age, and the First Prince of the Blood; and as such, he demanded the superintendence for himself. And he wound up with a compliment to the unmollified Villeroi, to whose experience and advice he looked for assistance in the exercise of these most important duties. This too passed, though there were at length signs that the outmanoeuvred opposition was recovering from its stupor–"All I can say," said Villeroi, "is that all the late king's arrangements are now subverted. I cannot witness it without deep sorrow. M. du Maine is very unfortunate."

But it was the Regent's lucky day, for at a moment when some sort of an opposition might have been got going, a messenger arrived with the startling news that the Parlement was debating as to whether it should obey the royal summons to the Tuileries. Every cock fights best on his own dunghill, and the First President much preferred that the coming battle should take place in their own hall, with the Paris mob at the doors. This First President is not our old friend Harlay; he has been dead since 1707, and this is President de Mesmes, an open supporter of the Sceaux clique, and consequently a strong opponent of the Regent, with whom he was to have many a tussle.

But not on this occasion. The Regent, for once in his life, was firm. He was possessed of the lazy man's short-lived spasm of energy today, seeing clearly that his own peace and quiet depended on following up his victory over the Council in the Parlement before that body had time to create an organized front. Parlement was notified that suspension would be the penalty for its refusal to obey; and Mesmes surrendered, for Parlement, like the Council, was taken by surprise. And with Mesmes' collapse disappeared the Duc du Maine's last hopes of a diversion in his favour, at least for the moment. D'Antin too, another of his supporters, gave up the struggle; he was on intimate terms with his half-brothers, Maine and Toulouse, but he saw the futility of attempting an improvised battle with the royal power. He contented himself with asking the Regent's permission to absent himself from the *Lit de Justice*, on the score of his relationship to the bastards, and leave of absence was immediately granted him.

At last came the eagerly expected news that the Parlement was crossing the great courtyard, marching two and two in their scarlet robes, as we can see for ourselves, for, says St. Simon, "we all crowded to the window, like so many children." The Regent hastily assembled his own procession, dukes, marshals, mace bearers, and so forth, and all passed to the Throne Room, where an uneasy and discontented Parlement was already awaiting them. Says St. Simon again,

"as I went in, I was so overcome with joy at the thought of the great scene I was about to witness, and the delightful moments so rapidly approaching, that I was forced to pause for an instant before I could see distinctly. I assumed an air of the deepest gravity and modesty."

The only fly in St. Simon's ointment was that the inexorable rules of precedence condemned him to sit between the dukes of Sully[18] and La Rochefoucauld;[19] the former he did not like, and the latter did not like St. Simon: "I could get nothing out of La Rochefoucauld but dry, surly answers, so I left off talking to him." However, "in my lofty position with nobody in front of me, I was admirably placed for scrutinizing the audience and I made the most of my

[18] SULLY, Maximilien Henri de Béthune, 5th Duc de, born 1669, second son of Maximilien Pierre, 3rd Duc, and of Marie Antoinette Servien.

[19] ROCHEFOUCAULD, François VIII, 4th Duc de La, 1663–1728, son of François VII, and of J. C. du Plessis-Liancourt; "a proud, surly man."

opportunities"–in fact, our star reporter is in the front row of the press gallery, horrified though he would be at such a sacrilegious description of himself. And we must admit that he gives us an admirable writeup of a historic scene, though it is far too long to be quoted here: the First President, with his "air of suppressed insolence," who "glares at the Duc de Sully and myself, seated in the places which the two bastards would have occupied:" the "dead silence, testifying to the eager attention, the curiosity, the fears and misgivings of the audience:" the king, "serious and majestic, and at the same time the prettiest little boy imaginable, his bearing one of becoming gravity:" the reading of the two declarations, done by the Keeper of the Seals in such a way that "not a syllable was lost, and every word told." For it is d'Argenson's day of triumph too; as Lieutenant of Police he had often stood bareheaded at the bar of the house to receive the orders of these gentlemen of the gown, who had made him feel the full weight of their hatred. And now it was his turn, as their master, to administer to them a public and stinging rebuke. And for St. Simon, oh joy of joys when the moment came for the legal gentlemen to salute the king.

"I revelled with inexpressible delight in the spectacle of these insolent lawyers who dare to refuse us the salute, kneeling humbly before the Throne rendering homage at the level of our feet, while we, with our hats on, occupied seats flanking the Throne. . . . I watched the Grand Bench, and the undulations of the fur-trimmed robes . . . robes trimmed with wretched miniver, trying to look like ermine. I gazed with delight on those bare heads bent humbly to the level of our feet."

There are times when St. Simon arouses in us the same disgust which we feel at the public misbehaviour of an exceptionally nasty child. There was no opposition from the Parlement worthy of the name; the First President did indeed speak in answer to the decree restricting the Parlement's right of remonstrance, but with the king present it could be little more than a token protest, whilst as regards Maine and Toulouse there was no protest of any kind. It is true that subsequently, behind the scenes, there was considerable indignation amongst the dukes not in the secret, who very properly complained that as a body they had been committed to the support of a decree of which they had never heard until it was read out at the *Lit de*

Justice; but this was of no help to the mutinous elements in Court and Parlement.

The king, already at seven a victim to the boredom which was to oppress him all his life, received the news that the Duc de Bourbon was his new superintendent without the slightest change of countenance, nor any sign of reluctance. From him, Maine could look for no support:

"(the king) never mentioned M. du Maine afterwards, except once, on the same afternoon, he asked him carelessly where he meant to go . . . but he had seen little of M. du Maine who, either from motives of policy or because he thought the king was not old enough, used to spend a short time by his bedside in the morning, and never go near him for the rest of the day."

The business of the session was now over except for the mechanical act of registering the decrees, which proceeded amidst a hum of conversation, the king "laughing and talking very prettily, having no more speeches to listen to." St. Simon retained his seat in order to be able to "dart looks of contempt and insult at the First President, which must have pierced him to the very marrow:" after which amusement, he returned home, "revelling in my vengeance; I rejoiced in the full gratification of the most constant and fervent wish of my whole life." Let us hope that the recollection of his ecstasy was with him when his own turn came to be hurled into outer darkness.

And what of the Duc du Maine, and still more, what of Ludovise? Left to himself, the unfortunate duke would have, I imagine, taken things quietly enough. He was still a wealthy duke and peer, and, as he well realized, to be such was a very comfortable thing; he knew the levity of his countrymen, and understood that he had only to lie close at home until the inevitable revulsion of feeling at the treatment accorded to him had time to do its work. Time and the Regent's good-nature were bound to combine to offer him some compensation. But it was hopeless for even the most insinuating of the Sceaux conclave to propose such measures to Mme. du Maine, who was in a rage which threatened in literal fact to send her insane; that she, Anne Louise Benedicte de Bourbon, Princess of the Blood, should find herself in such a situation! But a few short weeks ago, the Throne of France itself had not seemed beyond the reach of her high-mounting ambition, and what was she tonight? She had so far condescended as to marry a Prince of the Blood, and he had turned out to be an imposter: from potential Queen of France, she had fallen to the rank once described by Queen Victoria as that of "a common duchess:" and a duchess whose duke was a mushroom first peer of a new creation. The Rochefoucauld and the Rohan women, the Brissacs, the Noailles, a host of people whom she had hardly recognized as sharing a common humanity with herself, would now take precedence of her. And the storm rose once more to hurricane pitch as she realized it. A pleasant homecoming for a man who had just passed through the darkest and most humiliating day of his life! His duchess screamed for action, and something must be attempted. What that something turned out to be, we shall see in the next chapter.

13. *High Treason*

THE disasters which had just overwhelmed the Duc du Maine and his wife did not, as we have said, come as a bolt from the blue: though neither of them seems to have anticipated that the blow would have been so shattering, or the Regent so uncompromising. At first, Mme. du Maine was stunned–"it was an overthrow comparable only with loss of life itself"–but gradually she rallied herself to take stock of the situation

> "With head uplift above the wave, and eyes
> That sparkling blazed. . . ."

The situation was neither so unfavourable, nor the Regent's triumph so absolute as had been thought in the first moment of dejection.

France in 1718 was in a thoroughly restless and discontented state. The reduction of the Parlement to the status determined for it in 1667 had its opponents, even outside the legal fraternity, and the exile of some of its leading members, which occurred immediately after the *Lit de Justice*, had augmented the discontent; it was the heyday of that fool's paradise of paper and credit introduced by Law, and the poorer noblesse watched with bitter anger the piling up of vast fortunes by those who, like the Condés, had inside information and a pull in financial circles. But these were the privileged and unscrupulous few; the rest languished in impoverished boredom, casting sullen glances at a rising mercantile class from which they were excluded, and at those princes and dukes who were making fortunes on the stock exchange.

Then, on the crest of the wave of nostalgia for the "good old days," came the sudden discovery of the Memoirs of Cardinal de

Retz.[1] This book, which was soon in everybody's hand, had an enormous and easily understood success; these vivid, palpitating, breathless memoirs of the Fronde are among the very best of their century, stirring to read even today, and in them civil war, conspiracy, the seesaw of political and amorous intrigue, appears irresistibly attractive. There was just sufficient superficial resemblance between the minorities of Louis XIV and Louis XV to set everyone, nobles, lawyers, and commons, drawing the wrong inference from the book. Why not another Fronde, said everyone, consciously or unconsciously; those were the days, when there was cut and come again for anyone who could use a pen or a sword. Retz' heavily romanticized, but magical version of the days of seventy years ago had no small share in crystallizing a vague and widespread discontent.

On the practical side, there was serious trouble brewing in Brittany, where the Estates, taking advantage of the province's almost federal relationship with the central government, had in the previous year refused to vote subsidies; the government's retort had been to dismiss the Estates, impose taxation by edict, and to send a garrison to Brittany, with the result that the province was now on the verge of open revolt.

Looking nearer home, it was already common knowledge in Paris that the Regent was regretting his action in bestowing the superintendence of the king's education on the Duc de Bourbon, who, in the insatiable Condé way, was now asking for the command of the Household Troops. Nor were signs wanting that a revulsion of feeling in the Duc du Maine's favour might be expected at Court; on the very evening of the *Lit de Justice*, Villeroi had waited on the Dowager-Duchess de Bourbon, Maine's sister, to represent to her the indignities and injustices which had been heaped upon the Duc du Maine; we may here remind ourselves that this Dowager is the same lady whom we met, many years ago, acting comedies at the foot of the late king's bed to amuse him when he was recovering

[1] RETZ, Jean François Paul de Gondi, Cardinal de, 1614–79, son of Philippe Emmanuel de Retz; St. Vincent de Paul was his tutor; led the rebel party in the Fronde, 1648; arrested, 1652; escaped, 1654; pardoned and restored to favour, 1662; died, 1679; his famous Memoirs, which end in 1655, were first published at Nancy in 1717.

from an operation: who, even then, was a warm friend of her brother's, and whose influence over him Mme. de Maintenon so distrusted. On hearing Villeroi she was touched, burst into tears, and sent a message to the Princesse de Conti, her half-sister, to ask her to come up from Choisy to meet the Cte. de Toulouse, in order that they might might work out a joint scheme for assisting the Duc du Maine. Incidentally, the volume from which we quote gives us an interesting sidelight on how the Duc du Maine's disgrace looked to an observer midway between the event and our own times; it is Mme. de Genlis' edition of Dangeau's journal, published at Paris in 1817, and at this point she inserts a footnote– "The whole treatment accorded to the Duc du Maine was despotic and unjust." Finally, as Mme. du Maine reflected after taking stock, there were possibilities in Spain, despite Philip V's renunciation of the French Crown. Spain in 1718 was passing through a phase of attempted resurgence as a first-class power, under entirely new management. The exhausted Philip V, who, in a plain-spoken despatch from the French Ambassador, is described as caring for nothing in the world except to find himself "between the thighs of a woman" was, not surprisingly, suffering from what was politely called "vapours," and one Cardinal Alberoni[2] had become the de facto ruler of the Spanish Empire. This Alberoni, an Italian market gardener's son, was a man of some real ability, and an adventurous, audacious thruster, whose great mistake was his attempt to do too much in too short a time. Not content with introducing valuable reforms into Spain, he must needs adopt a "forward" policy in Europe, annoying England by his support of the Stuarts, and infuriating Versailles by fomenting a plot to make Philip V Regent of France: a plot which, probably at the instance of the Duchesse du Maine, was expanded to comprise the kidnapping of Orléans and his imprisonment in a Spanish fortress.

The date on which Mme. du Maine crossed the line dividing opposition from treason cannot now be determined; most probably

[2] Alberoni, Cardinal Giulio, 1664–1752, became secretary to the Duc de Vendôme, and accompanied him to France, 1706; in 1708, was Vendôme's publicity agent at Versailles; candidate for the Papacy, 1724; left vast wealth.

she could not have told us herself, but slipped insensibly into relations with Spain. One guesses that the first contacts with Spanish agents fishing in troubled waters were made some time after the Duc du Maine had been declared incapable of succeeding to the Crown, and some time before the famous *Lit de Justice*; it is worth noticing that the duke, after he had been stripped of his right of succession, exacted a promise from his wife that she would have no dealings with anyone who could reasonably be suspected of plotting against the government–a promise which, needless to say, Mme. du Maine made no attempt to keep.

Nor is it easy to tell what number of the discontented nobility continued to support the Duchesse du Maine after the actual plotting with Spain had begun; Buvat asserts immediately after the disclosures that fifteen hundred persons of quality entered into the intrigue, and that many were being arrested every day. But Buvat, we must remember, merely records the gossip of his fellow clerks in the royal library, without having access to any higher sources of information.

The first step into treason was not hard to make; society at Sceaux, as St. Simon sniffily tells us, had for sometime past been growing very mixed, and amongst the motley throng of poets, playwrights, and philosophers, were to be found men ready to turn their hands to anything. The eighteenth century is the golden age of the *chevalier d'industrie* and of the bogus nobility living on its wits in Paris, and a selection of these elements must have found its way to Sceaux: with, too, an admixture of that numerous class of foreigner, precariously settled in France, and wanted by the police of various European capitals. A miasma of conspiracy spread over Paris and the provinces, gradually settling at Sceaux, where it remained at its densest. But this is not to say that Mme. du Maine was in any sense the co-ordinator of the epidemic of conspiracies which harassed the Regent's government; all the groups had some contacts with each other, but never coalesced, except that the Duc de Richelieu's[3] private plottings

[3] Richelieu, Louis Armand du Plessis, Maréchal and 3rd Duc de, 1696–1788, son of the second duke; sent to the Bastille, on his father's petition, 1711; 3rd Duc de Richelieu, 1715; again in the Bastille, 1717; in 1719, in the Bastille again; largely responsible for victory of Fontenoy, 1745.

to hand over Bayonne to Spain overlapped with the Sceaux treasons. But Richelieu was kept a little outside Mme. du Maine's scheme, for he was a man holding an insurance policy covering himself only; amongst his many mistresses, the favourite was Charlotte Aglaé, Mlle. de Valois,[4] one of the Regent's daughters, so Richelieu could plot in the comfortable certainty that whatever happened, his head would remain on his shoulders.

Mme. du Maine's first step was to attempt to enlist the Cte. de Toulouse, a business which she set about with her usual energy. He could, she told him, only wash himself free from the stain put upon his honour by his special rank if he indignantly renounced it: and much more in the same strain. Toulouse at first hesitated; but he was under forty, ambitious, and had no taste for burying himself alive at his country house, Rambouillet; nor had he any particular liking for his brother, whilst he strongly disliked his sister-in-law. So, to her fury, he refused to resign his rank, much less enlist under the Sceaux colours. Poor Maine of course did what he was told, though his wife had a good deal of trouble with him; Mlle. de Launay tells us that it was only with great difficulty that he was brought to consent to Mme. du Maine's schemes, and that even then he was kept in the dark as to their full scope.

After some preliminary negotiations between Mme. du Maine and Philip V's confessor it was decided to send an envoy from Sceaux to Madrid with instructions "to seek His Most Catholic Majesty's support for the Duc du Maine," or in other words to invite Philip to assume the Regency of France, with Maine as his puppet at Versailles, taking his orders from Madrid. Such at least was the objective as visualized by Alberoni, but it is difficult to discover just how wide or how concrete was the plot as envisaged by Mme. du Maine; for, though engaged in a matter which might turn out to be one of life or death, the duchess was still the girl who could not grow up. To her, the mere fact that she was conspiring

[4] MODENA, Charlotte Aglaé de Bourbon, Duchess of, known before her marriage as Mlle. de Valois, fourth daughter of the Regent by his wife, Françoise Marie de Bourbon, born 1700; married, 1720, François III d'Este, Hereditary Prince of Modena, who became Duke of that Principality 1737; died 1761; "deceitful, untruthful, and horribly coquettish."

was as important as the success of the conspiracy itself. She was living as she loved to live, in a perfect whirl of excitement all round the clock, intensely enjoying all the stock properties of a conspiracy–midnight comings and goings, fêtes at which mysterious masked strangers murmured enquiries into her delighted ears; Laplanders, Hottentots, and Spirits of the Night, whom she knew to be disguised agents of the Spanish Embassy; whisperings in corners, hush, we are observed–great days for Mme. du Maine. The Baron Walef, a dubious adventurer of the Irish professional exile type, was selected to make the perilous journey to Madrid, whilst in the meantime Mme. du Maine, through her friend Pompadour, made overtures to the Prince de Cellamare,[5] the Spanish Ambassador to Versailles. On the web of moonshine which was spun as a result of these negotiations, the most refreshing comment is that of Mlle. de Launay, who was of course in the thick of it from the outset–"I won't explain their plot, for I never understood it; and perhaps they didn't either." It is not easy to disentangle in its earlier stages, and after the enrolment of Pompadour and Laval it becomes ever vaguer and more grandiose, more operatic.

These two were by no means of the bogus gentleman type of conspirator; to us, the name Pompadour brings only a vague recollection of the woman who was to disgrace it in the next generation, but the Pompadours were a good old family; the present man,[6] the second Marquis, married to a daughter of the Duc de Navailles, had held military, diplomatic, and Court posts. Not however apparently an exhilarating companion, or even the man for a plotter, for though well educated, he looked and talked exactly like an undertaker, and he was a notorious blunderer.

Laval had Montmorency blood in him, had served with distinction, and had for the past twelve months or so been active at Sceaux, where he was now Mme. du Maine's chief of staff. He had at some

[5] Cellamare, Don Antonio del Giudice, Duca di Giovenazzo, Prince de, 1657–1733, served under his uncle, Cardinal del Giudice, at Paris, 1714.

[6] Pompadour, Leonard Hélie, 2nd Marquis de (actually Marquis de *Laurière*, but always known in society as *Pompadour*).

time received an ugly wound in the face, over which he habitually wore a bandage, and was known in society as *Chincloth*, to distinguish him from others of his numerous clan.

The Prince de Cellamare, whose name the conspiracy bears, was as unwilling a participant as the Duc du Maine. A Neapolitan of over fifty, he was interested chiefly in his dinner and his library, mixed as little in society as he decently could, and disbelieved entirely in the possibility of overthrowing the Regent by means of the Sceaux clique. He had reported as much to his chief, Alberoni, but had been ordered to continue in the closest touch with Mme. du Maine, to whom he was to offer every assistance.

Rarely had any man a more distasteful commission; trained in the gravity of Spain, and of settled habits, he was equally irritated by the Duchesse du Maine's levity, and by her unreasonable hours. To be driven through the cold winter night to a rendezvous at Sceaux in the small hours of the morning, there to see the mountain give birth to a mouse amidst an ostentatious parade of secrecy, was to him not a delicious excitement but an intolerable nuisance; worse still, apt to be both undignified and dangerous, for Mme. du Maine's sense of fitness demanded that Laval, dressed as a coachman, should drive the Ambassador's carriage. And, on at least one occasion, Cellamare had the additional diversion of being overturned in a ditch, from which he was extricated, all unmollified by Laval's airy assurance that he was the first nobleman who could boast that he had been thrown out of a carriage by a Montmorency. Still, Cellamare was his master's loyal servant, and such coherence and practicability as the plot attained was his work rather than that of the duchess and her collaborators.

Unconscious of their doom, the little victims played.

Almost from its inception, the existence and nature of the plot was known to the Regent, who vainly tried to shut his eyes to a situation calculated to involve him in a disagreeably heavy amount of work; an occupation which, except at the head of an army, he regarded with distaste. Like so many men of his type, he found the day a desert which must be crossed in order to reach the oasis of evening, when business could be laid aside behind shut doors with his *roués*. Of his *roués* we have already spoken. They were as disreputable a collection of men and women as any age affords us, who interpreted their collective nickname as meaning that they would cheerfully be *roués*, broken on the wheel, for their master; but the Regent maintained that they were so called because they all deserved that punishment. The details of the Regent's supper parties we know chiefly from the satirists of the time, and theirs is evidence which must be taken with caution; but there is no other evidence available. No one with even the ghost of a reputation to lose ever attended these parties, and indeed would not have been admitted. It was the duty of Ibagnat, the palace porter, to light the Regent to the door of the supper room, and on one occasion the Regent laughingly invited Ibagnat to join them: to which that periwigged Jeeves replied austerely, "Monseigneur, my duty ends at this door; I must respectfully decline to wait on such bad company, and I am very sorry to see Your Highness in it." At which the Regent laughed more loudly.

As we have said, the Regent, left to himself, would fain have shut his eyes to the existence of any plot; indeed, to a man of his type, the potential danger must have seemed small in comparison with the amusement to be derived from the contemplation of the conspirator's antics, and especially from the thought of that grave and melancholy hidalgo, the Prince de Cellamare, sullenly shuffling round the ballroom at Sceaux in a mask and the medal of the Order of the Honey Bee.

But the Regent was not let alone, he was being driven on a road for which he had no liking by the Abbé Dubois, a man who, at least his equal in debauchery, was infinitely his superior in energy and statesmanship. If we were asked to make a choice of the worst subject of Louis XV, we might well draw back appalled in face of the throng of competitors for that bad eminence; but if we were asked to choose the worst half dozen, there would be few lists from which the name of Guillaume Dubois was excluded. Now in his sixties, he had been tutor to the Regent, and had impressed upon him that a contempt for the ordinary decorum of life was a sign of a man not afraid to think for himself: that honour and virtue had no real existence, but were the counters with which clever men and women raised the price of what they had to sell. He easily induced his pupil, by flattering his intelligence, to believe that religion was an invention of the wise to ensure docility in the ignorant: and, as soon as his pupil was of a suitable age, he had introduced him to the brothels of Paris. And with it all, Dubois was clever, witty, good company, and well read. Poor Philippe, what chance had he? The marvel is, not that he had vices, but that he had any virtues. Let us at least say this for Dubois, however, he was no coward; when in due course the time had come to take his pupil to the wars, Maréchal de Luxembourg noted with approval at Steenkirke, that "M. l'Abbé faced fire like a grenadier."

When Orléans emerged from the hands of this precious tutor, Dubois, who had completely achieved his object of becoming the indispensable man, stayed with him as his secretary and, when Philippe became Regent in 1715, Dubois was made a Councillor of State. And here let us say that as a politician he was worth his keep, showing himself to have no mean grasp of the European situation, and with decided ideas on the right course for France. Throughout 1716 he checkmated Alberoni at every turn; between July and September of that year he visited the Hague, Hanover, and Prussia, concluding defensive treaties which he early in 1717 succeeded in combining into the Quadruple Alliance, an important revolution in European politics, and a fatal blow to the new-fledged ambitions of Spain. His reward was the Ministry of Foreign Affairs, with which one would have thought the apothecary's son might well have rested content. But Dubois' greed and ambition were both insatiable. Not satisfied with his political reputation, he thirsted for ecclesiastical distinction, or at least for the loaves and fishes of the Church, and dreamt of the Tiara, with an Archbishopric and a Cardinal's hat as stepping stones. And, not to interrupt our narrative at a later point, we will here finish an outline of his career. When Cambrai fell vacant in 1720, Dubois, though a titular abbé, was not in Holy Orders; indeed, according to some accounts, he was a married man, who had got rid of his wife by robbing a sacristy and destroying the evidence of his marriage. However that may be, he certainly was not a priest. But the Archbishopric of Cambrai, worth over £60,000 a year, struck Dubois as just the thing for him. Even he, however, felt some diffidence in proposing himself to the Regent, and when he mustered up the courage to do so, Philippe's "What! You!" pierced even his skin. But it was unfortunately the old story, and it is the blackest stain on the Regent's memory; he allowed his old brothel comrade to talk him over, and in due course this engaging abbé was given the See which under Louis XIV had been occupied by Fénelon.

But he did not live long to disgrace it, or to enjoy its enormous revenues; in 1721 he was made a Cardinal, and in 1722, Prime Minister. On the 10th of August 1723, he died of syphilis, damning and cursing his doctors up to the last moment.

Such in brief was the man who was now the real ruler of France, and who was determined that his political schemes should no longer be at the mercy of irresponsible intriguers like Mme. du Maine and her clique.

As the plot took shape, Alberoni at the Spanish end naturally became insistent for detailed information as to the resources of the French malcontents, their number, the names of men of quality whose support could be relied upon and in short, he wanted a copy of Mme. du Maine's operation orders. Easy enough for Alberoni to ask for such a thing, but how were the papers to be conveyed from Sceaux to Madrid? Finally, a scheme which promised security for all parties was concocted by Cellamare and Alberoni. The Abbé de Portocarrero, coming on a holiday from Spain, and the Marques de Monteléon, en route from Whitehall to Madrid, were to meet accidentally in Paris and to return to Spain in each other's company; having of course, before leaving Paris, paid the usual call of ceremony at the Spanish Embassy. Here was no suddenly expedited Embassy courier to catch the eye of Dubois' police, just a couple of chance met Spaniards taking advantage of a lucky meeting to travel home together. What could be more innocent? So Cellamare brought the papers from Sceaux to the Embassy, where a certain amount of unavoidable duplicating had to be done by his clerks before the originals left for Spain, and done in the shortest possible time, for

Cellamare had no desire to retain the documents a minute longer than was necessary.

We may be sure that the Embassy clerks grumbled at the additional work, and none of them louder than a young gentleman who had, on that very evening, an appointment at Mme. Fillon's brothel. When at last he got away, his worst fears were realized; he was very late for his tryst, was roundly scolded by La Fillon herself, and got out of it by explaining to her that a sudden rush of confidential copying had resulted in all the Embassy clerks being detained long after normal closing hours. Spanish Embassy, rush of work? This, thought La Fillon, might mean a pound or two from her gossip, as she called Dubois. She was now all smiles for the laggard young clerk, introduced him to his lady, and slipped over to the Palais Royal. Something in it perhaps, thought Dubois, and in any case, easily investigated; for the two young men with the precious packet had, in all innocence, left Paris in company with an absconding banker, wanted by the London police, and it would be simple to apologize to the two Spaniards after their arrest as accomplices, should they prove to have no compromising documents in their possession. On the same night, the government courier set out with a *lettre de cachet* for Portocarrero and Monteléon, the three travellers were overtaken at Poictiers, and on the evening of 8th December, just as the Regent was leaving his box at the Opera, he was stopped by the breathless Dubois with a hasty summary of the plot against the Regent's government and person. "You cannot possibly have had time to examine the papers thoroughly yet," said the Regent soothingly, "tell me all about it tomorrow;" and he rapidly made his escape to the supper room where his *roués* awaited him. But on the following morning he was cornered, and forced to take action in what developed into the biggest sensation of the Regency.

For Cellamare, 9th December proved an unforgettable day. Hoping against hope that the arrest of his two messengers was due only to their being in the company of the defaulting banker, he made an early call on Leblanc,[7] and with as good a show of indif-

[7] LEBLANC, Claude, 1669–1728; praised for his handling of Paris riots, 1719; took a leading part in Villeroi's arrest, 1722; exiled, 1723; "invariably polite to the most humble . . . always obliging."

ference as he could muster, asked for the return of a private package which he had entrusted to these two stupid young men. But alas, Leblanc replied by saying that so far from restoring the package, he had to do himself the honour of reconducting His Excellency to the Embassy, in company with the Abbé Dubois. And His Excellency found on his return that the government had paid him the unwelcome compliment of surrounding the Embassy with the Musketeers.

For three hours Dubois and Leblanc ransacked the Spanish Embassy, Cellamare looking on with the utmost tranquillity. There was blood in him, and he supported a difficult situation with Spanish dignity; seeing Leblanc about to examine a small box of papers, he intervened politely–"Women's letters there only, I assure you, Monsieur. Leave that pimp's work to M. l'Abbé." And Dubois pretended to enjoy the joke.

With what agonies of apprehension the news was received at Sceaux we can easily imagine, though we have no account of it. Nor is it easy to understand why the blow was so long in falling on Maine and his wife. The last of the compromising papers, those in the Spanish Embassy, were in Dubois' hands by the evening of the 9th, yet nearly three weeks passed before he struck. It was not until 25th December that the Regent informed the Ducs de Bourbon and St. Simon that he had proofs in the handwriting of both the Duc and the Duchesse du Maine, seriously implicating them in the conspiracy, and explaining that he had summoned the two dukes to ask for their advice. There was no doubt in the mind of either of his counsellors; both advised the immediate arrest of the Maines, Bourbon urging in response to the Regent's objection that Mme. du Maine was a Princess of the Blood, that that was an additional reason for putting her somewhere where she would be out of mischief. The fate of the Maines was there and then decided upon by the three, and 26th and 27th December were devoted to making the necessary arrangements in all secrecy. But such secrets are rarely well kept. Possibly the Regent himself caused the Duc du Maine to be informed of what was pending; it would have been quite in keeping with his character to have done so. But at any rate,

Mme. du Maine was quick to seize her last chance, and the bulk of the original and most compromising documents were burnt, down at Sceaux, before the police arrived to search for them.

It is curious that in a matter which excited such universal attention, there should be any doubt about dates; yet so it is. St. Simon says the Duc du Maine was arrested on the 30th at Sceaux, "as he was leaving the chapel after Mass," whilst Buvat asserts that he was arrested on the 29th at an hôtel in the Rue St. Honoré. But on this occasion I believe St. Simon's version to be the correct one. St. Simon goes on to say that the duke was at once placed in a carriage, under the charge of Favancourt, Brigadier of the First Musketeers, and straightway conveyed to the fortress of Doullens. Poor Maine it need hardly be said made no shadow of resistance; he was, he asserted, entirely innocent, and very unfortunate, in that the Regent should listen to the slanders of his enemies, for he, Maine, had always been sincerely attached to the Regent. And, though his journey to Doullens took two days, he did not speak again, but sat sighing, dazed, but sufficiently conscious of the outer world to remember to make a low bow to every cross and church which they passed; remembering perhaps that long ago journey to Antwerp with Mme. de Maintenon, and recalling how she had told him then that one must never pass a church without bowing. Perhaps, too, almost glad that the blow had fallen at last, glad to be rid of his intolerable wife and her plottings, glad to be rid of his own ill-sustained pretentions, and numbly conscious of that broken satisfaction which comes with the casting away of all hope. The same unexpected confusion exists about the details of the arrest of the duchess; commonsense would seem to have dictated the arrest of all the conspirators on the same day and, as nearly as possible, at the same hour. But we are not certain that this was the case. Mlle. de Launay, who surely was in a position to know, states that the duke was arrested at Sceaux on the 29th, the duchess in Paris on the same day; Buvat agrees as regards the duchess, but St. Simon, who was a principal actor in the whole drama, says that she was arrested on the 30th, in a small house in the Rue St. Honoré which she had hired to serve as the Paris headquarters of the plot. And he adds the interesting information that the Duc du Maine had never entered this house.

To Ludovise, the discovery that restraint could and would be applied to her movements must have presented itself as a monstrous and unnatural portent, and we can easily believe St. Simon's statement that "she was very angry;" probably little consoled by the fact that in consideration for her rank, she was treated with more deference than her husband. And indeed the deference shown her seems but cold comfort to a modern reader, for it consisted in her being arrested and escorted to her destination by a Captain in the Life Guards, the Duc d'Ancenis.

The duchess, whilst she can hardly be said to have offered resistance, proved much more obstreperous than the duke; she wanted her despatch boxes; she wanted her jewels; she wanted this and that; until at last d'Ancenis, telling her "civilly but firmly" that she could have none of these things, handed her into a carriage, and they set out, the duchess protesting against the violent treatment to which she had been subjected. And, as the coach went through Paris, a horrid doubt may have crossed her mind as to whether she was the adored princess she had always assumed herself to be; the citizens were going quietly about their business, just as if the most infamous outrage in all French history was not transacting itself before their eyes; why was not the town in a blaze? Could it be, after all, that France did not regard her as the central figure in France? Disturbing thoughts, these. Her uneasiness increased as they travelled further and further from the capital, especially when she reached Burgundy; and when she had to enter the fortress of Dijon, and realized that she was the prisoner of the Duc de Bourbon, her fury knew no bounds. That she had shown vexation at there being no disturbance in the Paris streets perhaps indicates that her plans had provided for a riot in the event of her arrest; and some suspicion of this possibility was evidently in the mind of Dubois, for the journey was made in a plain hired carriage, and the principal streets were avoided in favour of a circuitous route under the ramparts to the Porte St. Bernard.

But if there was no émeute, there was at least a good deal of sympathy; two things about the arrest stuck in the public gizzard, first, the indignity of compelling a Princess of the Blood to enter a hired carriage, and second, the baseness of the Duc de Bourbon in consenting to act as his aunt's jailer. To a noble of the old school, the family was everything, loyalty to the House came before loyalty to the Crown, and Bourbon's conduct would appear to such as nothing less than domestic treason. Even Bourbon himself, thick-skinned and brutal though he was, felt the reproach of society; he had even been at first somewhat taken aback at the proposal to imprison his aunt in a fortress of which he was the Governor, though his protests to the Regent were so weak that they were evidently made only in order that he might put it on record that he had made them.

One by one the government laid its hands on the conspirators; the Advocate-General of the Parlement of Toulouse, who had written manifestos for the Duc du Maine, was taken to the Bastille on the 29th; as were most of the Maine household, including many old friends of ours, Mlle. de Launay and both the Malézieux amongst the number; Cardinal de Polignac escaped with exile to his abbey in Flanders; the Duc du Maine's family was carefully scattered, the Prince de Dombes being exiled to Moulins, the Cte. d'Eu to Gien, and Mlle. du Maine to the convent of the Visitation at Chaillot; Richelieu, whose little private plot to surrender Bayonne to Spain had come to light in the general collapse, was, for the second time in his chequered career, put in the Bastille; Cellamare, who was in one sense the most guilty of them all, but who was covered by his diplomatic immunity, was ordered to leave France, and was quit of the business at the price of being escorted to the frontier by a Life Guard unit.

This series of arrests, carried out with such unexpected vigour, produced a regular *sauve qui pêut* amongst those of the unarrested whose consciences were not at ease, and the Regent had to listen, with cynical boredom, to many protestations of undying love and loyalty. Amongst the earliest arrivals at the Palais Royal was a certain Marquis de Mesnil, armed with proofs that he was no relation to the Chevalier de Mesnil who had just been arrested at

Sceaux. "So much the worse for you," grunted the Regent, "the Chevalier is a man of quality."

The international and domestic repercussions of the plot were considerable. Friction between France and Spain had been increasing for some time past, and the discovery that Alberoni had presumed to dictate to France in a domestic matter, or indeed rather, had presumed to give France a new government, proved the last straw. On 17th December, 1718, England declared war on Spain, where Alberoni was openly preparing ships and troops for a Jacobite descent on Scotland; on 9th January, 1719, the French government entered the war as England's ally–an ironical comment on Louis XIV's life work. Only six years had passed since, at the price of his own country's ruin, he had placed his grandson on the Throne of Spain; and now, one Bourbon, as the ally of France's traditional enemy, was at the throat of the other one.

In twelve months, Alberoni's grandiose plan, which had embraced a battle front stretching from Hanover to the Scottish Highlands, was in ruins, and he himself had fallen from power. Philip V was forced to submit to terms dictated by his enemies on 17th February 1720, and this ended the dream of a Spanish resurgence. Many men had been drowned, shot, beheaded, and hanged, great treasure had been flung away, and Europe blundered on, much as before. It was a heavy price to pay for Ludovise's new game of conspiracies.

14. *Total Eclipse*

THE beginning of 1719 found all the principal conspirators behind bars, at Dijon, at Doullens, or in the Bastille. From Doullens came only rumours, from Dijon the muffled shrieks of Mme. du Maine, who was asserting her position as a Princess of the Blood in a stream of passionate but unavailing protests. To her it must have seemed as if the laws of nature had ceased to operate, as amidst vapours, fits, and paroxysms of rage, the truth dawned upon her that for the first time in nearly thirty years, her actions were controlled by an external force. And let us hope that for the first time in her life, she grasped what was meant by friendship, a word which was so often on her lips; for her disgrace revealed the fact that she had in the world one real and loyal friend. On 1st January 1719 her Lady of Honour, Mme. de Chambonas, who was in no way implicated in the plot, had come forward with what was rather a demand than a petition that she too should be imprisoned in Dijon fortress in order to carry out the duties of her appointment. Her conduct was greatly praised, says Dangeau, and well it might be.

Those who found themselves in the Bastille were the most fortunate. We who are old enough to have grown up on the cloak and rapier romance have never lost a dim but ineffaceable picture of lightless dungeons in each of which sat an imbecile in rags, chained, a rat for company, a pitcher of water and a "mouldering crust" for consolation. And nothing could be more extravagantly wide of the truth. Certainly there were dungeons in the Bastille, but they were places of punishment for refractory prisoners and never had permanent occupants; even as punishment cells they were used for short periods only, and that very rarely, if for no other reason than that their use involved the governor in a great deal of extra business. For he had no power to sentence a prisoner to the dungeons, but must report the matter to the government, giving full reasons for his recommendation of the punishment; his report was then considered by a legal committee, whose recommendations were submitted to the king for his decision.

The masked torturer too turns out to be a fictitious character; torture certainly was inflicted in the Bastille, but solely in the ordinary routine of preliminary judicial investigation, and I can find no trace of its ever having been used as a punishment; and as for the irresponsible sadism of the individual warder which now disgraces the prison camps of Europe, such conduct would have been regarded with horror by any prison officer of the ancien régime.

What was the Bastille of fact, as opposed to the Bastille of fiction? When Bassompierre[1] entered it in 1631, the governor told him at their first interview that he was to have every liberty, except of course that of leaving the prison; could move about inside as he pleased; and could bring in any of his domestics he chose; and Bassompierre is proud of his own modesty in "making do" with two valets and his cook, who were lodged for him at the king's expense. Admittedly Bassompierre was a Marshal of France, and therefore on the most select list of prisoners, but good treatment was the rule for all classes; Arnauld, a mere bourgeois, who was there at the same time, found himself among "as honest company as there was in France," enjoying "every liberty compatible with imprisonment," and adds that the governor became his particular friend.

The prisoner in the Bastille was in every way more comfortable than the prisoner in a modern jail; in fact it is no exaggeration to say that he was kept free in a very tolerable hotel. His time was his own, no two rooms were of the same shape or size, and each, in its furniture and amenities, reflected the taste of its occupant; he had books, writing materials, and musical instruments, whilst pets seem positively to have been encouraged. The day Mlle. de Launay arrived, her turnkey made her a present of a cat, which shortly afterwards littered, and of the kittens she has much to say. Rooms

[1] Bassompierre or Betstein, François de, 1579–1646; Marshal of France, 1622.

were apparently dismantled when not in use, though I am perhaps drawing a wrong inference from the fact that Mlle. de Launay arrived during a panic period when business was exceptionally brisk. Anyway, she was given an empty room, into which was brought at intervals during the day the necessary furniture, followed as the weeks passed by such of her personal belongings as she asked for from Sceaux. Her experiences in the Bastille are particularly interesting, for, as a poor dependent, she had no money with which to buy luxuries, and had to live on what the king provided; and her account has a further interest as a significant sidelight on life in the household of the Duc du Maine. She says succinctly that never before or since did she enjoy such liberty as when in the Bastille, and the whole prison passage of her memoirs breathes regret for a good time gone. She had her books and her music, the latter being of special service to her after the imprisonment of Richelieu in March; for from her window she could see his, and the two used to pass their mornings in singing duets from the latest musical comedies –with what satisfaction to the other prisoners we are not told.

Once a prisoner's judicial examination had been completed, he was given the freedom of the Bastille during daylight, which meant that he could play ball games in the courtyard, or stroll on the ramparts, gossip with his friends, or entertain them in his quarters. And for persons of quality, there was the governor's weekly dinner party and evening reception, at which a man could get as good a meal as was to be had in Paris, and in unexceptionable society.

Nor was the prisoner's own private table much, if anything, inferior to the governor's, for the "mouldering crust" is also a fiction. In fact the housekeeping of the Bastille was on an extravagant scale; déjeuner, following the custom of the time, was a mere snack, but midday dinner invariably consisted of soup, entrée, and two main dishes, followed by dessert, with which the prisoner had at his choice, and at the king's expense, either two bottles of champagne or burgundy, or one of each; which, as he had already been given a bottle of wine in the morning for casual use during the day, strikes us as tolerably handsome. In the evening there was a supper on the usual well-to-do Parisian scale. Those prisoners who were undergoing the punishment of deprivation of rations had to support nature as best they could on a dinner of soup, bread, meat, and half a bottle of wine.

There is no better testimonial to the king's hotel keeping than a still surviving petition from the inferior prisoners in the Bastille in the time of Louis XIV. In the preamble they complain of the injury to their digestions, caused by the richness of the food, and go on to ask that plainer diet be provided. And, on the other hand, the king took no offence at gourmets who complained of the inadequate quality or quantity of his hospitality; such could have their edibles and wine sent in from outside, and if they liked to buy their own wine, the "King's Arms" as it was often called, charged no corkage.

I can find no details of the scales of allowances for the various types of prisoner, but that they were generous, even excessive, is shown by the significant fact that the death of a first-class prisoner was a financial setback for the governor, whilst a shortage of prisoners was as distasteful to him as is a shortage of visitors to a hotel keeper. This implies a considerable profit on each of his compulsory guests, for we must remember that, contrary to the modern impression, the Bastille was a very small prison, having accommodation for only between forty and fifty inmates. To the excessive allowances paid for prisoners of the highest rank Bassompierre owed his release from the Bastille after Richelieu's death; the thrifty Louis XIII, now for the first time looking into his own affairs, was so appalled at the cost of boarding a Marshal of France that he gave orders for his instant liberation.

As is not uncommon in life, it was on the Duc du Maine, the least guilty of the conspirators, that the full weight of the government's severity fell. Favancourt, we are told, admittedly by Mlle. de Launay, "treated him with the incivility and harshness of a true jailer," whilst Doullens citadel was no Bastille; set in the dreary Flanders plain, with which some of us are only too familiar, the château was at this time falling into ruins, and had rooms whose walls were so full of cracks that it was difficult to keep candles alight in them. For company and surveillance, the duke had with him a

Gentleman of the King's Chamber, who never left him, day or night. January came in with a succession of the worst gales known for a century, which must have whistled eerily through the ruinous deserted château where there was neither hope for the future nor comfort for the present. Maine's request for an occasional day's hunting in the interests of his health was curtly refused, though after a time he was allowed to ride round the château on a "sorry hack," under escort, and never out of range of the muskets of the sentries on the wall.

In the meantime, the Crown lawyers were steadily continuing their examinations of the prisoners; Pompadour, in the Bastille, made a statement which ought to have been of considerable service to the Duc du Maine, but which, by a gross perversion of justice, failed to assist him. According to Pompadour, "when these matters (i.e. the plot) were discussed with the Duchesse du Maine she always broke off the conversation if M. du Maine came into the room." This passage in the cross-examination was calmly deleted by d'Argenson, the examining magistrate, as likely to damage the Crown's case against the duke. Luckily for Maine, however, there were influences working in his interest of which he knew nothing: "the best protection of the accused was to be found in the character of the Regent; services or disservices made little impression upon him."

And, even more important, Dubois, having crushed the conspiracy, began to wonder if it would be to his ultimate advantage to proceed to extremes against the Duc du Maine; he appreciated that public feeling was by no means unanimously behind the government, and began to realize that of the Duc du Maine he might make a political counterpoise to the Duc de Bourbon. He alone understood how precarious was the Regent's hold upon life, weakened as he was by debauchery and threatened with apoplexy. In the event of Orléans' death, Bourbon must become Regent, and as this was likely to happen, was he wise to extinguish a party whose services he might need to hold Bourbon in check? Dubois naturally did not represent matters to the Regent quite in this light; he in fact appeared as the representative of kindly Mother Church, pleading against the inexorable justice of the secular arm on behalf of her erring children, seasoning the whole with a few comments on the general conviction that the so-called conspirators had been led astray entirely by a passionate, though wrong-headed attachment to the person of the king. The Regent knew his Dubois thoroughly; he was not in the least impressed by this pathetic harangue, but he was quick to seize the pretext offered him to escape from a situation which was becoming an abominable nuisance to him:

"His laziness, and his dislike of having his pleasures interfered with, made him accept the Abbé's arguments, and he left Dubois master of the whole affair."

And Dubois, armed with complete authority, proceeded to extract all the information he could from his prisoners, whilst determining that there should be no trials, but that on the contrary, he would so manage matters that he could if necessary pose at some future date as the saviour of the Duc du Maine.

One thing however he was determined to have out of the duchess, and that was such a full confession of the ramifications of the plot as would put that enterprising lady completely in his power for the rest of his life; and he got what he wanted, though with a good deal of difficulty. The duchess was getting very tired of imprisonment; she had at last realized that so long as she continued to deny the plot, there was to be no escape from Dijon. She was a well-read woman, and there had come to her uncomfortable recollections, overlooked in the excitement of conspiring, of members of the Blood Royal who had spent a long life in captivity in remote châteaux, and there died forgotten by all their contemporaries. Though she was a courageous woman, the thought of life confinement in a provincial town was to her much worse than the thought of death itself; and after some three months of cross-examination, she admitted in writing that the conspiracy was a real one, designed to overthrow the Duc d'Orléans and make the King of Spain the nominal Regent:

"She spoke with great contempt of Pompadour and other persons who had been arrested; but admitted that Laval was one of the main springs of the conspiracy, through whom had passed all communications between herself and the Prince de Cellamare; he was also employed to manage the party among the nobility who favoured these designs."

Pleasant news for "Chincloth" Laval when in due course the lawyers arrived at the Bastille to cross-examine him afresh in the light of the Duchesse du Maine's revelations:

"He was furious with Mme. du Maine, calling her all sorts of names; he said she was the last person he would have thought capable of betraying her friends, and that it was she who had induced him to take part in the conspiracy. In his anger he let out a good many other particulars."

The immediate result of Laval's indiscretions was the arrest of Cellamare's secretary who, not covered by his master's diplomatic immunity, had been under police supervision since the beginning of the year; and from him too, much information was obtained. In fact, the game was up, and confession all round became the order of the day. Mme. du Maine, re-examined, made a further statement, in which she swore

"That owing to her husband's timidity, he had never been admitted into the secrets of the plot, and that one of her greatest difficulties had been to keep him in the dark; several times indeed, their plans had been delayed and important meetings postponed for this reason. He, on his side, declared that he had known nothing of what was going on, though, he said, he must have been an idiot not to have suspected something; he thought the scheme detestable, and expressed himself very bitterly against his wife, and those who had drawn her into it."

The confessions almost compensated the Regent for the nuisance of the plot, and for the Duc du Maine he showed a good-natured contempt which was more merciless than any anger. The duchess, though he disliked her more, he understood better, and of her he merely remarked sardonically that she was, quite sensibly, trusting to her native wit and her exalted rank to come out of the affair with flying colours. Society in general said that if the Duc du Maine felt greatly relieved at the establishment of his innocence, he could not feel very flattered by his wife's reasons for keeping him in the dark. Any lingering doubts about Maine's place in the plot were set at rest by Alberoni, who, on his fall from office in December of this year fled to France, and there gave all the information in his power to the French government; the Duc du Maine, he said, had not appeared in the plot at all, but the duchess was a she-devil; whilst as for her associates, he would not give a silver crown for the whole boiling of them.

It would be idle to pretend that as a prisoner of State the Duc du Maine cuts a particularly dignified figure; but if he was no Montmorency, to await the axe in the grand manner, he was at least, by general admission, sustained in prison by a fervent piety, tranquil and untroubled in his submission to God. We can all enjoy the luxury of vicarious chivalry and self-sacrifice; we feel impatiently that Maine would make a better show had he taken upon himself the sole authorship of the plot in an endeavour to shield his wife; not noticing perhaps the serious objection to his doing so, namely that as he was in ignorance of the details, he would have found considerable difficulty in exposing their intricacies to his judges. And after all, what right have we to demand such an effort from him? Each man knows where his own shoe pinches, and only Maine could know what provocation he had to leave his wife to stew in her own juice. Nor, let us remember, were the dangers faced by husband and wife equal; the duchess was a Princess of the Blood, whilst it had been more and more forcibly brought home to the duke that he was a simple peer. Royal heads had been safe even under Richelieu a hundred years earlier, and this was the eighteenth century. But for him there were no such safeguards. As he lay sleepless in his prison bed, the wind moaning through the long deserted château, his thoughts, in that cold hour before the dawn when courage runs low, must often have dwelt on those nobles who, within his own lifetime, had so suddenly disappeared for ever. Perhaps in twenty, thirty years time, he would still be occupying this room whilst at Versailles, old courtiers in a reminiscent mood would occasionally say, "The Duc du Maine? Probably dead I should imagine; it must be all of twenty years since he disappeared." Or perhaps Dubois might decide that he had better become the late Duc du Maine; easily done too. "Over-ate himself at supper," people would say, "sad business, died in the middle of the night." All things considered, it is hardly to be expected that he should have attempted to make himself the scapegoat for the disasters which his wife's levity and ambition had brought upon his house.

But Dubois, so far from having any intention of compassing the Duc du Maine's death, had, as we have seen, quite other plans for the future; in the early spring the minister had received disquieting reports of the Duc's health, which was rapidly giving way under the mental and physical strain of anxiety and unaccustomed confinement. Dubois had found out all that he wanted to know, and had decided not to proceed against the victims; he felt that the time was ripe for winning the gratitude of the Maines and their underlings with a view to future eventualities. One by one the prisoners began to trickle out of the Bastille, and on 30th March the monotony of life at Doullens was broken by the unexpected arrival of a detachment of the Life Guard; to Maine it must have seemed almost liberty when he heard that they had been sent to escort him from Flanders to his own château of Eu, in the neighbourhood of Le Tréport, where he was to live under house arrest during the king's pleasure. It was the first gleam of returning daylight.

But hardly had he been restored to this relative liberty, when a great sorrow fell upon him. Mme. de Maintenon died at St. Cyr at five o'clock on the evening of Saturday, 15th April, in her eighty-fourth year. The four years which had elapsed since Louis XIV's death had made of her a living legend rather than a contemporary. With her usual good sense she had retired to St. Cyr, and for ever, as soon as her husband was dead; she had always shunned general society, and it was not for her, she felt, to remain at Versailles, an object of contemptuous curiosity to a generation which was fast losing even the memory of the Great King. She never again came outside her convent walls, within which she devoted the last days of her life to the supervision of her beloved school:

"Nothing was done without her orders, and though her manner towards the elder ladies was invariably polite and gentle, and she was always kind to the young ones, they all trembled before her: yet nearly all the inmates of St. Cyr liked her."

What time and money she could spare from the demands of the community, were at the service of ex-officers and soldiers, particularly those of the Life Guard, who in trouble and poverty could always count upon receiving sympathy and alms from the lady of St. Cyr. She became difficult to see, and was from the first completely invisible to the common run of society whom an impertinent curiosity brought to her retreat. Mmes. de Caylus, de Dangeau, and de Lévis were allowed to visit her, as were Marshal de Villeroi, Louis XIV's oldest friend, and Cardinal de Rohan, who had rendered him the last offices. Once a week the Queen of England[2] would dine with her, and sometimes her diocesan, the Bishop of Chârtres; but even in the case of this privileged circle, there was no admission to be had without previous appointment. The only visitor who was allowed to come without an invitation and whom she always welcomed heartily was the Duc du Maine; up to the time of his arrest he never let a week go by without calling on her, and his visits usually lasted from three to four hours. Perhaps the pleasantest hours now left to either of them, when the years were rolled away, and he was once more her *mignon*, and she was his mother; for on those terms they remained until the end. What a pang must have shot through the duke's heart in his loneliness, as he realized that no living being would ever again address him as "mignon." Contemporaries tell us that Maine's imprisonment killed Mme. de Maintenon; but such language never means very much, and especially in the case of a woman of over eighty. Nor are we much more enlightened by the information that she died of a "languishing fever" which attacked her three months before her death.

For a few days she was a topic of conversation in the salons, where the smart young people reminded each other with sniggering incredulity that she had lived the first seven years of her life under Louis XIII, and the last four under Louis XV. She had overlapped the longest reign in European history, had herself been no small part of European history, and now she was gone.

She was buried under the choir in the chapel of St. Cyr, where her body rested undisturbed for seventy-five years; then in 1794 came the officials of a newer civilization to convert the ruined chapel into a hospital. They began proceedings by opening Mme. de

[2] Mary of Modena, widow of James II.

Maintenon's tomb, in which the body was found, perfectly preserved, and still odorous with the perfumes of the embalmer. A rope was placed around the frail throat, and the body dragged with kicks and shouts through the ruins of St. Cyr; after which it was mutilated and thrown into a hole in the grounds.

Mme. de Maintenon's descendant, the Duc de Noailles, writing in 1858, tells the story with an ironic restraint which would have won her own fastidious approval–"And so at last," he concludes, "she was publicly recognized as a Queen of France."

Early in August the Duc du Maine received a further mitigation in the conditions of his arrest, being permitted to move freely over his own considerable estate of Eu; and on the 7th of that month, "M. le Duc d'Orléans has ordered M. du Maine's equerry to send him two pages, two valets, two post chaises, six hunters, and a couple of dogs to amuse him." The proportion of hunters to hounds strikes us as odd, but no doubt the duke managed to extract some sport from them. On 22nd December, another relaxation is granted Maine; he may if he likes live at Clagny, a place we remember in the old days as being a suburban retreat of Mme. de Montespan's. And at the same time

"Another courier is being sent to Mme. du Maine, giving her permission to reside at Sceaux. . . . She is at full liberty, except that she is forbidden to visit Paris, and the same conditions apply to M. du Maine."

Thus Dangeau, who as usual sees only the back of the cards; for in fact a whole domestic drama lay behind this bald announcement.

It was nothing less than that the Duc du Maine was contemplating another revolt; by no means political, for of that he had had more than enough, but domestic. Such an opportunity for self-examination as rarely fell to a man in those bustling days had left him more than ever exasperated with his wife's childish inconsequence and its profoundly unsatisfactory sequel; life, he reflected, was not entirely over at fifty, and now or never was the moment to strike a blow for a quiet evening to his days. Why should not the restoration of his public liberty be made to coincide with a stroke for domestic freedom? Exhilarated by a twelve months' separation from his wife, he thought the thing possible. It does not seem that, even at this stage, he contemplated any such radical action as a judicial separation, for which indeed he had no grounds, but he felt that he had no desire to see his Ludovise again for a very long time, and that if he refused to join her at Sceaux, she might soon accustom herself to his permanent absence. And accordingly, as a first step, little though it was suspected by the public, and still less by Mme. du Maine, he persuaded the Regent to exile his wife to Sceaux, and himself and his children to Clagny. The Regent chucklingly acceded to the request; but Orléans was a gossip of the first water, and Maine showed more than his usual ingenuousness if he really thought that the Regent could keep such a good story to himself. The reasons for the Maines' continued separate exile were soon all over Paris, from where they were not long in reaching Sceaux. The offended fury of Mme. du Maine, who, up to the day of her death, believed that every man she spoke to was dying of love for her, can be imagined. All through 1720 the battle raged, and we must let Mlle. de Launay tell us of it in her own words:

"The Duc du Maine, very discontented at having suffered a harsh imprisonment for a whole year for an affair in which he had not been implicated, was determined to live at Clagny without seeing Mme. du Maine. The duke had let himself be persuaded that in openly showing his resentment against his wife, he would demonstrate his own innocence; which he had a great interest in establishing, in order to force the Duc d'Orléans to reinstate him in his rank and offices. In addition, he was annoyed at the state of his affairs, and the expense of his former way of life, wanted to fix an annual sum for his wife's upkeep and the payment of her debts, as well as to take precautions against her contracting any fresh ones."

At these unwonted signs of determination on her husband's part, and more especially at his financial programme, the duchess became seriously alarmed; she did everything she could to bring the duke back to her–short, of course, of offering any submission to his authority–but, Mlle. de Launay continues,

"M. le Duc du Maine was obstinate in his determination to stop at Clagny, and was even unwilling to see her. He made her the offer of an annual sum for household expenses, which was to be entirely at her own disposal. But all idea of a separation was odious to her, and she would not listen to any arrangement which tended to that end; on the contrary, she put every iron in the fire to draw them together once more. She got the Cardinal de Noailles[3] to attack him on the score of marital duty. The duke, pressed on all sides, felt unable any longer to refuse her at least an interview, which took place in the house of Landais in the Rue Vaugirard."

Did the duke, one wonders, on his way to the interview, pass his old nursery house in the Rue Vaugirard? The duke being once committed to an interview, we can guess what the result was. His wife was presented to him by the Princesse de Condé, but even now, wife, mother-in-law, and cardinal, all pulling together, had a very tough struggle to overcome him; but in the end he gave way. He returned to Sceaux, where he lived very much as he had always done, with one notable exception; there were to be no politics at Sceaux, and no politicians. And on this point he won the day; and it was not until many months had passed that he at last gave a reluctant consent to Malézieux rejoining his household.

If he had lost his first battle it had at least been worth the fighting; for once in his married life he had asserted himself, and he had given his wife a fright of which the salutary effects were not to be entirely dissipated during the rest of his lifetime.

One by one the remaining figures of the Grand Siècle are quitting the stage, and we would be ungrateful if we let Dangeau do so without some record of the fact; for he has signposted our road for us for nearly fifty years. One of Louis XIV's familiar friends, and known to our duke as far back as memory goes, he died on 7th September at the age of eighty-four, having passed his long life in a perpetual and disinterested adoration of the king. A man of whom Mme. de Montespan used to say that it was equally impossible to help liking him or laughing at him. His memoirs are invaluable and of a phenomenal dullness; there, day by day, year after year, are the externals of Court life under Louis XIV, with never a reflection upon, or a deduction from the facts he narrates. Would you know what Louis did or said on any day after Dangeau came to Court? He will tell you just that, and no more. But to us he is a sore loss, and we say goodbye to him with regret. The ground swell of the

[3] NOAILLES, Louis Antoine, Cardinal de, 1651–1729, second son of the 1st Duc de Noailles; Archbishop of Paris, 1695; on his deathbed, "characteristically signed two documents, one of which accepted the Bull *Unigenitus*, whilst the other rejected it."

storm in which the Duc du Maine had so nearly foundered subsided slowly in a wave of libels and pamphlets; of their authors, the most prolific and most savage was Legrange-Chancel, whose first Philippic, published in September 1720, apostrophized the Regent as "a monster vomited from Hell" and presented him to the public as a poisoner, an incestuous father, and a tyrant surpassing Nero or Tiberius. And to the extreme annoyance of the Duc du Maine, the concluding stanza of this precious production, after remarking that Maine's "great heart was not cast down by unjust persecution," implored him to yield to the groans of France and step forth as her champion. What made things worse was that Legrange-Chancel had been ostentatiously welcomed at Sceaux before the crash, and might easily be suspected of having written the verses on a commission from the Duchesse du Maine. A pretty thing, to be sure, this Philippic, for a gentleman under police observation to find on his library table; though even in his fright and indignation, Maine must have drawn some consolation from the stanza in which St. Simon is described as "nature's abortion, who, in spite of his obscure birth, has a prouder heart than yours."

However, no unjust suspicion fell upon Maine, who on the contrary was by slow degrees being restored to his old position by Dubois; on 25th June 1721 he took another step out of the shadow, when the Regent gave him leave to visit Paris and Versailles, as well as to make use of his town house, the Arsenal. And a month later he received a more striking proof that the past was to be forgotten, when by the king's orders he took the salute at a review of the Swiss Guards.

These favours did not pass unnoticed by his former associates and their pamphleteers; finding that fulsome praise elicited no response from their chastened leader, they now went on the other tack, and in February 1722 the duke had the mortification of seeing Paris flooded with advertisements of a forthcoming book–*Treatise on Christian and Political Patience, by M. le Duc du Maine, dedicated to the people of France*. But such flea-bites, though they doubtless caused irritation, could not goad him into action; such political ambitions as he had ever possessed had been effectually extinguished in the château of Doullens, and more than the jeers of Grub Street would be needed before he again entered that dangerous field.

Throughout his eclipse, and in spite of the greed of the Duc de Bourbon, Maine had been left in possession of his lucrative post of Grand Master of the Artillery; it was, as we have explained elsewhere, a sinecure, but one which conferred on its holder certain undefined privileges and a considerable prestige. To Dubois, it represented a valuable piece of patronage, which he felt would be better in his hands than in those of the Duc du Maine, and which he thought that that prince, in his deflated condition, would be easily induced to part with. "M. le Cardinal," we are told, "went to Clagny, where he proposed to M. du Maine that he should resign the Grand Mastership, in consideration of his doing which, the king would reinstate him in his honours and privileges; to which the prince replied that he would resign on condition that the honours and privileges descended to his children. The Cardinal replied that "his commission was limited to asking for the duke's resignation." There the matter rested, and a further suggestion that he should resign the Colonelcy of the Swiss Guard was no more favourably received.

Villeroi was the only figure still left from the Duc du Maine's halcyon days, and with his disappearance the seventeenth century is hull down behind us. He and the Duc du Maine alone survived of that little group which had gathered round Louis XIV in his innermost privacy, where the old king and the old marshal had provoked each other's reminiscences of the glorious days–"Do you remember, M. le Maréchal . . . ?"–whilst Mme. de Maintenon would from time to time drop a word of corroboration or contradiction from behind her knitting needles. Villeroi's banishment was to leave a gap in Maine's contracted circle which no one else was capable of filling.

Villeroi had no one but himself to thank for his disgrace; he had never succeeded in grasping the fact that the days of Louis XIV were over and done with, and he still saw in the Regent, not his master, but the deplorable young man over whose "goings on" he and the late king had so often shaken their heads. Not content with making this plain to Philippe, he provoked even Philippe's anger by his silly and ostentatious pose as the only protector of the little king's life. And finally, he was foolish enough to treat Dubois with unconcealed insolence and contempt. The Regent, clamorously canvassed by the two men, would gladly have ended his worries by exiling both of them, had this been practicable: which it was not. But on 10th August 1722, he did succeed in getting rid of Villeroi, who had, on the previous day, been stupid enough to refuse the Regent a private interview with the king. The old Marshal was banished to Lyons, and with him vanished the last trace of the Versailles of Louis XIV.

Dubois, though victor in his struggle with Villeroi, was however not without his own troubles; Louis XV was now ten years of age, already quite conscious of who he was, and already beginning to show likes and dislikes. And Dubois was no longer able to conceal from himself the fact that he was one of the chief objects of the king's aversion. He determined that, having failed to win the king's affection, he would at least shut him off from all contacts hostile to himself, and, with that end in view abolished the *grandes entrées* the right of access to the king's person, which every courtier, and indeed most of France, had enjoyed under Louis XIV; and at the same time he extended the *petites entrées* to the Duc du Maine, his children, and the Comte de Toulouse. St. Simon was furious:

"This paved the way for the restoration of the bastards, and M. du Maine's children, to all the honours and distinctions they had enjoyed at the king's death, except the succession to the Crown, the title of Prince, *and the privilege of crossing the floor at sittings of the Parlement* . . . we Peers made a formal protest, the last resource of the oppressed. . . . The event completed the breach between the Cardinal Dubois, the Duc d'Orléans, and myself."

In fact the time had come for our old friend St. Simon to follow Villeroi into outer darkness, and the Duc du Maine would have been more than human had he not rejoiced at St. Simon's disappearance in 1723. St. Simon, unlike Villeroi, was not exiled, he was simply snubbed into self-banishment by the Regent, to whom he had gradually rendered himself intolerable by his officiousness and his importunities. Not, to do him justice, that St. Simon was a beggar; that type the Regent was accustomed to, and could put up with, but St. Simon was something far worse. Not only was he a man with incalculable potentialities for starting a first-class crisis over a puerility–as witness the portentous *affaire du bonnet*–but further, he aspired to be the keeper of the Regent's conscience. There came a time when Orléans could stand St. Simon's lectures no longer, and St. Simon had to disappear into private life. He was to live another thirty years, completely forgotten by everyone, the last survivor of his generation and of his house.

The Regent was not to be left for long in the enjoyment of such tranquillity as he had won for himself by the disappearance of St. Simon. In years Philippe was only forty-nine, in body and in mind he was already an old man; he had been warned more than once by the doctors that death might claim him at any moment, but he refused to alter his habits, which indeed were by now unalterable. On 3rd December, whilst taking his usual midday chocolate with his wife, he complained of a heaviness in his head and a great weight on his stomach; he then rested in the duchess's room until three, when he went to his office until six. At six o'clock he entered his private room, taking with him for company a self-styled Duchesse de Falari, one of his mistresses. The Regent sat down, his head bent forward for a few minutes, as if in deep thought, then slid from his chair and fell in a heap on the floor. It was one of his private hours, and half an hour passed before the screams of the distracted mistress brought assistance. A surgeon pronounced the case to be hopeless; Philippe never recovered consciousness, and at seven that evening he died.

15. The Quiet Years

Dubois was dead, the Regent was dead, and the mantle of power had fallen on the shoulders of the Duc de Bourbon, Maine's bitterest enemy, who, with the aid of his shameless and insatiable mistress Mme. de Prie soon made France look back upon Orléans' regency as a golden age. More than ever it behoved the Maines to walk delicately, avoid the Court, and cultivate the Muses at Sceaux.

But even at Sceaux, the fetes and pleasures seem to have been darkened by the shadow of the new Regent; there is about this second, or post-exilic Sceaux, a noticeably *piano* tone as contrasted with its former noisy glory. If the silver age brings no change in the type or number of the entertainments, there is a hint of everything being staged on a more modest scale than in the days before the Cellamare conspiracy. I attribute this to the duke's revolt in 1720, and suspect that, if he had failed to seize the power, he had at least established himself in his wife's eyes as a formidable minority problem.

We get our best glimpse of Sceaux's silver age through the eyes of the President Hénault,[1] one of the most distinguished of the younger habitués, and a man of considerable reputation in his day. When he arrived at Sceaux in the early twenties, he was already a person of some eminence, having scored a big society success with his songs, published in 1712. Sceaux was, he tells us, when he first saw it,

> "very different to what it had been under the late king. In those days M. du Maine's credit was unbounded; and Mme. du Maine employed it solely for her own pleasures. Things were now greatly changed. But if her court was less brilliant, it was certainly not less agreeable."

[1] Hénault, Charles Jean François, 1685–1770; Member of the Academy, 1723; published his *Abrégé Chronologique*, 1744; a friend of Voltaire's.

The chief stars of the second period were, according to Hénault, the Duchesse de Luynes, Mmes. Lambert, Staal, Dreuillet, and du Deffand, MM. de Polignac, de Mesmes, and St. Aulaire. Walpole's friend, Mme. du Deffand, appears to have been the most favoured woman, for she alone had her own apartment permanently reserved for her in the chateau. To quote again from Hénault;

"I spent more than twenty years there (i.e. in the Maine circle), and, as my fate decreed, experienced ups and downs, crosses and vexation. God forgive me all the insipidities which I produced there in mediocre verse. If I am unfortunate enough to be outlived by them, people will think that Mme. du Maine was Beauty herself; that it was Venus who used to glide about on the canal; people will attribute charms to her face, which were in fact only in her conversation. She was the oracle of this little court. Impossible for anyone to have more wit, eloquence, badinage, or real politeness; impossible too for anyone to be more unjust or tyrannical. One of our chief pleasures was to have boating parties on the lake, midnight revels which gave birth to many a charming song. I remember a dinner once, at which there were only five of us, M. and Mme. du Maine, Cardinal de Polignac, young Malézieux, and myself. Cardinal de Polignac was the best talker of his day; Mme. du Maine told her stories with infinite gaiety, but M. du Maine effaced everybody by his simplicity."

And so Hénault rambles on to tell us of those winter gatherings when, at eight o'clock on Christmas Eve, the whole company would assemble in the great salon to sing carols, and of other evenings when the hostess would demand impromptus from her guests. At this sort of thing, the Duc du Maine was a practised hand, and the following, which was his effort one winter night, wins the approval of the critical Hénault:

"Cette chanson sera mauvaise,
Voici pourquoi;
C'est que, Madame, ne vous deplaise
Elle est de moi.
En vain j'ai voulu vous déduire
Mon embarras,
On s'est contenté de me dire:
Tu chanteras."

Or, for a change, the company would assemble on a summer evening at the Arsenal in Paris, where Mme. du Maine had built a pretty dining pavilion on the edge of the river. To Hénault, looking back down the vista of years, such nights seemed to have been idyllic, but to the Duc de Luynes, who like Dangeau kept a diary, the Duchesse du Maine appeared a less attractive hostess—"She has," he said, "a loud, strong voice, and can maintain that tone for three or four hours without any sign of discomfort."

Whilst France went steadily down hill, Mme. du Maine, now fifty, whose official lover was St. Aulaire, was indulging in the exciting infidelity of a platonic flirtation with La Motte,[2] who was fifty-four, and blind. It was an affair conducted mainly by correspondence, and correspondence which is, it must be admitted, very fatiguing to the modern reader; the last echoes of the Hôtel de Rambouillet in fact. The best that can be said for it is that La Motte shows all the tiresome ingenuity of the school in perfection, and there is a certain dexterity in his method of making each letter a declaration of love, without the word "love" ever being mentioned. He begs the duchess's signature in full, then writes in the course of a post or so for another signature, with apologies for not having made the first one last longer—the implication of course being that he has worn out the other one with his kisses; to which doubtless the fifty-year-old ingenue would reply "Oh, fie, Sir," or words to that effect. A pair of old fools, is our first verdict. And yet perhaps on reflection one is not so sure. Is there not after all a certain valiance in this determination to play the game out to the end in accordance with the established rules?

The 11th June 1726 must have been a joyful day at Sceaux.

For some time past a bitter struggle had raged at Versailles for the control of Louis XV, the rivals being the Duc de Bourbon and Cardinal Fleury, the king's old tutor.[3] Bourbon the young king had always disliked, whilst for Fleury he had as much affection as he was capable of feeling for anyone but himself; Bourbon, whose incapacity was exceeded only by his brutality, seems to have entirely

[2] La Motte, Antoine Houdar de, 1672–1731; opera, *L' Europe Galante*, 1697, his first success, and was followed by many others; published against the Ancients, 1707; defeated his enemy, Rousseau, in 1710 by getting a vacant chair in French Academy; published his abridgement of the *Iliad*, 1713, "a wretched performance;" started a campaign against poetry, 1730; calls poetry "ridiculous and mechanical labour."

[3] Fleury, André Hercule, Cardinal de, 1653–1743; entered Council of State, 1723; Prime Minister, 1726; a mild, peace-loving statesman.

miscalculated the strength of Fleury's hold on the king, and the strength of Louis' dislike of himself, and it was Bourbon who fell. On that 11th June he finally disappeared from the stage, into exile at Chantilly, leaving Fleury firmly installed as Prime Minister of France. But those in a position to judge seem to have regarded Fleury as a mere stopgap, and there was much intrigue on foot to provide the king with a new Premier. Amongst those considered eligible for the apparent vacancy was the Duc du Maine, who was sounded on behalf of an influential clique by no less a person than that same Mme. de Caylus, to whom nearly fifty years earlier he had made a childish declaration of love, and with whom, as Mme. de Maintenon's niece, he had been on friendly terms ever since. We have not her letter, but the duke's reply shows how completely he had abandoned, if indeed he had ever held, those political ambitions with which he is so often credited.

"Paris, 1st April 1727.

I am very conscious, Madame, as indeed I ought to be, of the kindness you show me in the letter with which you have honoured me, and I should not have failed to wait upon you today to express my gratitude, were it not that I must return to Versailles immediately after dinner. The favourable opinion of me which you acquired in your earliest years, from one whose memory will always be dear (i.e. Mme. de Maintenon), gives you altogether too flattering an idea of me. I am forty years older than the king, Madame, and it is miraculous that in view of the disproportion of our ages, he puts up with me without regarding me as an old fool; so I must be careful not to inspire him with a dislike of me; he will never have a subject more faithful, or more eager for his glory, but he will also never have one less anxious to fill one of those places whose deceptive *éclat* turns so many heads. . . . I find myself in these days in a way of life which is very comfortable, both for me and for my children; my reason and my inclinations give me an invincible distaste for those things which I imagine you do not care to trust to a letter. Do not despise me, I beg of you, and, if you blame me, at least believe that I do not sin through cowardice.

If you will continue to honour me with your esteem, I dare to assure you that you will never find me unworthy of it.

L. A. DE BOURBON."

We could hardly ask for clearer evidence of the burnt child's dread of the fire.

Death made another irreplaceable gap in the little Court of Sceaux this autumn by carrying off Nicolas Malézieux in his seventy-seventh year; that Malézieux whom we have known since the distant days of the trips to Barèges and Bagnières when he was the duke's tutor, and who was later on to play so big a part in determining his destiny. For it was Malézieux, we may remember, who by his elaborate entertainment of the Maines at Châtenay, had first given the duchess the idea of buying Sceaux; Malézieux too it was, who had borne a leading part in the follies of the Cellamare conspiracy, and whom the duke had been so reluctant to readmit to his household after his release from prison. It must have been with mixed feelings that Maine looked back over his half century of intimacy with the dead man; but he had shown him no lasting ill-will, and Malézieux had died as Chancellor of the duke's Lilliputian sovereignty of Dombes.

Ever ready to help a friend, the Duc du Maine secured one of Malézieux' offices for his new protégé, Hénault; the dead man had been Director of the French Academy, and Maine, says Hénault, "went to Cardinal de Fleury to beg the post for me. M. le Cardinal de Fleury made a point of waiting on the Academicians to propose me, and I was accepted."

Though the Duc du Maine's political troubles were all behind him, his dreams of domestic tranquillity were still to be disturbed by his children; his eldest son, the Prince de Dombes, seems to have been a man who in one way and another caused his father a good deal of anxiety. When we last met him in 1717, he had narrowly missed burning down the town of Châlons, and when we next come across him in 1729, his recklessness in the hunting field nearly costs the duke the life of both his sons.

"February, 1729. Some days ago, M. le Prince de Dombes and M. le Comte d'Eu were stag-hunting near the Abbey of Chelles. The stag jumped into the Marne and got across safely, as did the huntsman. The two princes also leapt into the river, but chose a bad place; their horses threw them in jumping, and they both went in head under. A miller, who came to their assistance, managed to pull them out, and they were carried to his mill, practically unconscious. There they were put to bed and brought round with brandy, and by good chance both did well. They were able to start for Marly next day."

14. THE DUCHESSE DU MAINE

From a print by Derochers

15. CARDINAL DUBOIS

It was at any rate a lucky day for the miller, for we learn from the same source that the Duc du Maine sent him fifty pounds, and settled eighteen pounds a year for life on him.

Though the Duc du Maine is now ageing, and is definitely a relic of the old Court–than which society can find no more damning term of abuse–he is far from being regarded as a man whose life is finished; he is still thought of as one who may yet be called upon to play a part in governing France. When in March 1732 the king announced that in view of Cardinal Fleury's infirmities, he had decided to give him Chauvelin,[4] Keeper of the Seals, as a coadjutor, some surprise was felt that Louis' choice had not fallen upon the Duc du Maine. "For a long time past," says Barbier in noting the appointment, "it had been thought that M. le Duc du Maine would get Cardinal de Fleury's place; so the Houses of Maine and Toulouse may well feel aggrieved at this." To what extent there was any serious body of opinion in favour of Maine's appointment we do not know, but that he felt any mortification at being passed over in favour of Chauvelin is unlikely. We have seen with what firmness he had rejected Mme. de Caylus' overtures in 1727, and nothing had occurred in the interval which could lead him to change his mind. The passage is however interesting as showing how much exaggerated is the idea of Maine's complete eclipse after Louis XIV's death; his later years may be barren of incident, but he evidently still bulked largely in the public eye. There was no ambition left in him however, no desire to keep himself before the king's notice; as we turn over contemporary memoirs his name catches our notice from time to time, but always as being at Court only on indispensable occasions of ceremony. What had he to do with Courts, he who remembered so vividly the great days of Versailles, and was now a disillusioned man in the middle sixties? How could he talk to these smart, slick young men, in their nasty little wigs and silk coats, youngsters whose very language he did not understand; all atheists too, sniggering and tittering in those noble rooms which he had seen filled with the glory of gold-laced broadcloth and the decent solemnity of *in folio* wigs. Young men who had

[4] CHAUVELIN, Germain Louis de; a man of "boundless energy and ambition."

hardly the civility to stifle a yawn if one tried to explain to them something of the glories of Racine and Bossuet, or of the great days of the nineties when France had held her own, single-handed, against Europe. Youths who belauded Voltaire, and considered Belleisle a better general than the Marshal de Luxembourg. And the women! No beauty, no wit, all charm and fragrance replaced by an easy, insolent vivacity, modelling itself on the wives of tax farmers and stock jobbers. Better live quietly at Sceaux among the ghosts of the past; and with such thoughts, he would return to his books, in which, if he could not relive his own youth, he could at least shut out the present. Or if the weather were fine, he would order out his steady old hunter and take a turn with his son's hounds; though hounds and horses, like everything else, were not what they had been.

In 1735, the routine of Sceaux was enlivened by a domestic marriage, highly characteristic of the Duchesse du Maine and her times. The bride was our old friend Mlle. de Launay, now well on the wrong side of forty. It was no Indian summer romance on her part, merely that it had occurred to her mistress that it would be convenient if Mlle. de Launay had a title. As the years passed, she had become more and more indispensable at Sceaux, had become as intimate a friend of the duchess's as perhaps it was possible for anyone to be. But one bar to complete intimacy remained. Even Mme. du Maine lacked the courage to break through the etiquette which debarred persons below a certain quality from eating at the table of the Blood Royal of France, and Mlle. de Launay was unfortunately ineligible for this privilege. But the matter was easily adjusted; marriage with a properly qualified noble would remove the bar, and the duchess set herself to find the man. We have, in the course of this story, met with not a few marriages of convenience, but Mlle. de Launay's, as told by herself, surpasses them all; she would one imagines, have displayed more interest over the betrothal of a chambermaid. A Swiss officer in the Artillery, the Baron de Staal, was selected, to whom the inducement held out was that the Duc du Maine as Grand Master of the Artillery would give him his patronage. The Baron accepted the offer, the marriage took place, and Mme. La Baronne de Staal, after spending a night in her husband's lodgings, returned to her normal life at Sceaux. Not indeed without a faint flicker of revolt; she hinted that she should perhaps live with her husband, but on finding that Mme. du Maine took the suggestion as a shocking piece of ingratitude, she let the matter drop.

The marriage had not been brought about without difficulty, for the Duc du Maine had raised objections. What his reasons were we do not know; perhaps nothing more than the elderly man's instinctive reluctance to face any change. He may, like Mr. Woodhouse, and with considerably greater justification, have arrived at the conclusion that all marriages were a mistake. His objection took a highly characteristic form:

"M. du Maine, with that address with which he customarily eluded a proposition which he had not the courage to reject, praised the idea of my marriage in general, and proposed several men whose consent was doubtful, or whose suitability was uncertain."

But the duchess, "accustomed to his evasions, pursued him until she had gained her object."

Maine certainly showed himself a true Bourbon in his inability to learn anything. He was now sixty-five, he had been married for more than forty years, and he was still under the youthful illusion that a woman in quest of the particular can be side-tracked by a discussion of the general; and that woman too, his Ludovise.

Between his release from prison and the beginning of 1736, the Duc du Maine had on the whole enjoyed tolerably good health, with nothing more to worry him than twinges of pain in the face, which were doubtless attributed to age and rheumatism; but in this year, the pain became constant and acute. Specialists were called into consultation; and the unfortunate man received his horrible sentence with courage and calmness. He was dying of an inoperable cancer.

"The disease, of which he had had warning for the last ten years, had been too long neglected, and had been aggravated by the extraction of a tooth. In the later stages, he would use no other remedy than the Sieur

Canette's plaster. This plaster, of which Canette alone knew the secret, is recognized as an excellent solvent; it is said to have prolonged the duke's life, and if he had lived by strict regimen, it would have kept him alive much longer."

From then on, with terrible steadiness, the disease pursued its ghastly course, "taking from him one after another all the functions of life, and finally life itself." One pleasant thing only is recorded of that dreadful sickroom, and that is the devotion of his wife, who nursed him with tender care, "undeterred by the horror of this frightful malady;" and in those pain-shot last weeks, both of them seem to have recaptured a glimpse of the long past days when they had been lovers.

A few days before his death, Maine sent in his resignation as Colonel of the Carabineers, which post the king immediately conferred on the Prince de Dombes, giving him at the same time his dying father's command of the Swiss Guard and his Governorship of Languedoc; to the younger son, the Cte. d'Eu, he gave the Maine Infantry Regiment, and the Governorship of Guyenne.

There remained only one thing for the duke to do, and that was to die in love and charity with his neighbours.

The worst result of the bitter, sordid business of his degradation in 1718 had been the breach which it had made between him and his well-loved sister, the Duchesse de Bourbon. The duchess, mother of the despoiler and sister of the despoiled, had, in a difficult situation, taken the part of her son; Maine, "wounded by the vivacity with which she took the side of the Princes of the Blood, had not seen her since." But a day or two before his death he sent his confessor to his sister to say that he asked her pardon for the past, and that he had forgotten it. The Duchesse de Bourbon replied with a loving prayer to be allowed to see him once more; but it was too late. He died, alone with his wife, at half past two on the afternoon of Monday, 19th May, having to the end excused himself from saying goodbye to his sisters, his brother, or even his own children.

So ended the first and last Duc du Maine; for his title died with him. It was time for him to be gone; within a twelvemonth of his death, we find d'Argenson writing in his diary,

"It is preposterous how little alacrity and civility there is among the courtiers. People are becoming republican, even at Court; they are getting disabused of all respect for Royalty."

By the Duc du Maine's will, the principality of Dombes, which of course passed to the eldest son, was charged with a pension of £850 a year for the widow; and double that sum for his daughter, so long as she remained unmarried. To the latter he also left his collection of snuff boxes, which were worth a considerable sum, for the duke had been a collector all his life.

The daughter had been a shadowy figure since her birth, and of her subsequent life we know little or nothing. At the time of her father's death she was apparently living at Versailles, and in May 1736 was given the late Duc du Maine's rooms there. In the following year there were rumours of her betrothal to M. de Guise, but apparently nothing came of it. Of his two sons, the elder, the Prince de Dombes, is one of those men whose career looks imposing enough on a tombstone, but is in fact a singularly empty one–Prince de Dombes, Peer of France, Knight of the St. Esprit, Grand Huntsman of France–this is his biography in brief, and indeed pretty much the whole of it. But he was, we are told, a scrupulously honourable man, lived on affectionate terms with his brother, and steadily devoted his life to the payment of his father's debts, an object which he had accomplished by January 1755. In itself a creditable life's work, even for a wealthy peer, for the Duc du Maine left debts amounting to about £145,000 of our money. The Prince de Dombes was struck down by apoplexy at Fontainebleau at six o'clock on the morning of 29th September 1755, and died without recovering consciousness a little after midnight on 1st October; and it was, in the hackneyed phrase, "a merciful release." For the last year he had been dying "of a total debility of nature, so great that he became mad and imbecile at fifty-five years of age, having used up his strength by hunting, in the pleasures of the table, and with courtesans."

He was childless, and there ensued the usual scramble for the dead man's posts:

"All the princes were at Versailles today to beg the places left vacant by the death of the Prince de Dombes. His brother asked for nothing, and the king gave him the command of the Swiss and the government of Languedoc . . . but asked him to surrender the Grand Mastership of the Artillery, to which the Comte d'Eu is much attached, and at which demand he was unable to hide his vexation from the king; but the king has asked for it for a particular reason, and he has granted the Comte d'Eu the government of the Arsenal, with the gift of all patronage depending thereon."

The life of the Cte. d'Eu presents even fewer features of interest than that of his elder brother, but from the little we do hear of him he seems to have been chiefly remarkable for a love of retirement and a devotion to field sports; a negative sort of man, not unlike that Count Zaehdarm on whom Carlyle's Teufelsdrockh wrote the Latin epitaph which was so unaccountably rejected by the family;[5] such a man in short as the Duc du Maine himself would have been, had fortune been kinder to him.

"The Comte d'Eu is a prince who likes to live private, loves hunting and building; he divides his time between Sceaux and his château of Anet, where he lives without ceremony, and without an establishment suitable to his rank, though he is scrupulous in paying his court to the king."

He reappears for a moment in February 1762, when he resigns the Colonelcy of the Swiss Guard and sells his principality of Dombes to the Crown–with reluctance, one gathers. Though the surprising thing is that the principality should have been allowed to exist so long; for this little sovereign state in the heart of the realm was more than an anachronism, it was an intolerable administrative nuisance. It had inevitably become an Alsatia of broken men and criminals, whose appreciation of Dombes as a place of residence depended upon the fact that the central government found it extremely difficult to extradite men from the principality. That it

[5] Hic jacet Philippus Zaehdarm . . . Zaehdarmi comes . . . qui dum sub luna agebat, quinquies mille perdices plumbo confecit: varii cibi centumpondia millies centena millia, per se, perque servos quadrupedes bipedesve, haud sine tumultu devolvens, in stercus palam convertit. Nunc a labore requiescentem opera sequuntur. Si monumentum quaeris, fimetum adspice. (Carlyle, *Sartor Resartus*, Bk. II. Ch. V.)

had survived Louis XIV's centralizing policy was due only to the fact that in his earlier days it had been the property of his cousin, *Mademoiselle*, and that she had bequeathed it to the Duc du Maine as part of the price to be paid for the release of Lauzun.

Charles de Bourbon, Cte. d'Eu, died in 1775, and with him ends the House of Maine.

The Duc du Maine's brother, Louis Alexandre, Cte. de Toulouse, remained a bachelor until 1722, when he married a daughter of the second Duc de Noailles. The issue of this marriage was the Duc de Penthièvre, a man of some note in his day as a patron of men of letters; Penthièvre's daughter fulfilled in a later generation the Duc du Maine's old ambition of a union between his branch of the family and that of Orléans, by marrying the then duke; by whom she had the misfortune to bring Philippe Egalité into the world.

And what of Ludovise, the ageless fairy queen of Sceaux? She survived her husband seventeen years, and until nearly the end the flame of her vitality burned with undimmed brightness. Two years after her husband's death we find her playing a leading part in a somewhat surprising agitation; surprising, that is, by reason of the volte-face of the Princess of the Blood:

"I hear that there is great talk about the strong request from *Mademoiselle* and all the legitimated princes, that an intermediate rank be granted the children, if any, of MM. de Dombes, d'Eu, and Penthièvre. All the Princes and Princesses of the Blood have joined in the petition, or have at any rate consented to it."

But if Mme. du Maine had hopes of the triumphant restoration of the rank of the bastards, she was doomed to disappointment; the matter seems to have dragged on until 1741, and then to have been dropped.

In 1742 Mme. du Maine lost her "shepherd," St. Aulaire, who died aged ninety, her "lover" to the last. In 1745 she entertained the queen at Sceaux, but in the same year declined to come to Court to meet the new Dauphine, on account of the expense involved. Can it be possible, we wonder, that on her widow's jointure, she was at last getting some dim idea of the value of money? Or was it an excuse to avoid some snub to her pretentions? We do not know.

In October 1747 she lost the "dearest friend" of the moment, the Duchesse d' Estrées, but two months later Sceaux was in full glory again: the occasion being a visit from no less a person than Voltaire, accompanied by his "divine Emilie." There were great doings in the private theatre, where Voltaire and Emilie played parts in one of Voltaire's comedies.

Mlle. de Launay–it is hardly worth while to call her Mme. de Staal–died in June 1750, having been an inmate of Sceaux for nearly forty years; and that winter we hear of Mme. du Maine being "seriously ill," for the first time in her life. The trouble was a continual cough, which she never again got rid of. In August 1752 she visited Versailles for the last time; and on the 23rd January 1753, she died at Paris. Three days later she was buried quietly, beside her husband, at Sceaux.

And now that the story is told, what of the Duc du Maine? can we dismiss him with that couplet from Hymns Ancient and Modern,

> "The roseate hues of early dawn,
> How fast they fade away."

or was there more in him than a precocious child who turned out a failure? Let us try to sum him up.

To begin with, we have written in vain if we have not managed to demolish St. Simon's duke, the crafty, limping hypocrite, devoured by ambition, treacherously fighting his way to the steps of the Throne behind the skirts of Mme. de Maintenon. And yet St. Simon's evidence, properly weighed, is not without its significance; however distorted the picture may be, the man who inspired it cannot have been a nullity, cannot have been as colourless a character as we have been sometimes tempted to think him. We must be on our guard against the identification of a weak character with a featureless one; weak the duke may have been, but featureless, no. Something of the brilliance of his early years he never lost, even by the testimony of his enemies, who grant him the polish of a man of the world, and a conversation which was delightful by reason of a well stored mind and a cultivated taste. But if this were all which could be put forward in his favour, it would be better left unsaid; that with so vast a start in the race of life, his flowering and culmination should have been that his company was sought after in the more intelligent salons and boudoirs of Versailles. That there was more in him than the agreeable *flâneur* we may safely postulate; amongst other things, a self-control, a toughness of moral fibre, which accords ill with the received conception of his complete lack of character. He was not one of those devitalized, thin-blooded men, who make a virtue of that purity which is in fact merely the result of a lack of impulse; his virility is proved by his entirely creditable insistence that his father should provide him with a wife. And, neither before or after his marriage, is there a hint from his contemporaries that he ever yielded to the temptations thrown in the way of a man of his rank, in a Court whose fundamental viciousness was but thinly disguised by a superficial varnish of religion.

And when we turn to the matter of his military career, what do we find? Here was a man who, in an age when soldierly prowess was the only legitimate object of a gentleman's ambition, found himself handicapped by physical disability, and an education which, so far as we can judge, had been markedly unwarlike; and yet his performances in the field are creditable, indeed more than creditable. I see no reason why he should not have attained the rank he did, even if he had not been Louis XIV's son; he was at least as brave and as efficient as the average amateur soldier of his day, and better in both respects than many whom we meet. Better for instance than his severest critic, St. Simon, who never rose above the rank of Colonel, did not deserve to, and fifty years later is still treating us to unmanly whimperings about his unmerited ill-fortune.

Were there potentialities in the Duc du Maine, whose development was checked by circumstances over which he had no control? I am inclined to think that there were, and that, had he been planted in a more genial climate, he would have blossomed into something more effective than the man as we now see him. It is impossible to overestimate the psychological damage done to his character by the misfortune of his withered leg, taken in conjunction with his father's determination that he should play the traditional part of a

Bourbon prince. Operating in a more restricted field, it is the same tragedy as that of the late Kaiser Wilhelm and his crippled arm, both men striving to fill rôles for which each was fundamentally unfitted. Had the Duc du Maine been the son of a great noble, his physical deficiencies, as we have noticed elsewhere, would have marked him down for the Church, and who can say how different his place in history might then have been?

But his lameness is only part of his handicap. He has often been hailed, rather uncritically it seems to me, as Mme. de Maintenon's masterpiece; and Mme. de Maintenon has often been hailed as the first governess of genius. But if her claim to that title rested on the upbringing of the Duc du Maine, I think we should have to disallow it. Had she been cooler towards the duke, more dispassionate, I feel it would have been better for her pupil; she would have then detected in him a certain ineradicable strain of weakness, and instead of letting her much stronger nature absorb him with a sort of hungry possessiveness, she would have concentrated on teaching him to fend for himself. And it is a further misfortune that Maine so readily responded to her devouring love; had her attitude towards him been such that he regarded her with respect and a faint dislike, he might have emerged from her tutelage a very different boy. But by the time he reached the hands of a governor, the harm was done; it is, we notice, never to his governor that he looks in moments of doubt and distress, but always to Mme. de Maintenon.

But the turning point in the duke's life, as I see it, was his marriage. Louis XIV's choice of a bride for his son puzzles me; the king disliked the House of Condé, always had disliked it since the Fronde, and he was a man who, though he could forgive, could not forget. And this consideration apart, he could hardly have made a worse choice; his son's character cannot have been hidden from him, and with his worldly wisdom, he must have known that for Maine, happiness and success lay in his having a wife of one of two types; either a wise, dominating, and understanding woman, not too much in love with her husband, who would have grasped the fact, evident long ago to Mme. de Maintenon, that the way to manage the duke was to suggest a course of action to him in such a way that he imagined that he had thought of it himself; or alternatively, a soft, clinging creature, whose very helplessness would have forced Maine to adopt the rôle of guiding destiny of the household. Louis chose neither, but fell between two stools, selecting a girl who was strong enough to dominate the duke, and too selfish to cultivate his potentialities.

Knave, fool, nullity, or the victim of frustration? Which was he? I have produced, and endeavoured to sum up, all the available evidence. The verdict I leave to the reader.

APPENDIX A

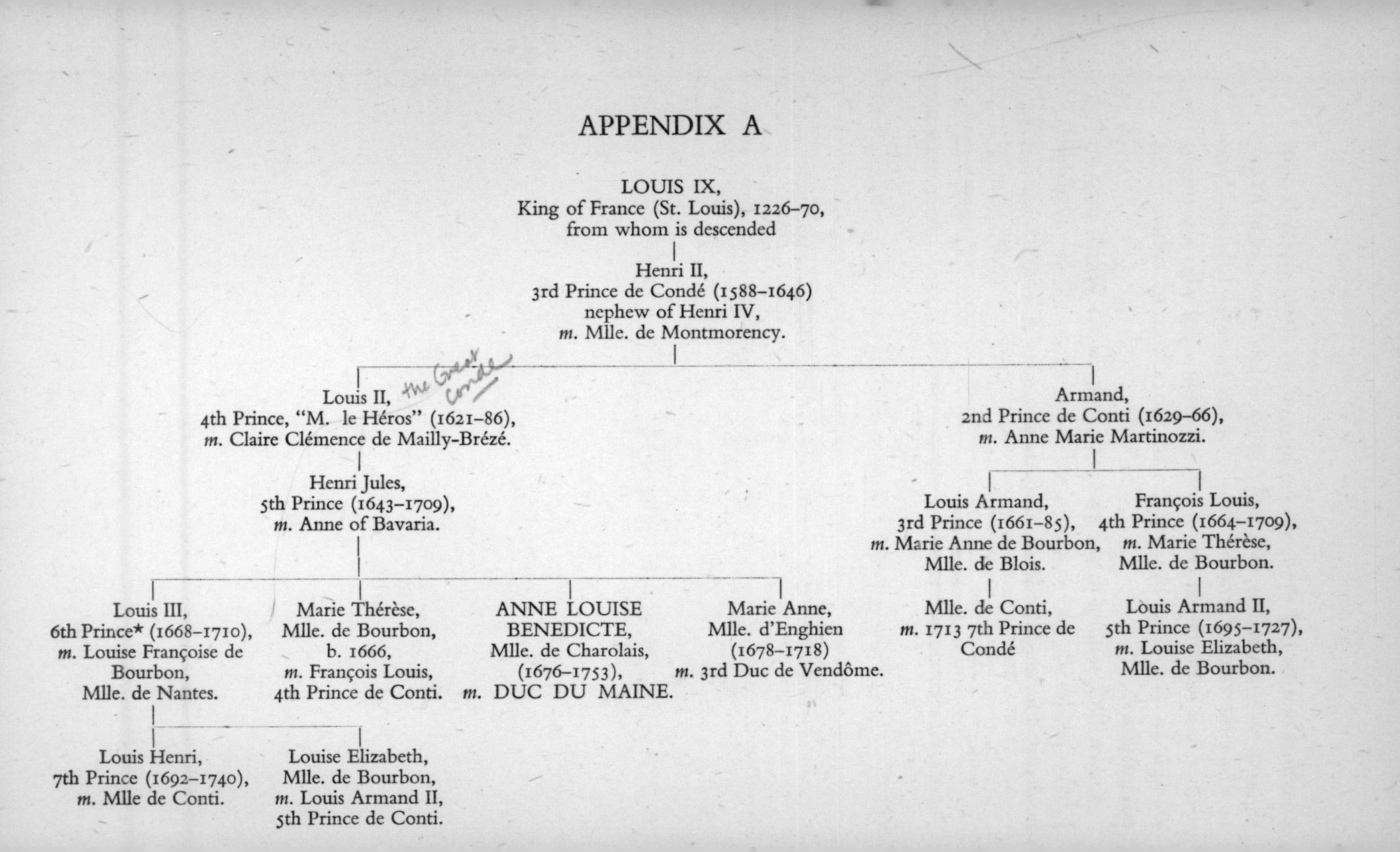
LOUIS IX,
King of France (St. Louis), 1226–70,
from whom is descended
Henri II,
3rd Prince de Condé (1588–1646)
nephew of Henri IV,
m. Mlle. de Montmorency.
Louis II,
4th Prince, "M. le Héros" (1621–86),
m. Claire Clémence de Mailly-Brézé.
Armand,
2nd Prince de Conti (1629–66),
m. Anne Marie Martinozzi.
Henri Jules,
5th Prince (1643–1709),
m. Anne of Bavaria.
Louis Armand,
3rd Prince (1661–85),
m. Marie Anne de Bourbon,
Mlle. de Blois.
François Louis,
4th Prince (1664–1709),
m. Marie Thérèse,
Mlle. de Bourbon.
Louis III,
6th Prince* (1668–1710),
m. Louise Françoise de
Bourbon,
Mlle. de Nantes.
Marie Thérèse,
Mlle. de Bourbon,
b. 1666,
m. François Louis,
4th Prince de Conti.
ANNE LOUISE
BENEDICTE,
Mlle. de Charolais,
(1676–1753),
m. DUC DU MAINE.
Marie Anne,
Mlle. d'Enghien
(1678–1718)
m. 3rd Duc de Vendôme.
Mlle. de Conti,
m. 1713 7th Prince de
Condé
Louis Armand II,
5th Prince (1695–1727),
m. Louise Elizabeth,
Mlle. de Bourbon.
Louis Henri,
7th Prince (1692–1740),
m. Mlle de Conti.
Louise Elizabeth,
Mlle. de Bourbon,
m. Louis Armand II,
5th Prince de Conti.

Bibliography

ALBERONI, The History of Cardinal etc., 1 vol., London, 1719.

ANSELME, de Ste. Marie (P. de GUIBOURS), Histoire Genéalogique et chronologique de la maison royale de France, des pairs, des grands officiers etc., 11 vols., Paris, 1712.

ARNAULD D'ANDILLY and L'ABBE ARNAULD, Memoires de, Vols. XXXIII and XXXIV, Collection Petitot, Paris, 1824.

AVAUX, Negociations de M. le Cte. d', en Hollande, 1679–1684, 4 vols., Paris, 1752.

BARBIER, Chronique de la Regence et du règne de Louis XV, 1718–1763, 8 vols., Paris, 1857.

BASSOMPIERRE, Mémoires du Maréschal de, 2 vols., Amsterdam, 1692.

BERWICK, Memoires du Maréchal de, Vols. LXV and LXVI, Collection Petitot, Paris, 1828.

BOSSUET, Jacques Benigne, a study. E. K. Sanders, London, 1 vol. 1921.

BOSSUET, Lettres de, edit. H. Massis, Paris, 1 vol. N.D.

BOURGOGNE, Le duc de, et le duc de Beauvilliers; lettres inedites, 1700–1708, edit. de Vogué, 1 vol., Paris, 1900.

BRIDGES, J. H., France under Richelieu and Colbert, 1 vol., Edinburgh, 1866.

BROCHER, H., Rang et l'etiquette sous l'ancien régime. 1 vol., Paris, 1934.

BRUYÈRE, Les caractères de Theophraste, traduits en Grec, avec les caractères et moeurs de ce siécle etc., 3 vols., Amsterdam, 1740.

BUSSY, Les lettres de Messire Roger de Rabutin, Cte. de etc., 7 vols., Paris, 1737.

BUSSY, Les Mémoires de Messire Roger de Rabutin, Cte. de etc., 2 vols., Paris, 1696.

BUVAT, Journal de la Régence (1715–1723), edit. E. Campardon, 2 vols., Paris, 1865.

BUZENVAL, Choart de, Bp. of Beauvais, 1651–1679. J. Gaillard, 1 vol., Paris, 1902.

CAMBRIDGE MODERN HISTORY, Vol. V, The Age of Louis XIV: Vol. VI, The Eighteenth Century.

CAYLUS, Souvenirs et Correspondance de Mme. de, edit. E. Raunié, 1 vol., Paris, N.D.

CHALLES, Mémoires de Robert, écrivain du roi, edit. A. A. Thierry, 1 vol., Paris, 1931.

CHÂTRE, Mémoires du Cte. de La, contenant la fin du règne de Louis XIII, et le commencement de celui de Louis XIV, Vol. LI, Collection Petitot, Paris, 1826.

CHOISY, Mémoires de l'Abbé de, pour servir à l'histoire de Louis XIV, edit. Lescure, 2 vols., Paris, 1888.

Churchill, Rt. Hon. Sir W. S., Marlborough, his life and times, 4 vols., London, 1933–8.

Clément, Pierre, Mme. de Montespan, Paris, 1868.

Condé, The Life of Lewis of Bourbon, late Prince of, digested into annals etc., 1 vol., London, 1693.

Condé, The Great, A life of. E. Godley, 1 vol., London, 1915.

Cosnac, Le Cte. de, Souvenirs du règne de Louis XIV, 6 vols., Paris, 1866–78.

Crump, L., Nursery life three hundred years ago, 1 vol., London, 1929.

Dangeau, Journal du Marquis de, various editions.

Dictionary of National Biography, O.U.P., 1920.

Dubois, Memoirs of Cardinal, trans. E. Dowson, 2 vols., London, 1899. (Spurious?)

Duclos, Mémoires sécrets sur le règne de Louis XIV, la Régence, et le règne de Louis XV, 2 vols., Paris, 1864.

Estrades, The Secret Letters and Negotiations of the Marshal d', 4 vols., London, 1690.

État de la France, various years.

Eugène of Savoy, Mémoires du Prince, écrits par lui-même, 1 vol., Paris, 1810. (Spurious?)

Europe in the Seventeenth Century. D. Ogg, 1 vol., London, 1931.

European History, chronologically arranged, 476–1920. Hassall, 1 vol., London, 1920.

Fénelon, François de, Viscount St. Cyres, 1 vol., London, 1901.

Feuquières, Memoirs, Historical, and Military, containing a distinct view of all the considerable states of Europe etc., 2 vols., London, 1736.

Fontenay-Mareuil, Mémoires du . . . Marquis de, Vols. L and LI, Collection Petitot, Paris, 1826.

France, The old regime in. Funck-Brentano, trans. H. Wilson, 1 vol., London, 1929.

France Galante, La, and Histoire Amoureuse des Gaules, Bussy-Rabutin, 2 vols., Paris, 1857.

Galland, Antoine, Journal Parisien, 1708–1715, edit. H. Omont, 1 vol., Paris, 1919.

Gramont, Mémoires du Maréchal de, Paris, 2 vols., 1826–7.

Haggard, C. P., Regent of the Roués, 1 vol., London, 1905.

Hénault, Mémoires du President d', Paris, 1855.

Hérouard, J., Journal du Roy Louis XIII . . . 1614–1615, 1 vol., Paris, 1838.

Histoire Amoureuse des Gaules, see "La France Galante."

Higham, F. M. G., King James II, 1 vol., London, 1934.

Hugon, C., Social France in the Seventeenth Century, 1 vol., London, 1911.

Hume, M., The Court of Philip IV, 1 vol., London, N.D.

La Fayette, Life and Times of Mme. de, L. Rea, 1 vol., London, 1908.

Lair, J., Louise de La Vallière, trans. Mayne, 1 vol., London, N.D.

LOISELEUR, J., Trois Énigmes Historiques, 1 vol., Paris, 1882.

LOUIS XIV, La morte de (Journal des Anthoine), edit. E. Drumont, 1 vol., Paris, 1880.

LOUIS XIV, Decline of the age of, 1687–1715. A. Tilley, 1 vol., London, 1929.

LOUIS XIV, Oeuvres de, edit. Treuttel et Wurtz, 6 vols., Paris, 1806.

LOUVOIS, Histoire de, et de son administration etc., C. Rousset, 4 vols., Paris, 1872.

LUYNES, Mémoires du Duc de, sur la cour de Louis XV (1735–1758), 13 vols., Paris, 1863.

MAINTENON, Mme. de, Correspondance générale, edit. T. Lavallée, 4 vols., Paris, 1865.

MAINTENON, Lettres inédites de Mme. de, et de Mme. la Princesse des Ursins, 4 vols., Paris, 1826.

MAINTENON, Histoire de Mme. de etc., Duc de Noailles, 4 vols., Paris, 1848–58.

MAINTENON, Mme. de, et la maison royale de St. Cyr (1686–1793). T. Lavallée, 1 vol., Paris, 1862.

MALPLAQUET, La bataille de, d'après les correspondents du Duc du Maine à l'armée de Flandre, M. Sautai, 1 vol., Paris, 1904.

MARÉSCHAL, Georges, Seigneur de La Bièvre . . . Cte. G. M. de La Bièvre, 1 vol., Paris, 1906.

MARINE FRANÇAISE, Histoire de la, Vol. V, C. de La Roncière, Paris, 1934.

MAZARIN, 1602–61. C. Federn, 1 vol., Paris, 1934.

MONTGLAT, Mémoires de F. de P. de Clermont, Marquis de etc., Vols. XLIX, L, and LI, Collection Petitot, Paris, 1825.

MONTPENSIER, Mémoires de Mlle. de, edit. Chéruel, 4 vols., Paris, N.D.

MOTTEVILLE, Mémoires de Mme. de, edit. F. Riaux, 4 vols., Paris, 1869.

ORLÉANS, Correspondence complète de Mme. de, née Princesse-Palatine, edit. G. Brunet, 2 vols., Paris, 1863.

ORLÉANS, Lettres inédites de la Princesse-Palatine, duchesse d', edit. A. Rolland, Paris, 1 vol., N.D.

ORMESSON, De l'administration de Louis XIV (1661–1672) d'après les mémoires inédites d'Olivier d', edit. A. Chéruel, 1 vol., Paris, 1850.

PERRAULT, C., Hommes illustres, Les, qui ont paru . . . pendant ce siècle, 1 vol., Paris, 1698.

PERRAULT, C., Mémoires de, edit. P. Lacroix, 1 vol., Paris, 1878.

RAVAISSON, Archives de la Bastille, 7 vols., Paris, 1866–73. (Vols. IV–VI.)

ST. MAURICE, Lettres sur la cour de Louis XIV, 1667–1670, 1 vol., Paris, 1910.

ST. SIMON, various editions.

STE. BEUVE, Causeries du Lundi, trans. E. J. Trechman, 7 vols., London, N.D. *The Duchess of Burgundy*, May 6th 1850; *Abbé de Chaulieu*, 26th March 1850; *The Duchess of Maine*, 23rd December 1850; *Mme. de Maintenon*, 28th July 1851.

SCIENCE des personnes de la cour, de l'epée, et de la robe, ou l'on trouve etc., 2 vols., Paris, 1707.

SEVENTEENTH CENTURY, The. J. Boulenger, 1 vol., London, 1920.

SEVENTEENTH CENTURY, Institutions, usages, et coutumes, 1590–1700. P. Lacroix, 1 vol., Paris, 1880.

SÉVIGNÉ, Lettres de Mme. de, edit. A. Martin, 6 vols., Paris, 1876.

SPANHEIM, E., Relation de la cour de France, en 1690, edit. M. C. Schefer, 1 vol., Paris, 1882.

SPANISH HISTORY, The, etc., 1 vol., London, 1678.

STAAL, Mémoires de Mme. de, Vol. LXXVII, Collection Petitot, Paris, 1829.

TEMPLE, Sir W., Works of, 4 vols., London, 1757.

TORCY, Mémoires de M. de, pour servir à l'histoire des negociations depuis le Traité de Ryswyck jusqu'à la Paix d'Utrecht, 3 vols., London, 1757.

TORCY, Journal inédit de J. B. Colbert, Marquis de, pendant les années 1709, 1710, et 1711, edit. F. Masson, 1 vol., Paris, 1903.

TREVELYAN, G. M., The Peace and the Protestant Succession, 1 vol., London, 1934.

TREVELYAN, G. M., Ramillies and the Union with Scotland, 1 vol., London, 1932,

TREVELYAN, M. C., William III and the defence of Holland, 1672–4, 1 vol.. London, 1930.

VILLARS, Lettres de Mme. de, 1 vol., Amsterdam, 1760.

VILLARS, Mémoires du Maréchal de, edit. Vogué, 3 vols., Paris, 1884.

Index

Mlle de Launay - producer at Sceaux

54	1672	Franco-Dutch War
	1678	Treaty of Nimeguen
	1688	James II out...
141	1695	5 armies ... Namur ... Wm of Orange
149	1697	Peace of Ryswick
152	1698	Compeigne
Pg 155	1700	Spanish Succession
	1702	Death of Wm ... Queen Anne
	1712	Congress of Utrecht